ALFRED BESTER

MODERN MASTERS OF SCIENCE FICTION

Edited by Gary K. Wolfe

Science fiction often anticipates the consequences of scientific discoveries. The immense strides made by science since World War II have been matched step by step by writers who gave equal attention to scientific principles, human imagination, and the craft of fiction. The respect for science fiction won by Jules Verne and H. G. Wells was further increased by Isaac Asimov, Arthur C. Clarke, Robert Heinlein, Ursula K. Le Guin, Joanna Russ, and Ray Bradbury. Modern Masters of Science Fiction is devoted to books that survey the work of individual authors who continue to inspire and advance science fiction.

A list of books in the series appears at the end of this book.

ALFRED BESTER

Jad Smith

UNIVERSITY OF
ILLINOIS PRESS
Urbana, Chicago, and Springfield

1 2 3 4 5 C P 5 4 3 2 1
∞ This book is printed on acid-free paper.

Frontispiece: Alfred Bester circa 1968. First published in *SF Symposium/FC Simpósio*, edited by José Sanz for the Instituto Nacional Do Cinema, Brazil, 1969.

Library of Congress Cataloging-in-Publication Data
Names: Smith, Jad, author.
Title: Alfred Bester / Jad Smith.
Description: Urbana : University of Illinois Press, 2016. | Series: Modern masters of science fiction | Includes bibliographical references and index.
Identifiers: LCCN 2016021556 | ISBN 9780252040634 (hardback) | ISBN 9780252082139 (paperback)
Subjects: LCSH: Bester, Alfred—Criticism and interpretation. | Science fiction, American—History and criticism. | Bester, Alfred. | Authors, American—20th century—Biography. | BISAC: LITERARY CRITICISM / Science Fiction & Fantasy. | BIOGRAPHY & AUTOBIOGRAPHY / Literary.
Classification: LCC PS3552.E796 Z85 2016 | DDC 813/.54 [B]—dc23
LC record available at https://lccn.loc.gov/2016021556

For Staci and Staz
and
In memory of
Cuyler W. "Ned" Brooks Jr.
(1938–2015)

Contents

Acknowledgments

The staffs of several libraries and archives provided me with invaluable assistance as I conducted my research, and I am grateful for the help of the Special Collections Research Center at Syracuse University; the Lilly Library at Indiana University, Bloomington; the University of Pennsylvania Archives; the Rare Book and Manuscript Library at University of Illinois, Champaign-Urbana; and Booth Library at Eastern Illinois University. Institutional support for this project included a grant from Eastern Illinois University's Office of Research and Sponsored Programs and release time awarded by the College of Arts and Humanities dean's office. Ned Brooks, who passed away in August 2015, was a valued correspondent who provided research advice and scans of fanzines on several occasions, and I thank him with a heavy heart. I am indebted to Richard Moulson and Ken Biggle for helping me track down rare books and magazines, and to Stephen Swords for many stimulating conversations about SF. Gary K. Wolfe and James Gunn offered insightful feedback that improved my manuscript, and my editors Marika Christofides and Willis Goth Regier have been a wellspring of guidance and support. Special thanks to Staci and Anastazy—my magnificent mainstays in life—for their help, encouragement, and patience.

ALFRED BESTER

INTRODUCTION

ALFRED BESTER
The Insider's Outsider

Like Isaac Asimov and Robert A. Heinlein, Alfred Morton Bester (December 18, 1913–September 30, 1987) began his career in science fiction as a pulp fictioneer and finished it as a Grand Master, but he followed a far more curious path to the field's highest honor than either of his big-name contemporaries. He focused on SF only intermittently during his nearly fifty years as a professional writer and, at times, maintained few ties with the field. He started his career in SF and finished it there as well, but in between, he kept to a pattern of voyage and return, putting SF aside for two extended intervals, first to script comics, radio mysteries, and teleplays and later to work as a magazine columnist and editor. Even during his most concentrated burst of activity in SF, the fifties, he resembled broad-based writers with close ties to the arts-and-entertainment industry such as Charles Beaumont, Richard Matheson, and William F. Nolan more so than a dyed-in-the-wool SF author, and his output remained fairly small by the field's standards. However, his work from that decade proved definitive, including not one but two landmark novels: *The Demolished Man* (1953), an SF–murder-mystery hybrid that won the first-ever Hugo Award for Best Novel, and *The Stars My Destination* (1956), a sleekly savage and adult space opera that gained a cult following among readers and a reputation in some circles as the "single greatest SF novel" ever written.[1] Widely revered for their splendor of invention and stylistic innovation, these novels alone assured Bester a lasting place in the annals of post–World War II SF, but he also penned a string of brilliantly conceived and widely anthologized short stories during the same period. Perhaps the most celebrated of these, "Fondly Fahrenheit" (1954), accomplished a blackly deranged but wholly logical circumvention of Asimov's Three Laws of Robotics, using mixed point of view to portray a murderous instance of human-android projection.

If these contributions to the field during the fifties made Bester's name, his reputation nonetheless remained that of an outsider. Even before Bester's second hiatus from SF, Damon Knight still afforded him rather less than professional standing in the field, likening him to a "hobbyist" constructing teetering but elegant art out of the genre's refuse; and during the next decade, on similar grounds, Sam Moskowitz classed him as an "admired dilettante" rather than a major writer.[2] But over time and partly in his absence, Bester's reputation grew into more than just that of an outsider: he became the quintessential insider's outsider. Movers and shakers among later generations of writers—Michael Moorcock, Samuel R. Delany, Harlan Ellison, M. John Harrison, William Gibson, and Bruce Sterling, among them—came to regard Bester's work as pivotal to SF's development, as a harbinger of movements ranging from New Wave to the seventies space-opera revival to cyberpunk and beyond. Brian W. Aldiss once placed him on a short list of "mad" writers whose unique creative energy had hit the field with an electrifying jolt.[3] By some accounts, the beat and pulse of Bester's fiction entered into the very lifeblood of SF. In the eighties, Michael Bishop asserted that young SF authors with little or no knowledge of Bester nonetheless absorbed his influence indirectly, often at several removes, and K. W. Jeter claimed that just about every "new thing" in SF stemmed at least in part from cyclical rediscoveries of Bester's work.[4] More recently, Barry N. Malzberg neatly encapsulated such lavish appraisals of Bester's impact. He suggested that if Bester were removed from the history of science fiction, the resulting void would be on par with the one that would be left by the erasure of legendary editor John W. Campbell Jr.'s legacy. According to Malzberg, without Bester, the "innovative and progressive edge of science fiction" would be virtually unimaginable as it existed during the latter half of the twentieth century. It is telling that even in the midst of such extravagant praise, Malzberg also emphasized Bester's outsider status, portraying his work as "still marginalized," a bright but underappreciated beacon on the periphery of the field, recognized by a select few.[5] Remarks such as Malzberg's make it almost unnecessary to say that when Bester returned to SF during the final stage of his career, he found himself to be SF's favorite antihero, a wayward talent welcomed back into the Hall of the Greats.

* * *

In thinking about Bester's career, the notion of the outsider effect—that the introduction of an outsider into a group often shakes things up in a productive way—is especially appropriate. It provides a framework for understanding not only the reception of Bester's most influential work but also Bester's disposition as a writer when he decided to return to the field during a bout of mid-career crisis. In the late forties, as Bester made the transition from radio to the new medium of television, he felt increasingly hemmed in as a script writer; more and more often, he submitted story ideas that producers and watchful sponsors rejected as too novel or demanding for mainstream audiences. Although Bester was a seasoned professional who understood markets all too well, his frustration with such artistic limitations began to spill over. He wanted to write for the sake of creative release rather than for a core audience. In consequence, he turned to SF, his "first love," as an imaginative outlet.[6] Having been an avid fan of SF in his youth, a writer for the pulps during the late thirties and early forties, and an on-again, off-again reader of the genre throughout his adult life, Bester was quite familiar with the idiom of science fiction but also at a remove from it. He brought valuable skills with him from comics, radio, and television—including a highly developed sense of pacing, a flair for both comic and hard-boiled dialogue, and a strongly visual approach to narrative—and he combined them with his own freewheeling imagination. To boot, he had a hip, iconoclastic New York attitude. Bester was perhaps the ideal outsider to crash the gates of Golden

Bester circa 1953. First published in *The Demolished Man*, Shasta, 1953.

Age SF, and an unhappy encounter with John W. Campbell himself would further solidify that status.

Bester's most significant stories from the forties, including "Adam and No Eve" (1941) and "Hell Is Forever" (1942), appeared under Campbell's editorial auspices, and when Bester ended his first hiatus from SF by writing the short story "Oddy and Id" (1950), he naturally picked up where he had left off, submitting it to *Astounding*. In turn, Campbell accepted the manuscript and invited Bester to his office in New Jersey for a story conference. Bester held Campbell in the highest regard and relished the chance to meet him for the first time, but within minutes of arriving at Campbell's office, his attitude toward the "Great Man" would change drastically. As Bester told the story of their meeting, it was a fiasco. Bester had sent Campbell a story based on Freud's notion of the id as an unconscious seat of desire, a theme no radio or TV show he wrote for would let him fully explore. Campbell, much in the thrall of L. Ron Hubbard's forthcoming *Dianetics*, more or less greeted Bester by informing him that Hubbard's ideas had wholly discredited modern psychology. When Bester took pause, Campbell pressured him to read a chunk of galley proofs from Hubbard's manuscript on the spot, and Bester did—at first carefully, then halfheartedly, and finally inattentively, just moving his eyes across the page to keep up the illusion of reading. According to Bester, matters went downhill from there. At lunch, Campbell urged him to use the principles of Dianetics to purge his mental blocks and trace his emotional traumas back to the very womb, a request that left Bester somewhere between dismayed and bemused. As one might expect, when the two got down to business after lunch, Campbell asked him to remove all the allusions to Freud in "Oddy and Id," including the one in the title. Although Bester saw psychology as one of the most exciting avenues for the development of SF and the requested edits as "absurd," he recognized right away that the changes affected the story only superficially. Wanting a quick escape, he consented to them and, as he put it, "got the hell out of there."[7] The story appeared in *Astounding* under Campbell's title, "The Devil's Invention" (1950), sans Freudian references, but when Everett F. Bleiler and T. E. Dikty bought the story for *The Best Science Fiction Stories: 1951*, Bester took advantage of the reprint to revert to the original version—and with that token of refusal, he parted ways with Campbell for good.

Bester perhaps overreacted. As Harry Warner Jr. would later point out in response to Bester's anecdote, Campbell was widely known to make a sport of subjecting people to odd and eccentric opinions in order to get a rise out of them.[8] There is little doubt, however, that Bester's meeting with Campbell occurred at exactly the wrong moment for Bester. In returning to SF, Bester had hoped to gain a freer hand and a sympathetic ear but instead came up against an overzealous blue pencil. In reflecting on this incident later in his career, Bester pointed out that as a reader, he would always "worship" Campbell for his historic role in advancing science fiction; but he also made it clear that as a writer, he never sang Campbell's praises again. In fact, he admitted that after meeting Campbell, he grew "contemptuous" of him and that, on that basis, a mutual sense of "*antipatico*" developed between them.[9] Bester accepted the lion's share of blame for the continuance of this antipathy, but that very gesture underscores that he, of his own accord, took up an adversarial position in relation to the most powerful editor in the field. In a step few dedicated SF writers could afford to take, Bester simply shunned the *Astounding* market throughout the 1950s. Fortunately for him, new and edgy markets such as *The Magazine of Fantasy and Science Fiction* and *Galaxy* welcomed old hands with fresh takes on the genre, writers such as himself, Theodore Sturgeon, and Edgar Pangborn. As Bester shifted his focus toward these emerging markets, he took on the role of outsider in earnest, finding there the freedom to make his fiction, more than ever, a self-conscious commentary on specific aspects of the SF tradition.

⋆ ⋆ ⋆

Bester's fiction during the middle stage of his career most clearly bears out this point, but his essays on SF from the fifties provide a helpful point of departure in understanding his approach, not in the least because they obviously criticize the brand of so-called engineering SF closely associated with Campbell's *Astounding*. Bester, it should be noted, came late to critiques of SF of this sort. He arrived on the SF scene amid voices not only clamoring that SF was "growing up" but also debating just where Campbell and *Astounding* stood in relation to that process. In point of fact, in February 1949, well before Bester met with Campbell about "Oddy and Id," Rog Phillips opened his popular "Club House" column for *Amazing Stories* with the quip, "Everywhere you hear that science fiction is growing up, whatever that means," and then went on to say that the idea had been repeated so often and so incongruously that it had started to sound almost "meaningless."[10]

The backstory of the debate Phillips mentions is necessary context for understanding Bester's essays on SF, and perhaps fittingly, Campbell himself launched the first sally in that debate. Not long after he took the helm of *Astounding* in October 1937, he outlined his editorial policy in a short speech, which associate editor R. V. Happel read in his stead at the Third Eastern Science Fiction Convention in Philadelphia later that fall. After taking a moment to dispel an unkind rumor about the circumstances of F. Orlin Tremaine's departure from the editor's chair, Campbell's speech went straight to the heart of the matter, indicating that by way of "gradual change," he hoped to nudge *Astounding*, and possibly the field as a whole, in a "more adult" direction.[11]

Needless to say, he accomplished this goal admirably, demanding plausible science and extrapolation, lived-in backgrounds, and rounder characters from his writers. Asimov once pithily captured the nature of Campbell's intervention in the field by suggesting that he had single-handedly "blotted out the purple of pulp."[12]

From the mid-forties on, however, there was a sense that SF approached a new watershed moment. The field, to be sure, stood increasingly in tension with Campbell's science-centric vision. A common observation of the time—namely that advances in science and technology followed ever closer on the heels of the SF imagination and might soon outstrip it—pointed toward an underlying concern that Campbell's approach was slowly but surely painting SF into a corner. Perhaps surprisingly given his later reputation as a staunch member of the old guard, Donald A. Wollheim was among the first to issue a challenge to the paradigm Campbell had played a central role in establishing. In the introduction to his pioneering anthology *Novels of Science* (1945), he commented on the rapid rate of scientific and technological change, asserting that the "racing minds of writers" could "barely keep ahead" of such developments—but he did not stop there. Despite the prominence of "science" in the title of his anthology, Wollheim concluded that this encroachment of science fact on science fiction ultimately meant very little because the best SF dealt "first with mankind itself, rather than with machinery" anyway. For him, clever gadgetry and "believable prognostication" mattered less than exploring the human dimensions of scientific and social change. The future of the field, he asserted, lay not in the direction of action-adventure and scientific thrillers such as those written by "Robert A. Heinlein, A. E. van Vogt, and John W. Campbell"—however entertaining those might be—but in that of stories and novels that "set the reader thinking along concepts vaster than his own petty life." According to Wollheim, British writers such as H. G. Wells and Olaf Stapledon had led the way in producing SF of notable emotional texture, social insight, and cosmic perspective, but American (or, in the latter case, American-based) authors such as H. P. Lovecraft and John Taine had also followed suit in addressing adult themes.[13] That *Novels of Science* would appear as part of the esteemed Viking Portable Library surely influenced Wollheim's selection and outlook, but his views went beyond playing up SF's literary value to satisfy an upmarket publisher and audience. He had his finger on SF's pulse, and only a couple of years later, Campbell himself would agree that it was "man, not the idea or machine," that held the greatest interest for readers of the genre.[14]

Despite this concession, Campbell's editorial policy remained much the same throughout the forties, and the perception of *Astounding* as calcifying and in decline became entrenched in some quarters. In a column in the August 1949 issue of the *Bloomington News Letter*, Redd Boggs mourned the passing of the "golden age" of *Astounding* and the magazine's leveling off into middle-of-the-road fare full of "ideas and scientific doubletalk" that was utterly lacking in "human interest." From Boggs's point of view, even if *Astounding* catered to "technicians and Oak Ridge scientists," Campbell would do well to cultivate a lineup of regulars who were "fiction writers first, and technologists on the side, rather than the other way around." Such a shift in focus, Boggs implied, might even return *Astounding* to its former glory—or at least restore its relevance for a readership he suspected of having "grown up" since the magazine's heyday from 1939 to 1943.[15] Another commentator, William Hines, positioned *Astounding* as a key player in SF's coming-of-age story but not as the locus of the genre's greatest maturity. In "Belles-Lettres Go out of This World as Science Fiction Grows Up," he credited *Astounding* with introducing sound science into the field but portrayed the fledgling *Fantasy and Science Fiction* as the magazine "most significant from the literary point of view."[16] Naturally, Campbell's vision for SF also had its staunch defenders. Phillips's "Club House" column, which represented the chatter about SF growing up as so much empty buzz, fell into this category. Phillips acknowledged the anxiety most commonly associated with Campbell's speculative-science approach—that science would simply pass SF by, stripping it of its ability to create a sense of wonder—but he met that concern head on. After reiterating Campbell's notion that science-fictional extrapolation could serve as a prologue to scientific discovery, he added the caveat that as science forged ahead and the SF tradition grew more complex, some avenues for extrapolation narrowed or closed altogether, making the job of the writer a whole lot harder. For Phillips, that was what growing up meant—a predictable raising of the bar in the field as it matured.[17]

* * *

Enter Bester, by all appearances itching for a fight. He weighed in on the idea of SF growing up in "The Trematode: A Critique of Modern Science-Fiction" (1953), an essay ostensibly addressed to the SF world at large but arguably shaking a finger at Campbell specifically. Bester's assessment of the field leaned in the direction of Wollheim's, but he bared his teeth and got down to the nitty-gritty details of craft. Characteristically, rather than accepting the premise that SF was growing up, Bester took a waggish and polemical stance, focusing on SF's unnecessarily prolonged adolescence, or what he dubbed its "Three Immaturities." The first of these, intellectual immaturity, he chalked up to an unsavory enthusiasm for "fads" and "nostrums," adding ironically, "I need mention no names"—and indeed, he did not, given the scandal then surrounding Campbell's championing of Dianetics.[18] The second and third of these immaturities, the emotional and technical, Bester linked to a type of SF that prided itself on scientific "extrapolation" but took "refuge in science to the detriment of its fiction" (15–17). In Bester's view, SF of this stripe encouraged readers to make science—rather than emotionally developed characters—the main point of identification, and it also leaned on science like a crutch in terms of plotting, employing it more often than not as a bogus means of resolution. As a result, such SF broke little new ground in terms of technique despite the robust possibilities of the genre itself, and in essence, it pandered to the willfully escapist reader. Once again, fairly or not, Bester presumably made Campbell his target. In 1947, Campbell had used the phrase "prophetic extrapolation" to distinguish SF from fantasy, and afterward, "extrapolation" was popularly associated with him and *Astounding*, a fact Bester himself recognized later in his career when he said in cutting tones that Campbell had "used the word like he owned it."[19]

In Bester's view, at their worst, these three immaturities interlocked in a pattern of arrested development. Intellectual naiveté led to escapist scientism, which in turn stifled craft opportunities. Bester singled out for special censure the scientist-hero so common to the pages of *Astounding*, the "One Man with the One Invention," arguing that far too much of the science in science fiction still rested on the cracked narrative foundations of thirties super-science—on thinly-conceived "supermanism," "supermachinism," or some mixture of the two (15–16). Whether realized in Van Vogt's superman, Heinlein's messianic figure, or the unabashed optimism of gadget SF, these one-man-to-save-the-world and science-as-talisman plot devices amounted, for Bester, to prefabricated dei ex machina—to pointless exercises in self-fulfilling prophecy. They involved readers in forms of secondhand wish fulfillment but did little more than that. To Bester's way of thinking, the pervasive effects of World War II propaganda—a lingering mentality of "popular villainism"—was partly to blame for this state of affairs (16), but writers and editors in the field had also ridden the wave of SF's "novelty" rather than tackling adult themes suited to its "maturing" audience (21). This complacency had fostered insularity, or a tendency among many writers and readers alike to treat SF like a cozy, privately owned enclave that afforded prescribed thrills and spills but few genuine opportunities for measured reflection.

Bester's essay reads like an arm-chair psychiatric evaluation of engineering SF, one that pronounces it neurotic—a self-serving and unrealistic way of viewing the world and humanity's place in it. According to Bester, this variety of SF rarely acknowledged that "the universe is most probably entirely indifferent to our aims, ideals and fears, to our virtues and sins; and, what is more, should be" (15). Undeniably, as a critic, Bester did not have a pleasant bedside manner—Knight would a few years later label him the "caustic satirist of neurotic science fiction"—but in effect, he turned the debate about SF coming of age around one hundred and eighty degrees.[20] If scientific advance had nipped at the heels of SF, SF in Bester's account rode on its coattails, counting on the wider interest in new technologies to hook its audience. If SF writers and editors had once pushed SF toward the leading edge of imagination, they now balked as the field experienced growing pains, hanging back in the well-established comfort zone of the juvenile market. SF readers had grown up, but on average, the genre lagged behind, too often vexed by an "inability to understand human beings on an adult level" (17). Bester covered quite a bit of ground but emphasized this last point—the need for adult themes—above all else.

Bester, it is important to note, knowingly cultivated his status as an outsider in this essay—and not only in relation to engineering-style SF but also to the field in general. He closed the essay with a striking image of SF as a trematode that had wriggled its way into the minds of its readers, including his. At once grotesque and comic in its reversal of expectations, this comparison of SF to a parasitic worm conveyed Bester's ambivalence about SF, placing him among the infected but not quite in the camp of the devoted. It also underscored his opinion that SF approached a make-or-break developmental threshold. A trematode infests a mollusk and either spoils it or forces it to produce a pearl. From Bester's standpoint, only time would tell whether SF would yield a lustrous gem or turn to rot, succumbing to what he personally saw as its own self-incurred immaturity. He had his doubts but, for his part, hoped for the pearl (22).

Not surprisingly, "Trematode" won Bester few friends. Although it originally appeared as the introduction to *The Best SF of the Year: 1953*, the editors buried it at the back of the volume in later reprintings. Even *Fantasy and Science Fiction* editor Anthony "Tony" Boucher, one of Bester's most enthusiastic allies, disliked it intensely and told Bester that it made him sound like "[Arthur] Koestler & the other outsiders" who generalized about a narrow sliver of SF as though it represented the whole.[21] But Bester stood by it. He refused to quarrel with Boucher about it because he said they sounded like two parents arguing about how best to discipline a dearly loved child, and he explained away his rigid attitude, saying that, if anything, it suggested he in fact loved "the baby more."[22]

* * *

Bester revisited this line of argument about a year and a half later, in a 1955 guest editorial for *Science Fantasy*. He once again commented on the future of the field but, because he wrote the editorial during an extended visit to the United Kingdom, he helpfully recast his ideas in the context of the American and British SF scenes, adopting a very evenhanded tone. In a somewhat tongue-in-cheek comparison, he suggested that each of these SF cultures closely reflected its milieu. Americans he portrayed as upstarts, a "nervous, high-strung people, anxious, insecure, generous but confused, eager to get places but not exactly sure where."[23] As such, American SF brimmed with movement and apprehension and, to make up for a lack of clear bearings, fetishized answers. It exceled at exciting readers, but its constant chasing after "definitive prophecy" and "pat answers" often left readers who valued richly developed ideas or characters dissatisfied (4). By contrast, Brits possessed a deeper and more staid sense of cultural heritage, and in consequence, British SF showed greater self-assurance. It moved at a more relaxed pace, lingering over questions of character and giving readers opportunities to contemplate the finer points of human behavior. Its maturity in this area had nevertheless fostered a weakness. In Bester's view, British writers tended to approach plotting with diffidence, working over standard plots for new bits of meaning rather than reinventing them (3–4).

As in the case of his "Trematode" essay, Bester's editorial is of interest as much for its subtexts as its surface statements. Bester could not but assume the stance of an outsider with respect to British SF, but he also distanced himself from what he saw as the mainstream of SF in the United States. He boiled it down to one of his incisive mock equations: M + P = A, or Man plus Problem equals the Answer. Bester's equation is best understood in the context of a comment Frederik Pohl once made about the state of magazine SF in the United States before the launch of *Galaxy* in 1950: "Problems were meant to be solved. There were always solutions, once you found the right scientist to look for them, and when a problem was solved it stayed solved. Its solution did not generate new problems."[24] Bester clearly meant his equation as a crude approximation of this sort of SF, the sort associated with the problem-solving scientist-heroes and scientific rationalism of Campbell's *Astounding*. His own fiction—including a *New Worlds'* reprint of "Disappearing Act" (1953) likely to be fresh in the minds of many U.K. readers—plainly did not show such a "tendency to reduce life to round numbers" (4). Instead, it sought after ambiguity, whether it be moral, psychological, or literary. Incidentally, even though Bester considered British SF to be more mature than its American counterpart, he remained partial to the American style and gainsaid any desire to crossbreed the traditions. He preferred that the two cultures remain "friendly rivals" and, by implication, that American SF be allowed to move forward on its own terms (5).

This last point is worth dwelling on. However much Bester distanced his approach from the style of SF associated with Campbell's *Astounding*, he sought no hard-and-fast break with the broader imperatives of the American tradition. He relished its bustling and overheated plotting and the entertainment value stemming from its action-adventure and thriller elements. His trademark antihero, sometimes referred to as the "Besterman," shared characteristics with the superman, as the critical catchword implies.[25] He produced dynamic and memorable characters but, despite his interest in psychology, shied away from lyrically rendered portraits of characters' interiority. He reveled in restless invention and made use of gadgets and McGuffins with the best of them—"Rhodopsin Ionizer" flash grenades and "PyrE" demonstrate that. That said, pointing out that Bester's approach in some ways intersected with the broader contours of American style is not a way to downplay his difference but to highlight it. What Bester brought to SF was not a radically new template but an idiosyncratic self-reflexivity about the writing and reading protocols of the genre—about how stories were being told and consumed. To him, that was what it meant for SF to grow up, a shift in point of view.

* * *

As Bester himself declared in a speech from the same period, he was not a crusader for change.[26] He simply called it as he saw it and went his own way. His way involved cultivating a self-conscious narrative style, one stemming in part from his admiration of decadent and modernist fiction in the vein of J. K. Huysmans's *À Rebours* and James Joyce's *Ulysses*, but also playing off of SF's own built-in tradition of self-referentiality. Bester pushed his fiction in the direction of literary satire and metafiction, producing stories that at once recycled, reimagined, and commented on the machinery and motifs of genre SF. Take, for instance, Bester's account of the genesis of the time-paradox story "Of Time and Third Avenue" (1951). Later in his career, Bester indicated that he wrote it out of irritation with clichéd plots in which a book or newspaper is mysteriously displaced into the past and brings with it not only dreams of wealth and power but also a curse, either foresight of the recipient's death or some equally miserable circumstance. According to Bester, he set out to handle this story pattern definitively. He even implied that he wanted to use it up in the process, to generate new problems that would make it hard for any writer after him to take it up, especially idly. By his account, he failed to recomplicate the plot to that degree, but his pursuit of this goal is still instructive.[27] He courted a different kind of comprehension and consumption, writing especially for readers who knew SF reading protocols well—who could take pleasure in watching a writer read between the lines of the idiom and reflect their own knowledge of the genre back to them in unexpected and challenging ways.

It is tempting to discuss Bester primarily as a stylist, one of a different sort than Sturgeon or Ray Bradbury, but as a stylist nonetheless. However, much like these other notables of his generation, Bester's broader vision encompassed more than the sum of its stylistic parts. Bester made no bones about aiming first and foremost to entertain readers, or even about dealing in shock and dazzlement, but he also concerned himself with the reader's agency in an uncommon way. He thought that the "mature fan" of SF, by which he meant a reader steeped in the genre's idiom, deserved an experience resembling that of a theatergoer, who "shares a play in its making." Escapist fiction, which Bester associated with reader passivity, barred such sharing, offering up little more than a place to "communicate with un-dead things," mere revenants of SF's past. For his part, he wanted to write "arrest" fiction, or open texts "full of romantic curiosity and impractical speculation" that left ample opportunity for the reader to cogenerate meaning and thereby experience the euphoria of raw imagination—to experience a feeling akin to what he felt while writing.[28] Bester very likely adapted this idea from one of his favorite authors, Leo Tolstoy, who made a similar argument in *What Is Art?* (1897), but Roland Barthes later coined a term that better captures the drift of Bester's argument. Barthes would describe open texts as "writable" rather than merely "readable," and note that their openness depended on a writer not only consciously fostering a certain level of meaningful indeterminacy in a text but also engaging in a kind of knowing parry-and-thrust with readers' expectations for a particular genre.[29] This excess within the text was a risk for the writer—it recognized the reader as a free and individual agent in resolving narrative ambiguities—but it also served as a possible source of heightened pleasure for that very reason.

Bester brought precisely this sort of writable quality to his SF. On the one hand, he chipped away at the easy, capital-A answer. Far from a catch-all means of plot resolution, science generally functioned as a metaphor in his work, often for the inexplicable or irrational, as in the case of Bester's use of π to figure pattern compulsion in "The Pi Man" (1959). His fiction fostered and did not neatly resolve psychological ambiguities; it instead focused the reader's attention on them, leaving plenty of questions to be asked and answered based on the reader's line of identification. Both his use of mixed-viewpoint narration in "Fondly Fahrenheit" and his doubling of hero Lincoln Powell and antihero Ben Reich in *The Demolished Man* attest to that. On the other hand, he bent genre expectations in all kinds of thought-provoking ways. He undertook surprising reversals of common assumptions, from making the visceral creativity of the poet, not the specialized knowledge of the scientist, the only way to end a world war in "Disappearing Act" to undercutting pretty much every power fantasy associated with time travel in "The Men Who Murdered Mohammed" (1958). He experimented with formal techniques, including parallax, pastiche, and synesthesia, as a means of distorting reading protocols, particularly those associated with narrative time, as in the case of *The Stars My Destination*. Bester sometimes even half buried metafictional elements in his fiction, just deep enough to become inside jokes with savvy readers. The tribe of Scientific People, whose naive worship of scientific relics in *Stars* so belies their name, was this type of gambit, gently satirizing what Bester saw as the all-too-common tendency of some SF writers to treat science as a magic talisman and of certain readers to accept it as such. Bester walked a fine line between parody and pastiche, poking fun at and paying homage to the SF idiom all at once. He hijacked readymade genre machinery, turning it to novel ends time and again, and he prided himself on achieving this sort of dislocation within genre writing's imperative to entertain, viewing the distinction between the "serious" and working writer as little more than a "portentous concept of the literary establishment."[30]

Of course, Bester was not ploughing a lonely furrow. Many others in the field were also writing against the limits, so to speak—so much so that Mike Ashley has suggested that the "early fifties were just as much a Golden Age as the early forties, possibly more so."[31] Newly launched magazines and expanding markets for hardcovers, paperback originals, and anthologies fostered this swell of creativity, but at the heart of it lay a larger trend toward recomplication of the genre, one which found expression in the work of an oddly incongruous assembly of writers: newcomers such as Philip K. Dick, Philip José Farmer, Walter M. Miller Jr., Robert Sheckley, and Judith Merril; mid-career standouts such as C. M. Kornbluth and Frederik Pohl; and transforming veterans such as Sturgeon and Pangborn, to note just a few signal examples of change in the American context. Perhaps more so than any SF writer of this period, Bester brought to his writing a measured sense of excess, of operating all at once inside and outside of the specialized idiom of genre SF.

Bester's SF has an overdetermined quality, one similar in effect to bricolage. Bester paid little heed to the supposed divide between literary and popular fiction, and proved eclectic in his range of allusion, but he also consciously played off of genre SF's sense of identification with a subculture, engaging in what Umberto Eco has called the purposeful "extra-coding" of metatexts.[32] The asteroid-cum-space habitat occupied by the Scientific People in *Stars* provides a ready example of this practice. It is drawn just as much from a pulp story, such as John Beynon Harris's "Exiles on Asperus" (1933), as from the grand academy of Lagado in Jonathan Swift's *Gulliver's Travels* (1726), and the result is electric—at once comic and serious, familiar and strange. Bester's writing crackled with this sort of excess, with an atmospheric intertextuality capable of inflecting reading protocols and drawing readers (and other writers) into a dialogue about the genre itself. Although Bester employed extra-coding less as a distancing mechanism than later writers, his pioneering work straddled the boundary between the markets for genre SF and contemporary fiction in a revelatory way and stood in the lineage of later writable SF—especially novels such as Anthony Burgess's *A Clockwork Orange* (1962) and Thomas M. Disch's *Camp Concentration* (1968), both of which focused intently on reading protocols and the reader's agency, employing self-conscious narration to elicit self-conscious reading, even to force rereading.

CHAPTER 1

BEGINNINGS
Early Life and First Stories

Bester's story as an outsider writer, perhaps not surprisingly, began with the pedigree of an insider. In fact, he witnessed the birth of genre SF firsthand. Although only twelve years old at the time, he was "hungry for ideas" and searching for imaginative outlets suited to his curious turn of mind but struggling hard to find them. He even remembered borrowing Andrew Lang's *Blue* and *Red* fairy books from the library and sneaking them home under his coat, feeling self-conscious about reading fairy tales at his age.[1] Then, in April 1926, the first issue of Hugo Gernsback's trailblazing *Amazing Stories* debuted on newsstands, and Bester's eyes opened wide. He would later characterize the emergence of the science fiction magazine as a major cultural event that was, in its own way, every bit "as revolutionary as the talkies" of the same era. No one who learned to read afterward, he once remarked, could fully understand "what a gap science fiction filled" for his generation, "what an imaginative need it answered."[2]

In some respects, Bester's initial encounter with SF followed a common pattern, one documented anecdotally by a host of writers and fans over the years: he fell for SF hard and fast and young. However, his origins story differs instructively from those of other writers of roughly the same era, as the examples of Frederik Pohl and Damon Knight serve to demonstrate. On the one hand, a ten-year-old Pohl took just one look at the sensational art on the cover of a pulp magazine and saw in SF a form of escape from grim, Depression-era realities. On the other, Knight was drawn in by stories that extrapolated scientific trends into the future and stirred feelings of awe and wonder. Both Pohl and Knight characterized SF as an all-consuming addiction. Bester, by contrast, thought of SF as a gateway. He admired it for its ability to serve as an "agar for thought" and open up a larger "world of ideas."[3] Not long after he discovered SF, his nightstand was piled high with reading, not only an assortment of science fiction magazines but also books ranging from Sir Isaac Newton's *Principia* (1687) to Nikolai Gogol's *Dead Souls* (1842) to Camille Flammarion's *Mysterious Psychic Forces* (1907) and well beyond. Bester cut his teeth on science fiction, as far as ideas went, and he would never forget the excitement of that moment or the importance of SF to his intellectual development.

Bester's outlook perhaps seems unremarkable, a variation of the commonplace notion of SF as a literature of ideas, but his understanding of the genre grew out of an early fixation on the Renaissance thinker, the *Homo Universalis* with a broad range of intellectual interests and expertise. Bester once placed his idealization of figures such as Leonardo da Vinci and Michelangelo into context by relating a series of incidents that occurred in his youth, some of which involved—much to his parents' dismay—the conversion of household objects into raw materials for projects. When a piece of linoleum flooring came loose, he turned it into moveable type and quietly allowed its disappearance to be blamed on the housecleaner. He destroyed his family's Victor phonograph by using it as a potter's wheel and, in an effort to start up the Bester Barometer Corporation, fashioned weatherglasses out of water-filled light bulbs. He ruined yards and yards of wrapping paper composing symphonies with a hole-punch, wrote a verse history of the Spanish Armada that his sixth-grade teacher scoffed at because of his messy handwriting, and made a plaster-of-Paris life mask of a friend, who did not undergo the process without real danger of suffocation. Almost needless to say, his veneration for Renaissance thinkers also led him to more conventional pursuits such as chess and microscopy, and in 1925, soon after witnessing an eclipse from the rooftop of his New York City apartment building, he developed what became a lifelong fascination with astronomy and telescopic instrumentation. Bester was, in his own words, a "Renaissance kid."[4] It is not surprising that when Gernsback's *Amazing Stories* came along, with its emphasis on popularizing science, invention, and new ideas in general, Bester found in it a lively counterpart to his varied interests—or that he came to view SF as a Renaissance genre, as a medium especially suited to mixing and marrying various influences and branches of knowledge.

Bester's preoccupation with the Renaissance thinker inflected not only his view of SF but also his early intellectual trajectory in general. He was raised in a middle-class Jewish family with a lax attitude toward religion. His father James had grown up in Chicago, a city that Bester described as having "no time for the God bit," and his mother Isabelle was a convert to Christian Science. In light of their own unorthodox views, his parents gave him the option of choosing his own faith. Not without an early hint of contrarian humor, he settled on a common precept of Renaissance thought: Natural Law.[5] As a pre-med student majoring in zoology at the University of Pennsylvania, Bester ran up against what he remembered as the "grim specialist days of the early thirties," but for his own part, he bucked the norm of specialization. He elected as many classes as possible in art, music, and psychology and recalled hurrying from science labs to his other classes, feeling self-conscious about the lingering scent of formaldehyde and sulfur-dioxide on his clothes.[6] Outside of the classroom, he ran himself ragged with extracurricular activities. He served as moderator of the campus Philomathean Society and president of the cartooning club; joined the German, economics, and drama clubs; and chased after varsity letters, rowing on crew and playing football but distinguishing himself in particular at fencing, a fact of perhaps more than passing significance given that he named his most famous character "Foyle."[7] On top of all these other undertakings, he "went mad" in the library, reading anything and everything from Persian poet Ferdowsi's verse epic *Shahnameh* (ca. 1010) to French novelist Anatole France's satirical fantasy *Penguin Island* (1908).[8] Looking back on this period, Bester admitted not only to spreading himself too thin but also to graduating from Penn in 1935 without high-enough test scores to attend medical school. (Apparently, he did not suffer this fate alone. His senior yearbook noted that on December 7, 1934, the "Pre-Med Seniors took their examination," and as a result, there would soon "be a bunch of lawyers."[9]) As it turned out, Bester did go on to study law, entering the program at Columbia University in the fall of 1936 and transferring to New York University the following year, but despite the rigors of law school, which he enjoyed, he ultimately decided that law did not suit him. In his own words, he was "just stalling" because he did not know what he wanted to do with his life.[10] When all was said and done, Bester's college experience had fostered an intellectual versatility that would later serve him well as a writer, but it left him somewhat at a loose end, working in advertising.

Bester's attitude toward SF changed in important ways during college. He had continued to read the genre regularly but felt that the magazines' horizons were shrinking at the same time that his own were expanding. His Renaissance ideal, in other words, became a kind of measuring stick for SF. Bester understood the emergence of Buck Rogers–style space opera in the late twenties and knockoffs of it such as Anthony Gilmore's Hawk Carse series in the early thirties as unfortunate signs of the field's "dissolution into pulp."[11] Fiction of this type often featured clean-cut heroes who were bare-knuckled champions of humanity and so indistinguishable from one another that Bester derisively lumped them all together under the alias "Brick Malloy," an amalgam of the names of William Ritt's comic-strip space adventurer Brick Bradford and Lester Dent's crime-solving Chance Malloy. As Bester remembered it, some fare of this sort merely borrowed formulas from pulp Westerns, translating cattle ranches into alien planets and rustlers into space pirates. The very worst of it oozed with paranoia or racism that left him cold. To his way of thinking, it was this broader watering down of the genre, even more so than Gernsback's questionable emphasis on SF as popular science, that gave birth to the SF ghetto. He did still observe high points in the field—he cited Stanley G. Weinbaum's "A Martian Odyssey" (1934) as one of them—and he also enjoyed the grand-scale "blood and thunder" of E. E. "Doc" Smith's Skylark and Lensman series despite feeling guilty about reading them.[12] However, his most important reading experiences occurred outside the pages of the SF magazines. He would later note offbeat speculations such as Olaf Stapledon's *Last and First Men* and *Odd John*, and the fiction of fin de siècle and modernist writers such as J. K. Huysmans and James Joyce as his major influences during this period.

After school, as Bester put it, he "drifted into writing." He tried his hand at SF because he liked reading it, knew its idiom, and mistakenly believed it would be "easy to write."[13] In 1938, while still working at a publicity office, the twenty-five-year-old Bester submitted an unsolicited manuscript titled "Diaz-X" to Standard Magazines. It ended up in the hands of Mort Weisinger and Jack Schiff, two editors at *Thrilling Wonder Stories*, and when the three of them met to discuss Bester's manuscript, they hit it off because of their shared interest in Joyce's *Ulysses*, which the idealistic Bester had recently read and would "preach . . . enthusiastically without provocation, to their great amusement."[14] A couple of years earlier, Standard Magazines had bought the unprofitable *Wonder Stories* from Hugo Gernsback, adding it to its existing line of "Thrilling" titles aimed at the juvenile market, and according to legendary literary agent and comics editor Julius Schwartz, Weisinger not only liked Bester's story, he envisioned it as the basis for a promotion that could both boost the magazine's circulation and launch the young writer's career. His plan was to partner with the Science Fiction League, whose list of executive directors included Forrest J. Ackerman, Edmond Hamilton, and Ray Cummings, among others, to run an amateur story contest with a prize of $50. According to Schwartz, Weisinger later confided to him that he had set Bester's "story aside for a while, announced the contest, and then pretended to rediscover the story as a contest entry" before declaring Bester the winner.[15] However, Bester's memory of the details differed from Schwartz's. He indicated that even though the contest was in the works before he submitted his manuscript, he did not intend "Diaz-X" as an entry. Having received no suitable submissions, Weisinger and Schiff approached him, told him his story "might fill the bill if it was whipped into shape," and helped him revise it.[16] Whatever the actual course of events leading up to its publication, the story became Bester's first in print. After being retitled "The Broken Axiom," it appeared in the April 1939 issue of *Thrilling Wonder* alongside stories by notables such as Clifford D. Simak and Henry Kuttner. The "Meet the Author" boxout announcing Bester as the contest winner left little doubt about his continuing pursuit of the Renaissance ideal. The editors listed Bester's hobbies as "telescope making, painting, photography, playwriting, composing, and interpreting James Joyce" and revealed that when they had asked him which of the arts he would pursue given a free choice, he had replied, "all seven—or however many there are."[17]

An additional circumstance surrounding Bester's first publication makes for an interesting side note. Years later, Bester interviewed Robert A. Heinlein, who revealed that a notice for the *Thrilling Wonder* contest had inspired him to write his very first story, "Life-Line" (1939). After Heinlein learned that he stood to make more money publishing his seven-thousand-word story in *Astounding*, which paid one cent a word, he submitted it there—and earned an extra $20 when John W. Campbell accepted it. At hearing this news, Bester shot back in mock anger, "You son of a bitch . . . I won that *Thrilling Wonder* contest and you beat me by $20!"[18] It is interesting to consider what might have happened had Heinlein entered the contest. Bester's story, which is about a physics professor who slips into a liminal space between realities during a failed attempt to test a matter transmitter, definitely lived up to the standards of *Thrilling Wonder*. It even pointed toward Bester's penchant for breathless suspense and psychological realism, given that it included a long interlude of altered perception. Schwartz has suggested that Bester's story, in addition to its own merits, already had the "fix" and Heinlein's "probably would have been automatically rejected."[19] However, Heinlein was somewhat older than Bester, and perhaps for that reason, "Life-Line" showed a greater maturity of theme, examining the social and economic ramifications of the invention of a machine for predicting life expectancy. Heinlein's story holds up much better today than "The Broken Axiom," and he may well have taken the prize even if Bester had an inside track. Another possibility is even more mind-boggling: that Weisinger might have declared Bester and Heinlein co-winners and discovered two of the most important SF authors of the twentieth century simultaneously.

Weisinger would publish three more of Bester's stories within the next year or so. The first of these, a short short titled "No Help Wanted," fit on a single page of the December 1939 *Thrilling Wonder* but, regardless of its brevity, saw Bester rummaging around the writer's toolbox, exploring the use of point of view in particular. The story begins with a common-enough Depression-era scenario—a displaced, unemployed man is searching for work—but it hinges on a quick reversal of the reader's expectations, revealing the narrator to be quite different from an ordinary, down-on-his-luck drifter. He is an observer from Mars grappling with the difficulties of life on a "planet of savages."[20] The second story, "Guinea Pig, Ph.D.," appeared in the March 1940 issue of *Thrilling*'s new companion magazine *Startling Stories* and resembled "The Broken Axiom" in an important way. It turned an episode of psychological disorientation into the basis for an interval of purple prose laden with swimming sounds and colors, high-pitched emotion, and exaggerated irony. In a nutshell, a biology lecturer is snatched up into another reality, where he learns he is a mere lab rat for a higher being. Both of these efforts, like "The Broken Axiom," employed universities as settings, suggesting that in his early days as a writer, Bester drew on his recent experiences as a student in conjuring up backgrounds and dialogue.

By contrast, the third story, "Voyage to Nowhere," represented a real breakthrough on at least two levels. For one, the novelette earned Bester a small byline on the cover of the July 1940 issue of *Thrilling*, and in the magazine's regular "Story Behind the Story" column, the editors announced that with their encouragement, Bester had gone on from winning the magazine's first amateur story contest to become a full-fledged staff writer. Though he rarely even saved his manuscripts, much less memorabilia related to his writing, Bester kept the cover of this issue (and a few others stamped with early credits) until late in life, as nostalgic reminders of having made the transition from amateur to professional writer.[21] The other step forward occurred at the level of craft. "Voyage" represented Bester's first foray into pastiche, a writing practice central to his approach throughout his career. Pastiche, of course, encompasses a range of practices—from relatively straightforward imitation of another work to truly transformative borrowing of techniques and motifs. In this instance, Bester leaned in the direction of imitation. As he pointed out in his author's comment, his story paid homage to Irvin S. Cobb's "Faith, Hope, and Charity." Cobb was a regionalist writer who sometimes dabbled in horror, and in his story, three international criminals meet with grisly but poetic forms of justice. As they are transported by train through a barren stretch of New Mexico, on their way to deportation, they escape only to fall prey to strange accidents that resemble the forms of capital punishment awaiting them abroad in France, Spain, and Italy. By and large, Bester merely

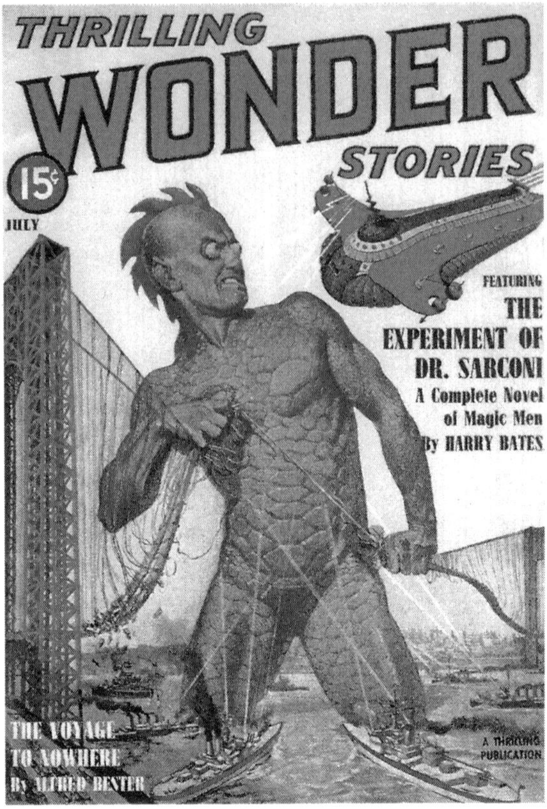

Bester's cover credit for "The Voyage to Nowhere," *Thrilling Wonder Stories*, July 1940. © Better Publications/Standard Magazines/CBS Publications.

transposed this plot into space and followed Cobb in interlacing fast-paced action with slower, accruing bits of character study meant to suffuse each criminal's comeuppance with a sense of irony. Be that as it may, Bester also elaborately fleshed out the plot with science-fictional color and content, for instance, using the prison break and ensuing chase sequence to bring into play various gadgets, space hazards, and alien landscapes, and treating the disparate origins of the fugitives as a vehicle for close description of Mercurian, Venusian, and Martian physiologies and customs. In other words, even though "Voyage" bordered on a practice that Bester later came to deplore—simple translation of existing genre plots into the SF idiom—it also showed sparks of Bester's growing talent for generous invention and the adept synthesis of SF tropes.

Between the sale and publication of "Voyage to Nowhere," Bester reached yet another professional milestone with Weisinger's help: securing an agent. Weisinger and Schwartz had co-founded a literary agency called the Solar Sales Service before Weisinger became an editor, and the two remained on friendly terms. Schwartz now represented a host of well-established science fiction and fantasy writers on both sides of the Atlantic—Weinbaum, Hamilton, Henry Kuttner, Leigh Brackett, H. P. Lovecraft, John Russell Fearn, and Eric Frank Russell, to name a few. Schwartz hardly needed to take on a relative unknown, but after Weisinger talked Bester up during a workaday lunch, describing him as a "promising and prize-winning science-fiction author" sure to "make it big in the pulps someday," he decided to take a chance on him.[22]

Bester delivered two manuscripts to Schwartz almost immediately but surprised him in the process: the stories both fell into the category of action-adventure rather than science fiction. Although taken slightly off guard, Schwartz quickly sold both manuscripts to a single editor. At the time, Raymond A. Palmer edited both *Amazing Stories* and the struggling *South Sea Stories* for Ziff-Davis, and he snapped up Bester's stories on June 28, 1940, in a frantic effort to fill out the fifth (and final) issue of the latter magazine, which ceased publication in October 1940.[23] A common editorial policy of the day decreed that no author appear in an issue's table of contents more than once, and as a result, Palmer published the novella "Treachery on Camoia" (1940) under Bester's byline and the short story "The White Man Who Was Tabu" (1940) under the pseudonym Alexander Blade, a Ziff-Davis house name used over the years by the likes of Hamilton, Robert Silverberg, John Jakes, and Randall Garrett, among others. Together, these two sales doubtless represented Bester's highest payday to date, earning him $195, the equivalent of more than $3,000 today. They perhaps also offered the earliest glimmer of Bester's career-long conception of himself as an *"everything writer."*[24]

"Treachery on Camoia" is a predictable and overwritten tale featuring a hot-tempered hero named Johnny Maverick who growls his dialogue, learns a valuable lesson, and gets the girl, and it ranks as little more than a curiosity today; but the "The White Man Who Was Tabu," at present hardly even known as Bester's work, occupies a notable place in his early output. Though it employs stock elements of the South Seas adventure—forbidden love, a race to retrieve sunken treasure, a gold-digging femme fatale, and a

Cover of *South Sea Stories*, October 1940. © Ziff-Davis Publishing Company.

Polynesian knife dance, to name a few—the story is Bester's first attempt to use depth psychology to transform the typical genre hero into an edgy antihero. It centers on a mysterious white man who has washed up on the island of Motu Atua with a scar across his forehead, unable to remember his own name, much less his origins or the circumstances that brought him there. The natives refer to him as Tane Heva, or the "man who is wrong in the head," and come to regard him as a "Sacred Hermit" because he wanders the island's jungles and beaches in isolation. He suffers from amnesia, but his thoughts reveal him to be rational, except under one circumstance.[25] In the presence of women, he shows signs of a dual personality and is overtaken by feelings of revulsion and hatred that quickly spiral into an uncontrollable urge to kill. These moments of misogynistic rage fill him with a sense of detached horror, turning him into a powerless "spectator" to the violence of the alter ego that possesses him (123); and the psychological plot takes shape around the idea that he labors under an irresistible compulsion, one mixed up with basic survival instincts and primal bloodlust in the depths of his unconscious mind.

Counter to the usual reader expectations for this type of story, action takes a backseat to psychology. The adventure plot gets underway entirely in the background. A group of whites has arrived on the island offering to buy it in exchange for a rich cargo of guns, tobacco, rum, and other goods, but readers learn of this unusual circumstance indirectly, as the native leader Laana meets with Tane Heva to ask his opinion about their proposal. Laana hopes the "mad one" might provide some insight into the motives of the strangers, but Tane Heva responds in terms that underscore his own mysterious illness and sense of personal displacement. He advises the Chief not to accept the offer for the simple reason that "It is bad not to have a home" (118). This guileless answer affects Laana deeply, and he not only concurs with Tane Heva but invites him to serve as interpreter, so that no misunderstanding occurs between his people and the whites. At this point, the psychological and adventure plots begin to build off of each other evocatively. When Tane Heva meets the strangers, especially their leader Luke Swanson, his mind roils with suspicion. Swanson calls for a Miss Marsh, and Tane Heva snaps under ballooning psychological pressure, fleeing into the jungle before she appears.

After an unspecified break in time, the narrative resumes, wholly filtered through Tane Heva's isolated viewpoint. The action plot now begins in earnest, but once again at a remove. Tane Heva thinks he hears branches snapping nearby but soon recognizes these noises as distant gunshots—lots of them—and realizes that Swanson and his crew are taking the island by force. During a series of deadly skirmishes, Tane Heva slowly regains snatches of his memory, partly with the help of Laana's daughter Nania, who reaches out to him despite the very real threat he poses to her. For the bulk of the narrative, it is difficult for the reader to know how to respond to the protagonist, who does indeed experience a psychotic break and attempt to kill his potential love interest. The ambiguity shrouding Tane Heva complicates and disrupts the possible line of identification with him even as it heightens the suspense of the action plot. Bester, in other words, purposely disturbs the relationship between the main character and the reader, employing psychological realism as a distancing device.

The parallel plots reach a turning point when Tane Heva finally meets Swanson's companion Goldie Marsh. As he stands and faces her, he realizes that his strange antipathy toward women relates to her specifically—that it in fact functions as a "substitute for his hatred" of her. Contextual clues such as this one hint that Tane Heva's condition goes well beyond simple amnesia, approximating what psychoanalysts at the time called "traumatic neuroses," a dissociative disorder brought on by repression of a harrowing experience. (This condition is now referred to as Post Traumatic Stress Disorder, or PTSD.) After Tane Heva painfully acknowledges Marsh as the trigger for his misogynistic rages, his memory floods back. He is Captain John Chalmers, the sole survivor of a ship that wrecked off the coast of Motu Atua with a fortune in gold bullion in its hold. He tried to report the wreck's whereabouts, but Swanson and Marsh decoyed him, tricked him into revealing its location, and attempted to murder him in order to obtain clear salvage rights. The unveiling of a hidden backstory was, of course, a common device in this type of story—but not as it is handled by Bester. Positioned at the intersection of psychology and adventure, this climax affords the reader a writable moment—that is, an active role in puzzling out the nature of Chalmers's affliction and recovery. Regrettably, one of the editors at *South Sea Stories*, perhaps Palmer himself, responded to the novelty of Bester's approach with a no-reader-left-behind measure, inserting an intrusive and clumsily worded footnote. Nothing will capture its impact but quoting it in full:

> There are many cases where pressure on the brain—the impact of a bullet across the forehead, as in this story—will cause any one of a number of queer reactions. In Tane Heva's case, he was injured just at the time his mind was seething with bitterness toward a woman who had betrayed him. His memory being impaired through the injury to his head, he was able to remember only this one thing. (125)

Attributed to the editor specifically, this clinical-sounding note not only explains the matter away, it deflates the climax entirely, treating psychological ambiguity as a flaw rather than a desirable element of story logic.

Chalmers continues to puzzle out the source of his amnesia and compulsion while locked in the cabin of Swanson's schooner, and in a further twist that at once bolsters the suspense of the action plot and infuses it with tense humor, he makes the most of his situation by continuing to play the madman and aiding the natives in a surprise attack. As they approach in outriggers, he creates a distraction by simpering inanely and writhing like an eel on the deck of the ship, coolly ignoring the jibes of Swanson, Marsh, and the crew. Soon after, he shifts into heroic action mode proper, saving the day and winning the girl; but these outcomes amount to little more than a tailpiece of conventional heroism tacked onto an otherwise intriguing experiment in characterization, a point underlined by the fact that the off-center humor of Chalmers's feigned lunacy carries over into the resolution of the romantic subplot. As the story closes, Chalmers passionately kisses Nania against the lush backdrop of the island, but Bester inflects the potential exoticism of the ending by bringing into play an extra layer of coding. The islanders leer with astonishment at Chalmers and Nania, at the "foolishness" of the foreign custom of kissing (142). The introduction of their point of view pushes the scene into the territory of comedy, a final twist that interrupts and surprises readerly expectations. In other words, Bester deforms the usual payoff of the exotic adventure story without denying it entirely. He plays consciously with the expected reading protocols.

If the "The White Man Who Was Tabu" represents Bester's first foray into writable fiction and foreshadows his use of psychological ambiguity in later stories such as "Hobson's Choice" (1952) and "Fondly Fahrenheit," it also speaks to the origin of his distinctive antiheroes. Tane Heva is clearly a prototype for Bestermen such as Ben Reich and Gully Foyle, who struggle with their own sinister doubles in the figures of The Man With No Face and The Burning Man. This character particularly anticipates Foyle, who adopts the sometimes clownish guise of eccentric circus-owner Geoffrey Fourmyle in order to hide his real identity and motives. In an interview late in his career, Bester even hinted at a possible connection between these two characters, acknowledging that he, some fifteen years later, recycled bits of his research for his South Sea tales as he drafted *The Stars My Destination*.[26]

Compared with his adventure stories, the first SF manuscript that Bester sent to Schwartz fared less well. "The Pet Nebula" (1941) bounced in top markets and eventually worked its way down to Frederik Pohl's fledgling *Astonishing Stories*, which paid only half a cent per word. However, even though the story brought in a mere $17.50, it did prove significant in other ways, winning Bester his first cover illustration and resulting in his first appearance outside the Standard Magazines market. Schwartz sold Bester's "Life for Sale" to *Amazing Stories*, a slightly better market, in August 1940, but for reasons unknown, the story failed to appear in the magazine until 1942. Meanwhile, as a staff writer at *Thrilling Wonder*, Bester also continued to sell stories directly to Weisinger, with both "The Mad Molecule" and "Slaves of the Life-Ray" seeing print during 1941.

Considered together, these stories look a lot like a backlog of older material that Bester reworked into passable shape before taking on a more ambitious project. All four focus on weird science, two of them on experiments gone wrong and two on mad scientists who attempt to take over major cities through doomsday schemes involving death rays and toxic gasses. The blandly sensational titles of the stories give a good indication of their run-of-the-mill plots, and they form a curious juxtaposition with Bester's next publication, "The Probable Man" (1941), which advanced leaps and bounds in terms of craft and earned a spot in the field leader, *Astounding*. Although Bester later spoke dismissively of his early career, describing all of his stories written before 1950 as "miserable" and chalking up their publication to the influence of "two kindly editors at Standard Magazines," his work showed great promise from this point forward—and none of it appeared by virtue of his association with Weisinger and Schiff.[27]

CHAPTER 2

OF THINGS TO COME
The *Astounding* and *Unknown* Stories

To understand the breakthrough that "The Probable Man" represented, it is first necessary to consider the importance of a non-genre piece that Bester published at roughly the same time, a detective story titled "The McGrabb Bag" (1941). In it, Bester would take the emphasis on contextual clues in conventional mystery-and-detection stories and ratchet it up a notch through the introduction of a split viewpoint. The story features a father-and-son police detective team who notice and comment on a variety of early clues, all but pointing them out to the reader. However, unlike a typical Holmes-and-Watson exchange, their continual back-and-forth does not serve to disambiguate those clues in the least. Quite to the contrary, the father, referred to only as Old McGrabb, has cracked the case early in the story; but in a manner both cranky and comic, he badgers his son Lium with questions and purposely withholds even the thinnest sliver of a conclusion. The dueling viewpoints of Old McGrabb and Lium open up an intellectual side game with the reader, one that extends well beyond solving the mystery of the jewel heist and racketeering ring that lies at the center of the plot. Old McGrabb frames his refusal to share his knowledge with Lium in no uncertain terms, calling his son a "sucker for romance" and telling him he goes to the "movies too much."[1] In other words, Old McGrabb questions his son's reliance on conventional reading protocols and does so in a teasing way that similarly implicates any reader also lagging behind in solving the mystery. His paternalistic grousing becomes a kind metafictional taunt, one that calls attention to the matching of wits between writer and reader at the same moment that it serves as a vehicle for displacing or—more properly in this instance—deferring the usual mystery-and-detection reading protocols.

Even though *The Saint Detective Magazine* would reprint "The McGrabb Bag" in the fifties after Bester made his name, it does not actually amount to much as a story: the tension Bester creates through the conflict between Old McGrabb and Lium culminates in a very ordinary action scene and a concluding infodump. Nonetheless, Bester's venture into detective fiction taught him lessons that strongly inflected his approach to SF. If he used one character's viewpoint to satirize another's and showed an overt concern with the reader's agency in "The McGrabb Bag," he would soon initiate similar intellectual side games in his SF. From this point forward, he tended to plot his SF by introducing subtle contextual clues and narrative incongruities early on and employing self-aware style or metafictional references to invite the reader to notice them. Bester played fair with readers—that is, in accordance with the rules of detective fiction. He made sure that these sorts of odd details, which often read like pulp hash or continuity errors, played off of one another and locked into place logically during the story's climax or final twist. Long before *The Demolished Man*, mystery plotting was the source of what Bester would later call a "strong structural compulsion" in his work, and even at this stage in his career, it would serve as a vehicle for the transformative recycling of genre tropes and motifs.[2] What looks like a sudden leap forward in Bester's craft ability at this moment actually stemmed from a writerly attitude that he developed as he worked across mediums within the larger domain of genre writing.

"The Probable Man" was very likely written at the same time or just after "The McGrabb Bag." The two stories, in fact, open with a near-identical scene: a mysterious "black car" pulling alongside and cutting off a fleeing roadster.[3]

Not surprisingly, "The Probable Man" proves similar in approach to the detective story, marking a strong turn toward the type of self-conscious narration that would become Bester's stock-in-trade later in his career. The novelette also added to Bester's repertoire a theme he would return to again and again: time travel. Like Ross Rocklynne's "Time Wants a Skeleton" (1941), Heinlein's "By His Bootstraps" (1941), and many other stories published that year, it came on the heels of a May 1940 *Amazing Stories* contest that urged readers to come up with inventive endings for Ralph Milne Farley's open-ended short story "The Time-Wise Guy." The interest that the contest stirred among fans left in its wake a vogue for time-paradox stories among pros, who took up the challenge in their own right.[4] And of course, the time-paradox theme presented a perfect opportunity for Bester to engage in an intellectual side game with the reader through self-reflexive play with existing plot types.

Time-paradox stories of this period typically employed one of two devices: a causal loop or an altered timeline. The former worked by a closed logic, in which time travel or an anomaly in time resulted in a forward event on the timeline either becoming its own cause or seeming to lack causality altogether. In this scenario, exemplified by the Rocklynne and Heinlein stories noted above, the timeline typically did not change, functioning in the end as a kind of self-fulfilling prophecy. Stories involving altered timelines, popularized in particular by Nat Schachner's "Ancestral Voices" (1933), followed another tack. They opened out onto alternative history, postulating that even minor changes to the past would amplify and compound over time, radically altering the future. Thus, in Schachner's story, after a time traveler kills a single man in the distant past, fifty thousand people in the present simply vanish. However, a third model was also emerging, to some extent in response to pioneering work on quantum field theory by physicists such as Werner Heisenberg and Niels Bohr. David R. Daniels's "The Branches of Time" (1935), for instance, embraced the possibility of probable timelines and coexistent realities, moving toward the idea of a multiverse. In "The Probable Man," Bester seized on this latter notion to hybridize the two most common variants of the time-paradox story. The story's protagonist David Conn travels back in time and, by virtue of that act, creates a fork in time, but even as he manages to close a loop in his timeline proper, he witnesses a "probable" Conn departing into an indeterminate future.

Though the reader does not know it at the outset of the story, which begins in the middle of an action sequence, Conn is a "journalist in Time" who has returned to April 1941 from a millennium in the future to document a crucial juncture in history: World War II (87). It is now April 1942, about a year after his arrival, and he and Hilda—a Dutch heiress with whom he has fallen in love several months before—are fleeing Nazi spies who hope to capture her and use her as a political pawn. Unbeknownst to Hilda, Conn also pursues another agenda: he must reach his time machine before its power levels dip too low for him to return to the future. Building on his use of shifting perspective in "The White Man Who Was Tabu," Bester here fades in and out of Conn's viewpoint by alternating free indirect style that represents his thoughts with an objective third-person account of the action. Through the filter of Conn's mind, readers not only learn his true identity but also get direct access to an ongoing internal struggle, one that develops alongside and in response to the raw empirical facts of his battle with the Nazis. The truth is that Conn does not want to leave. In the future, *his* future, technocracy thrives, and that is a bad thing. The landscape of 2941 glistens with ultramodern cities, and machines provide for every convenience, making life "smooth and easy," far too much so for Conn's taste. The prospect of returning to the automated comforts and bland safety of home fills Conn with ennui. He relishes the danger and "breathlessness" of a more primitive age and cares deeply for Hilda, who will run a greater risk of falling into the hands of the Nazis after his departure. As he kisses the confused Hilda goodbye, he thinks, "This . . . ought to be the last paragraph. Nothing else comes after this but 'They lived happily ever after' and then 'The End,'" but his sense of duty prevails, and he boards his time machine with a vague hope of coming back for good after delivering his rucksack of notebooks and film to the future (77).

This story setup differs in important ways from the "mad science" approach Bester used in his four previous SF stories in that it foregrounds the main character's psychology rather than driving the plot forward based on the ins-and-outs of a dangerous device or mysterious object. Although Conn's journey is an experiment destined to go wrong, the inventor of the time machine (a scientist named Dunbar) and the mechanics of time travel remain in the background, while the effects of technology on human psychology, evident in Conn's hesitation, take center stage. The winking metatextual reference to fairy-tale endings—remarkable and oddly out of place in pulp SF of this era—highlights this psychological focus and brings Conn's dilemma to a head. Is he giving up romance and adventure in favor of a sterile existence? Has his society, a fully realized technological utopia, already done just that? Or is he caught up in self-indulgent nostalgia for the past and romantic illusions about a woman long since crumbled to "dust and ashes"? (76) Bester here draws attention to narration as narration, driving a wedge between science and romance and putting them in contest as SF story elements. Conn stands at a writable juncture, apparently in possession of the power to choose the ending of his own story—and the reader is invited to stand there with him, not only considering the possibilities but weighing them against each other.

Because of the way this hook involves the reader, it is all the more humorous and ironic when the next turn of events completely disrupts the reader's expectations, abruptly derailing the reading protocols that have been invoked. Conn steps out of his time machine into an unrecognizable future and realizes that he has misread his situation entirely. Where Dunbar's lab and a high-tech cityscape should be, he finds barren fields stretching away in every direction. In one of Bester's signature moves, time travel becomes just another contingency rather than a determinant of history or of an individual's destiny. Conn arrives neither here nor there but in an inscrutable elsewhere, lost and isolated.

The arrival of this unexpected elsewhere requires the construction of a second narrative framework within the first, and it is established through fairly conventional means: an action sequence ending in Conn's capture and interrogation, which provides a perfect scenario for exposition. On exiting his time machine, Conn witnesses a strange scene, a skirmish between two knights and a horde of rabbit-like men. With all the impetuosity of a blustery hero, he jumps into the fray on the weaker side and helps the knights to a victory, but once again, he misreads the situation before him. The knights Schiller and Horst—whose names very likely allude to Friedrich Schiller and Horst Wessel, two icons of Nazi agitprop—make him realize his mistake soon enough.[5] They reveal themselves as Swasts and turn on him after finding books in his knapsack, denouncing him as a Reader spy. Conn makes a narrow escape from the Swasts, and his subsequent capture by the Readers brings about a lengthy interrogation, one heavy with information that winches down the plot in preparation to catapult it forward. Conn suspects that "Swast" derives from "Swastika," and the Readers confirm as much: in this alternate reality the Nazis won World War II and proceeded to occupy the United States for nearly a thousand years. The Readers represent the last vestiges of a resistance movement that has gone underground—literally. They live in a vast underground cavern with artificial light and other conveniences, but they avoid the surface as much as possible, moving around by means of an elaborate network of tunnels resembling a rabbit warren—thus, their fur garments.

This nested storyline clearly invokes Charles R. Tanner's subterranean pulp adventure "Tumithak of the Corridors" (1932), but it also riffs on the Eloi-Morlock plot in H. G. Wells's *The Time Machine* (1895), portraying above- and belowground remnants of humanity who are divided for the most part by the partial forms of knowledge they possess. At some point in the distant past, both the Swasts and Readers lost the art of mechanical engineering but continued to carry on the war using a remainder technology, the now barely understood uranium particle lance. In the meantime, the Swasts have regressed into an almost theatrical state of feudalism, one descended from Nazi idealizations of medieval orders such as the Knights Templar and the Teutonic Knights, while the beleaguered Readers have advanced only one abstract branch of knowledge, becoming grossly overspecialized in theory. This latter circumstance, it should be pointed out, proves of much convenience to the plot. The Readers, it turns out, know the crux of Conn's predicament right away. In planning Conn's trip to the past, Dunbar overlooked a fundamental law governing all backward time travel: the traveler always returns to an alternative time track and is barred from returning to the future he left. Traveling to the past adds factors to the timeline that cause it to fan out into alternative branches, a phenomenon that the Readers' leader Rollins explains to Conn by way of a mathematical proof. If ABC, or the past, equals abc, or one set of probable futures, then ABC + b equals abc + b, or a different set of probable futures. After adding "b" to "ABC," the traveler cannot undo that action and go back to the "abc" time track (89). The self-consistency of space-time simply will not allow it. Nonetheless, according to Rollins, Conn does have one option: to return to the past he left—and to Hilda.

Not surprisingly, given the story's publication in *Astounding*, the interior storyline hinges on a long interval of applied science amenable to John W. Campbell's editorial policy at that time. Conn possesses exactly what this future lacks, mechanical expertise, and decides he will use it to win the Readers' war for them if that is the only way to get back to Hilda. With the Swasts blasting at the gates of the Reader complex, he becomes the consummate problem-solving hero, mixing batches of liquid explosive and leading a counterattack on the Swast stronghold, which turns out to be an age-old museum that is home to a perfectly preserved tractor. In a sequence that reads like a paean to farm machinery crossed with a how-to manual, Conn converts lamp oil to fuel, devises a method to crank-start the tractor, and employs it as a tank against the Swasts, helping the Readers to a decisive victory. He then uses the tractor's engine to recharge the depleted cells on his time machine; and amid fires and cave-ins generated by his homemade bombs, he escapes to the past without a hitch, with a uranium particle lance in hand—yet another factor that will alter the timeline. Interestingly, it is after this sensational spectacle that the real pyrotechnics begin, at least in terms of storycraft.

With Conn's reemergence into the broader narrative frame, the story takes on a more contemplative tone appropriate to the exploration of paradox and the psychological implications of time travel. The final section opens with the lines: "The silver-apple moon had slipped toward the eastern horizon when Conn at last came to the surface. It was blood-red and vast. The sky around it was steel-blue. He leaned on the lance he had brought with him and felt sick and weary." The Homeric epithet "silver-apple moon" and repetition of compound-adjectives introduce a new sort of lyricism into Conn's viewpoint, a dreamlike sense of disbelief and experiential overload. By some odd chance, Conn has gotten back just a few minutes before he left and sees the Nazi spies closing in on Hilda and his other self. As a sense of déjà vu sets in, a "most peculiar idea" occurs to him: that he should help himself out. And he does, calmly picking off five of the seven Nazis and leaving the other two to his earlier self, who he knows can handle them.

Bester first introduced this scene in a mixed-up welter of physical action juxtaposed with Conn's thoughts, and now he repeats it from Conn's time-wise point of view. He closes a causal loop within the narrative, not only through exposition but in the structure of the story itself. In the original scene, Conn noticed but rationalized several discrepancies. For instance, there were strange flashes of light just before his unlikely defeat of the Nazis (77), and Hilda inexplicably and joyfully exclaimed "David!" as he trudged off toward his time machine (78). These loose ends, which the reader has perhaps passed over as the kind of hash all too common to pulp SF, now take on new significance, recognizable as carefully planted clues. Whether the reader puts two and two together or flips back to reread, the story logic comes full circle: Conn simultaneously waited in the wings, in effect already reunited with Hilda, *and* trudged hesitantly toward the time machine in a purely probabilistic or superpositional state, resembling nothing so much as Schrödinger's cat. Bester undercuts the possibility of a "Gosh Wow" response to this surprise through humor and the layering of philosophical complications. In a campy parody of juvenile excitement, future Conn watches himself tramp away and imagines running up to himself to exclaim "Hi!" and shake hands; but instead he returns to Hilda, not without a twinge of sadness for his earlier self, whom he quietly permits to take the time machine into an unknown future. As a telling repetition of the earlier metatextual reference indicates, the story ends here for time-wise Conn: he reaches "the last paragraph for real"; but "probable Conn" enjoys no such luxury (104). He departs into yet another elsewhere, caught in a paradoxical regress into the future, perhaps an infinite one.

Whether or not this split-in-time-creates-nine resolution of the plot makes any sense theoretically is probably a question for physicists and philosophers to decide, but Bester's careful circumvention of the problem of chronology violation through what physicist David Deutsch would some fifty years later dub "asymmetric separation" certainly makes for interesting plotting and point of view.[6] In the end, the two Conns hold divergent subjective viewpoints, one satisfying the reader's need for closure and generating a sense of wonder at the vastness of space-time, the other treating the reader to a built-in alternate ending that opens out indefinitely. The story reads like a narrative version of a double-slit experiment, creating an interference pattern that all at once delivers the usual genre payoffs and a writable moment of the first order. A reader can focus on Conn's romantic return to Hilda and time-wise perspective, or speculate on the likely fate of probable Conn, or puzzle over the paradox formed by the juxtaposition of these outcomes. The ending of the story is a feast at which Bester gives readers the opportunity to have their cake and eat it, too, by placing a fairy-tale ending alongside an enigmatic repetition of the interior storyline's new beginning. In essence, Bester achieves this effect by engaging the reader in a moment of parallax, the re-representation of a narrative event through a divergent point of view. Bester probably borrowed this technique from Joyce, who used it in *Ulysses*, but he puts a perfectly science-fictional spin on it, combining it with the device of time travel to allow a single character to experience the same event from two different vantage points, his proper and probable timelines.

What is more, a reader who looks back at the rest of the story from the vantage point of the ending finds subtly overdetermined meanings on par with the clues to the resolution throughout. Even Conn's name is overcoded. He himself speculates as to whether his name could be a future corruption of the Jewish surname Cohen, offering an empirical explanation of its origin, but it also brings to mind a "con" or "cheat." Does Conn con time? Does Bester attempt to con the reader with a smile and tilt of the head, hoping to get caught? And what of that group of characters called Readers who help Conn cheat time by way of their speculative knowledge? Should the reader identify with them? The ironic self-awareness pervading the story makes it difficult to rule out that Bester intended Conn's name as a metafictional reference, as an inside joke with the reader about the kind of cat-and-mouse game he plays as author.

"The Probable Man" roundly beat out Anson MacDonald (pseudonym of Robert A. Heinlein) and A. E. van Vogt stories in *Astounding*'s "Analytical Laboratory" reader poll for July 1941, and it gave the first installment of Heinlein's *Methuselah's Children* stiff competition for the top slot. Although one critic has dismissed "The Probable Man" as shallow and outdated, a simple good-guys-versus-bad-guys adventure tale that was perhaps relevant in the context of World War II but holds little interest for the modern reader, it in fact rivals "Adam and No Eve" (1941), a later story typically recognized as Bester's first praiseworthy effort.[7] "Probable" doubtless has its faults, including coincidence-driven plotting and relatively thin characterization, but it does contain the seeds of Bester's writable approach and represent a decisively modern take on the time-paradox theme, especially in terms of technique. Bester used asynchronous timelines and recursive structure to move away from linear, cause-and-effect plotting—a staple of Golden Age SF—and to weave paradox into the very fabric of the story. He also showed a great deal of market savvy in nesting a typical techno-adventure storyline within a headier philosophical one, at once meeting the core demands of the *Astounding* market and tapping into an excess just beyond it. Most important, Bester concerned himself with the reader's agency, with creating a possible interplay of meanings that could transform reading into a pleasurable form of metacognition rather than just a vicarious experience, and he made a strikingly philosophical statement about perception and the changeability of personal identity due to experience as a result.

The reason "The Probable Man" remains lesser known today than "Adam and No Eve" very likely stems from the fact that it did not share the latter's charmed publication history. Raymond J. Healy and J. Francis McComas selected "Adam and No Eve" for *Adventures in Time and Space* (1946), an

Cover of *Astounding* (U.S.), July 1941. Copyright © 2016 by Penny Publications/Dell Magazines (Analogsf.com). Reprinted with permission of the publisher.

early anthology that became a much-reprinted classic, and it was the only of Bester's early stories widely known from the forties on. "The Probable Man" would go on to grace the cover of the July 1941 U.K. edition of *Astounding*, but only because Atlas Publishing's license with Street and Smith did not include rights to serials and thus dropped Heinlein's *Methuselah's Children*. In all likelihood, Bester's story won the cover because it fit best with Hubert Rogers's time-themed cover art for Heinlein's novel, which the British edition retained (although, again due to licensing limitations, as repainted by an uncredited artist). After this appearance in the United Kingdom, "The Probable Man" fell out of print for almost thirty years until Sam Moskowitz bought it in August 1969 for his collection *Futures to Infinity* (1970). It then fell out of print for another thirty years until its inclusion in *Redemolished* (2000), which collected Bester's lesser-known stories along with some nonfiction, interviews,

Bester's "Probable Man" appears on the cover of *Astounding* (U.K.), July 1941. Copyright © 2016 by Penny Publications/Dell Magazines (Analogsf.com). Reprinted with permission of the publisher.

and other odds and ends. While certainly no lost masterpiece, "The Probable Man" deserves to be better known, if only as a definitive milepost in Bester's career.

At this pivotal moment in his development, Bester's frustration with a specific SF cliché, the Adam-and-Eve trope, bubbled to the surface. His next two stories—"The Biped, Reegan" (1941) and "Adam and No Eve" (1941)—amounted to a rather impolite confrontation with this shopworn gimmick. The use of the Adam-and-Eve trope in fantastic literature dated back at least to M. P. Shiel's *The Purple Cloud* (1901), but Bester's dissatisfaction with it probably stemmed from a more immediate example: Robert Arthur's "Evolution's End," which appeared in the April 1941 issue of *Thrilling Wonder*. Authors typically employed the trope as a means of plot resolution, and over the forty years between Shiel's and Arthur's stories, Adam-and-Eve endings had changed very little. They went something like this: in the wake of an apocalypse, a single man and woman survive, destined to repopulate the earth as the new Adam and Eve. All too often, the device bore little real relevance to the plot, functioning as a weightless deus ex machina, an easy way out of any narrative hinging on a global catastrophe. Arthur had perhaps brought the device to a new low, broadcasting the conclusion of his story by naming his protagonists Aydem and Ayveh. Already losing its impact in Bester's day, the Adam-and-Eve trope eventually became so hackneyed that Brian W. Aldiss dubbed it—and all other stories that simplistically transfigured religious myths into ready-built surprise endings—"shaggy God stories."[8] By cleverly reversing the middle term of "shaggy dog story," a phrase used to describe a joke with a lengthy lead-in and no clear punchline, Aldiss emphasized the profound sense of anticlimax that readers experienced at the end of these stories.

Although "The Biped, Reegan" appeared in November 1941, a month after "Adam and No Eve," Bester surely wrote it first, perhaps even before "The Probable Man." In some respects, it resembles his early stories for *Thrilling Wonder*, with their nondescript heroes and plots built around weird science, but it also reads like a self-conscious parody of that type of story. In other words, it bears all the marks of a transitional piece, either an older manuscript snatched from the bottom of the drawer and revised with a cynical eye, or an early attempt to satirize super-science that bounced down to a lower market—

in this instance, to *Super Science Stories*, the fledgling companion magazine of Fictioneer Inc.'s *Astonishing Stories*. Bester's story harks back to entomological SF such as David H. Keller's *The Human Termites* (1929) and Frank Belknap Long's "The Last Men" (1934) but screws up the intelligent-insects-take-over-the-world plot to a comic pitch, largely by means of an unlikely and unreliable narrator: a smug ant commander filing a detailed but amusingly inaccurate report to its queen concerning the final victory of the ants over humanity. The humor of the story derives from the ant's faulty point of view: specifically, it misunderstands matters obvious to the reader, ranging from the import of human technologies to the basics of human anatomy and reproduction. The ant's most grievous misinterpretation occurs at the triumphant climax of its report. It mistakes the launch of a rocket and the scorched earth it leaves behind as a sign that the hero Reegan and his female companion Dinah have "destroyed themselves" out of despair.[9] In fact, they have made a daring escape and will become the new Adam and Eve. This ending probably sounds groan-worthy, but in context, it actually works well as satire—not of the ant mindset, of course, but of the Adam-and-Eve trope itself, which Bester turns into little more than a campy and largely throwaway punchline for the ant's conceited palaver. By the end, the story takes the form of an inside joke between author and reader, one depending not only on the reader filling in gaps in the ant's point of view but also recognizing the purposely strained humor and insincere handling of the resolution. Though it most certainly falls into the pulp category, "The Biped, Reegan" achieves a level of self-parody that Bester's early stories, and much pulp SF of the day, did not. It becomes a "shaggy ant story," as it were, with its humor derived from the ersatz treatment of the overripe story elements. Although not likely to be of particular interest to modern readers, the story does read well alongside other entomological tales of the period such as Milton Kaletsky's "Revolt of the Ants" (1940), a creaky and humorless political allegory that plays the super-science straight. It should also be noted that Bester's story appeared in esteemed company in this particular issue of *Super Science Stories*, which contained a Lyle Monroe novella by Heinlein and Ray Bradbury's very first professional publication, the short story "Pendulum" (1941), which he co-authored with Henry Hasse.

If Bester gently nudged the Adam-and-Eve trope into the territory of self-parody in "The Biped, Reegan," he revisited it with a sledgehammer in "Adam and No Eve." The very title of the story declares the trope its focus but also begins to generate a number of questions around it: how, exactly, do we have an Adam and no Eve? Will the last man die alone? If so, in what sense is he Adam? If not, will he attempt to create his own Eve or find some other way around this obvious dilemma? The opening gambit of the story itself echoes these ambiguities. The story begins in the middle, with a striking scene and no clear premise, although this hook perhaps leans toward the most bleak of the possibilities suggested by the title. Readers see a filthy, crippled Stephen Crane dragging himself across a desolate, ash-and-cinder landscape that looks more like a forbidding alien planet than earth. He flees from a vague menace but also struggles forward, filled with an enigmatic yearning to reach the sea. Periodically, he experiences ultra-vivid hallucinations—is visited by the phantoms of a belligerent scientist named Hallmyer and of his concerned but strangely distant wife Evelyn. The one gives voice to his guilt, implicating him in the tragedy at hand, the other to his fear and grief. The action, such as it is, is less important than the ebbs and flows of Crane's unstable mind. Although readers soon learn the basis for his deranged viewpoint—the combined effects of fatigue, starvation, septic shock, and acute stress—the narrative initially reads like a ghost story, placing readers inside the mind of a protagonist unable to distinguish between fantasy and reality.

Bester more than once noted that he chose character names with great care, and he very likely intended Crane's name as an allusion to writer Stephen Crane, whose Civil War novel *The Red Badge of Courage* (1895) focused more on the inward experience of its protagonist Henry Fleming than on the external trappings of war.[10] Bester commonly used metatextual references to signal his approach, and this one is appropriate to the story's perspectivism—to the fact that it places greater emphasis on the psychological effects of disaster than on the disaster itself. The filtering of narrative events through Crane's disoriented and sometimes faltering viewpoint allows for nonlinear development of the plot through episodes of altered perception, and the backstory of the catastrophe emerges midway through the story during a long, lucid flashback that Crane experiences when he stops to rest and weather an ash-and-cinder storm.

This backstory—a clear holdover from the annals of improbable super-science—involves mad ambition, an experimental rocket, and a conflict between scientists. In what now seems like a former life, Crane developed a super-efficient but extremely volatile catalyst capable of bringing a rocket to escape velocity, but his desire to achieve spaceflight blinded him to the catalyst's dangers. His chief scientist Hallmyer warned him of them repeatedly and even tried to sabotage the project by setting fire to their workshop, but Crane rushed into the flames and brashly launched the ship anyway. As Hallmyer predicted, the catalyst leaked into the atmosphere and, as it settled, set off a global iron-oxidization reaction that left nothing in its wake but scorched earth and water choked by toxic ash.

In terms of technique, "Adam and No Eve" is a companion piece to "The Probable Man," and this flashback functions more like a distinct story within a story than a seamless part of the narrative whole. Bester employs standard super-science but largely for the purposes of straight exposition. Seeing that the narrative machinery of super-science afforded narrow possibilities for character development, he here worked around that problem by invoking a particular character-related stereotype of super-science in the flashback—the maverick scientist's egomania—and carrying it forward as the focal point for the rest of the story. That is to say, within the wider post-apocalyptic-cum-gothic frame, he examines this undercoded aspect of character in detail and attempts to unlock its broader potential. He puts science, per se, to the side, refocusing attention on *why* rather than *how* Crane's egotism has turned science to horror, the earth to a ruined world.

With the end of the flashback and return the narrative present, readers find Crane buried in cinders after a spell of rejuvenating semi-unconsciousness and slowing realizing that the menace at the edge of his consciousness is real. During the hurried launch, his dog Umber ended up on board the rocket, and now mad with hunger, it stalks him. Crane wants nothing so much as the dog's company, but his harrowing encounter with it turns into a life-or-death struggle that signals an end to human values and a return to the primal laws of nature. The scene focused on their encounter—in which Crane kills and burns the remains of his dog—is suffused with a nightmarish emotional texture reminiscent of Lord Byron's "Darkness," and afterward, Crane finally understands his irresistible compulsion to reach the sea. If he once harbored delusions of grandeur, he will now realize his ambitions in a darkly ironic way: by throwing his broken body into the ocean, where it will drift, fester, and decompose. With this final act, he will become a creator of sorts, providing the bacteria and other raw materials necessary to spawn a new cycle of life. At this moment in the narrative, Crane's determination to jumpstart evolution serves as a double image of his destructive egotism, and the two become opposite sides of the same coin, aspects of one deep-seated drive much like Freud's life and death instincts; but despite this paradox, Crane's worldview has also shifted. He accepts at face value impersonal natural forces much greater than himself, much greater even than humanity as a whole.

This irruption of hard science in the story, although withheld as a closing strategy, does not come across as a gimmick at all. In fact, in bringing Crane's internal conflict to a head, it helps to round out the psychological portrait of him. At the same time, it also forcefully undercuts the Adam-and-Eve trope, pointing out the irrelevance of the human cycle of reproduction to nature—that is, to evolutionary processes requiring only a decomposing body and the mechanism of biogenesis to continue on their way. Bester, who wrote this story twelve years before the historic Miller-Urey experiment demonstrating the likelihood of abiogenesis as the origin of life, would later note with casual amusement that even Crane's body was unnecessary.[11]

Doubtless, Bester's background as a major in zoology prepared him to take the Adam-and-Eve trope to task in this way, but his approach perhaps also owed something to his abiding interest in the decadents during this period of his career. Crane's fate recalls Charles Baudelaire's "A Carcass" (1857), in which the speaker represents decay in aesthetic terms, as a blossoming of life that gives "great Nature back a hundredfold / All she together join'd."[12] If Baudelaire's well-known poem presents the reader with a curious paradox, a grisly *memento mori* alongside images of death as the transfiguration life, Bester does much the same, forcing the reader to step back from Crane's death and view it with an objective eye, as a kind of rebirth bound up with the workings of a larger reality.

By the end of the story, Crane has brought humanity to the brink of extinction, where it faces the prospect of becoming little more than a lost origin based in a biogenetic reaction, but the final lines of the story redeem him somewhat and strike a note of long-term optimism: "Crane smiled up at the stars, stars that were sprinkled evenly across the sky. Stars that had not yet formed into the familiar constellations, [and] would not for another hundred million centuries."[13] This reference to ancient star patterns, of course, forces a shift in the reader's perception of narrative time. Crane's months of determined crawling toward the coast have paid off, and his act of creation, though not particularly grand in terms of his role, succeeded long ago, indeed resulted in the world that the reader now inhabits—a world descended from Adam alone.

This last twist could be read as a sellout to a gosh-wow sense of wonder—and perhaps it is. It backs away from the darker implications of the hard science involved, ignoring the improbability of evolution following such a similar course after an extinction event, and unlike the rest of the story, these final lines do not stand up well to rereading—they feel artificial, like a cheat that fails to emerge organically from the established story logic. Nevertheless, in other respects, this twist finishes Crane's transformation from a mere egomaniac into a full-fledged antihero, underscoring the ambiguity of his final act. Is Crane despicable or admirable? The question hardly matters couched in such simple, either-or terms. The story, being less a satire of so-called "neurotic" science fiction than a dazzling recomplication of it, does not really attempt to answer it. Rather, it generates more complex questions in a grey area surrounding Crane's character. Is egotism a necessary but dangerous part of scientific advance? Is human fallibility an ineradicable part of science that makes it destined to fail? Is Crane's final act a testament to the human spirit? Does it simultaneously point toward nature's superiority to man? A certain kind of reader could ignore such overdetermination and happily soak up the sense of wonder that the final gimmick supplies; another sort could turn the story's ending into an immensely writable moment, especially at that particular historical juncture, which bordered on American involvement in World War II and the dawn of the nuclear age.

With Healy and McComas's classic anthology *Adventures in Time and Space* (1946) as its transport after its initial appearance, "Adam and No Eve" reached a fairly wide readership. Bester once even recalled meeting with a television producer who said to him, "There's one story I've never forgotten, and I'm hoping you can tell me who wrote it. I'd like to get hold of that man." Then, much to Bester's delight, the producer went on to describe the plot of "Adam and No Eve." Later in his career, however, Bester viewed the story as a relic of his juvenilia. When he introduced it for the story collection *Star Light, Star Bright* (1976), he described it as "jejune" and said that it appealed mainly to SF fans on a "nostalgia kick"—that is, to those who remembered the stir it caused when it first appeared in *Astounding*.[14] Nonetheless, it did have considerable impact on the field, helping to establish organic evolution at the molecular level as an enduring trope. As such, the story stands in the lineage of Greg Bear's Hugo and Nebula Award-winning "Blood Music" (1984), in which human bodies become little more than a stepping-stone in the evolutionary advance of nanotechnology, and even of Ridley Scott's recent film *Prometheus* (2012), which portrays a biogenetic reaction involving a member of the enigmatic race of Engineers as the lost origin of the human race.

Despite his decisive handling of the Adam-and-Eve trope, Bester would nonetheless revisit the genesis mythos one more time in his next story, but from a more oblique angle. "The Push of a Finger" (1942) hinges on a couple whose union will result in the birth of a Cain-like figure, a cursed genius whose theories will divide the scientific world ever after and bring about an appalling event, the very collapse of space-time. This catastrophe will not occur for about a thousand years, but the Stability, an institution charged with overseeing social balance, already knows about it due to developments in prognostication, a form of predictive sociology rooted in mathematics. The Stability possesses an Integrator that converts raw data into live images of the future, and the story focuses on an attempt by Stability officials and a reporter named John Carmichael to work backward from future events to identify the couple and prevent them from meeting.

This premise perhaps sounds very serious, given its vague similarity to that of Isaac Asimov's Foundation series, but Bester develops it in the direction of comedy, again exploring the use of voice as a vehicle for satire as he did in "The Biped, Reegan," but with much greater sophistication here. Carmichael, the first-person narrator, tells the story to a group of reporters, often breaking off to address them directly, but Bester deliberately obscures the identity of his audience until the end of the story, making it easier for readers to imagine themselves as auditors listening in real time. Carmichael speaks in streetwise slang that is passed off as the argot of beat reporters, and he is variously cheeky, witty, and confessional—a pitch-perfect raconteur. Right from the outset, he engages in metanarration, explaining in no uncertain terms how he will tell his story:

> I think it's about time someone got all those stories together and burned them. You know the kind I mean—X, the mad scientist, wants to change the world; Y, the ruthless dictator, wants to rule the world; Z, the alien planet, wants to destroy the world. Let me tell you a different kind of story. It's about a whole world that wanted to rule one man—about a planet of people who hunted down a single individual in an effort to change his life, yes, even destroy him, if it had to be. It's a story about one man against the entire Earth, but with the positions reversed.[15]

Carmichael positions himself as an insider who knows the sort of story he will tell all too well but chooses to go against the grain of the common formula. In essence, he tips off his listeners to how he will change the rules of the game. At the level of story, his caveat stresses for his audience the importance of viewpoint, that his tale will reverse the usual line of identification; but at a second, metafictional level, it invites the reader into a side conversation about the conventions of genre fiction, SF in particular. This second level of meaning becomes increasingly important as the story develops.

The plot proper begins with Carmichael's account of how he ended up on the Stability team trying to track down the ill-fated couple—namely, through his insatiable curiosity and a bit of slick maneuvering. He was on the beat at Stability headquarters in Manhattan and noticed that because of confusion related to an undisclosed crisis, Stability officials had left a door leading from the press room to the restricted areas of the mysterious Prog Building both unlocked and unguarded. As chance would have it, he likewise had a way around the Stability requirement that news agencies work always in tandem, presenting all stories in point and counterpoint. The reporter from Carmichael's opposition outlet had quit unexpectedly that day and had not yet been replaced. Afforded a perfect opportunity to slip away unnoticed, Carmichael proceeded to create a distraction and to do just that—not necessarily in search of an exclusive scoop, mind you, but indulging a juvenile fantasy that he might catch an entertaining glimpse of a Hyperman or a Fighting Robot. Inside, he found the Integrator instead and learned the secret of his world's doomed timeline. Worried that the truth would get out, the Stability had made him press secretary to the Chief Stabilizer, Groating.

Throughout his story, Carmichael admits such foibles as his dubious motive for wheedling his way through that unlocked door, but he brings off these confessions with a boyish charm designed to entice rather than estrange the reader. This same quality, if one trusts Carmichael's account, improves his standing with Groating and allows him to assume a leadership role in the effort to alter the future. With the Stability team at a loss concerning how to begin, Carmichael suggests tracing the chain of causation backward from the fatal event. He sells Groating and the other officials on this idea through a diverting, hook-and-grab explanation of Charles Darwin's anecdote about old maids and clover, and follows up with an analogy to detective fiction: "The reason I imagine you gentlemen have been slightly bewildered up to now is that you're busy men with no time for foolishness. Now I'm not so busy and very foolish, so I read detective stories. This is going to be a kind of backward detective story" (119). As this deft display of false modesty demonstrates, Carmichael is a consummate performer, a little full of himself but also disarming and firmly persuasive. His voice draws in the Chief Stabilizer, who obviously admires his verve, but it also tempts readers to understand this second moment of metanarration—the comparison to a "backward detective story"—as a hint at the reading protocol best suited to deciphering the story. In fact, Carmichael's affect comes so far into the foreground of the story by this point that it begins to seem like a central concern—to raise the question of whether readers should fall in line, as Groating does, or suspect Carmichael of feeding them a line.

With Carmichael's help, the team soon makes a major breakthrough in the case, identifying not only the couple's son, a renegade scientist known only as FitzJohn, but also the source of the faulty axiom responsible for the accident that obliterates space-time. According to one of FitzJohn's lectures, the formula $i = (b/a)\,\pi\, i\, e/\mu$ originated with his father, who had an epiphany and blurted it out to his mother in Central Park on the evening of February 9, 2909. It so happens that for Carmichael and the others, that moment lies just a few hours in the future, and they scramble to prevent the conversation from taking place, clearing out Central Park and surrounding it with a cordon of guards. A tense moment occurs when a helio lands in the park, and Groating and Carmichael rush to turn it away, but when they learn that it carries only the press corps, they let out a sigh of relief and allow it to land. At this point, a clue lingering in the background of the story since the beginning resurfaces with force. Carmichael's new opposition, Halley Hogan, disembarks the helio, and the surprise of seeing *her* causes him to mutter, "I'll be a pie-eyed emu" (129).

Those taken in by Carmichael's charisma have been had. His meddling has caused and perpetuated all the trouble, bringing about the very timeline that the Stability sought to forestall. The very fact of the matter serves as a counterpoint to Groating's express faith in the Stability program and predictive sociology, and here again, Bester portrays the human element of scientific endeavor as an indelible threat to its success. This twist occurs not only at the level of story but also at the metanarrational level. Early in the story, Carmichael has issued a directive, "Don't ask questions now. I'll explain as I go along"; and now, his admission of his role in the predicted disaster suggests that listeners who consented to such a guided tour have been set up (108). His story is proleptic in the sense that it attempts to anticipate and answer objections in advance. That is, his lofty buildup to the climax, full of self-congratulatory appraisal of his role in the effort to avert the ill-fated timeline, now looks absurd, as do his claims for the distinctiveness of his story. His tale differs only superficially from a typical closed mystery that hides key clues in plain sight and employs misdirection to discourage readers from latching on to them, and his reversal of viewpoint within the "one man" formula is clearly self-serving, hiding his identity with an eye toward preemptively slanting the story in his favor and garnering sympathy for himself. For a moment, he even takes on an uncharacteristic trace of self-pity and victimhood: "I—innocent me. I was X, the mad scientist and Y, the ruthless dictator, and Z, the alien planet—all rolled into one. I was the one guy the Earth was looking to stop" (129).

If Carmichael attempts to bamboozle his audience, Bester has nonetheless played fair with the reader. At its broadest level, the narrative has offered up plenty of subtle reasons to consider reading against the grain of Carmichael's story. Most obviously, it places the reader in a rhetorical situation and makes the possibility of interrupting his narrative clear. It also offers space for the reader to develop a critical distance from Carmichael—to take note, for instance, of his casual attitude toward duplicity and worryingly self-centered mindset. With the climax of Carmichael's story, this other layer of clues that the reader has not been handfed takes on primary importance. In fact,

Bester's choice to crown Carmichael's story with a paper-thin gimmick—that FitzJohn's dangerous axiom stems from a corruption of Carmichael's glib remark—bursts the inflating bubble of narrative urgency, giving his whole performance the feel of a well-told but ultimately empty shaggy dog story.

And from there, the potential to identify with Carmichael and his reliability as a narrator diminishes rapidly. "Old Groating," for whom Carmichael now shows open contempt, has undertaken another measure of "protective promotion," exiling him to a "God-forsaken" asteroid where he serves as editor of a piddling two-sheet weekly. Carmichael knows that his penchant for treating the world as his playground got him in this mess, but despite that, he has not changed an iota and nonchalantly admits that he finds himself in the grips of a new obsession, one much more intense than his desire to learn the secrets of the Prog Building. His mind constantly wanders to an attractive prospect that affords a way out of his present circumstances—Hogan herself. "I keep thinking about her and I keep thinking how easy it would be to stow out of here on an Earth-bound freighter—change my name—get a different kind of job. To hell with Groating and to hell with Stability and to hell with a thousand years from now. I've got to see her again—soon" (129).

The story ends by setting the scene for an errand of seduction, one that the charismatic Carmichael seems all too capable of accomplishing. If "The Push of a Finger" does represent an extension of Bester's erstwhile interest in the Adam and Eve story, he arguably revisits the mythos within the context of rabbinic lore, particularly texts such as the *Pirkei de-Rabbi Eliezer*, in which the satanic figure Samael, not Adam, fathers Cain through the seduction of Eve. Carmichael reads in the end like a darkly comic version of Samael—comic because he is not evil as much as hopelessly compulsive, perhaps even the hapless agent of the self-consistency of space-time.

Of course, not even these final shadings of Carmichael's character guarantee that every reader will gain distance from his viewpoint, but the layering of story-level and metafictive reading protocols serves as a built-in satire of readers who do not, much as Carmichael's ability to insinuate himself into Stability affairs satirizes Groating's egotism and naiveté. Bester does deliver a backward detective story of sorts, though not according to the terms Carmichael lays out. For readers who do see through Carmichael, either early or late, the story brings additional pleasures, ones derived from sharing in an authorial self-awareness related more to the telling of the story than to its content. As such Carmichael precedes a character such as Alex in Anthony Burgess's *A Clockwork Orange* (1962), whose streetwise teenage slang blends neologisms, multilingual puns, and portmanteau words to set up a seductive veil of personality between the reader and the reality of Alex's self-serving and often brutal mentality. Although Bester explores this use of voice on a smaller scale, he achieves a similar effect, employing an enticing but unreliable voice to destabilize reading protocols and present the reader with the choice of whether or not to identify with the narrator.

It is tempting to read Bester's story as a satire of the Foundation series—of Asimov's notion of psychohistory in particular; but amazingly, "The Push of a Finger" appeared in *Astounding* alongside "Foundation" (1942), the original story in the series. (Asimov would later rework this novelette into "The Encyclopedists," the second chapter of the 1951 novel *Foundation.*) This coincidence likely resulted from Campbell's ongoing interest in future history, which began as early as 1936. In that year, Campbell published the time-paradox story "Elimination," which centers on a "Probability Time Wave" receiver or "PTW tube" that foretells the future with tragic results.[16] Specifically, the scientists who invent it attempt to influence their own time tracks, disrupting the natural progression of their timelines and destroying themselves in the process. Although in a manner less subtle than Bester's, Campbell's story employs a frame narrative, presenting the reader with an earnest patent attorney who tries to dissuade a young inventor against the development of a similarly dangerous device. Whereas Asimov took up this style of future history via the route of extrapolation, displacing the thin scientific premise supplied by the "PTW tube" with psychohistory and the Seldon plan, Bester opted for satire, placing the time-viewer at the center of an ironic time-paradox plot demonstrating the danger and futility of attempts to influence the future through scientific intervention. Harry Harrison and Brian W. Aldiss, who included the long-out-of-print "Push of a Finger" in their collection *The Astounding-Analog Reader* (1972), called it a "miracle" given that it simultaneously fulfilled and subverted Campbellian imperatives, and they cited its publication in *Astounding* as evidence that Campbell could still at that point in his career recognize a "good joke," even if it was at odds with his editorial stance.[17]

In 1941, well before "The Push of a Finger" appeared, Bester had already begun moonlighting at DC.[18] His departure from the SF field for comics perhaps prompted him to publish "The Unseen Blushers" (1942), a roman à clef—or story with a key—that thinly masked the identities of the real SF authors it represented. Bester's story took as its subject a loose coterie of pulp writers who were referred to as the Steuben's group because they met weekly for lunch and shoptalk at Steuben Tavern in midtown Manhattan. Many of the writers in the group were Schwartz's clients, and Bester first met the group (with Weisinger having yet again run interference for him) not long after Schwartz became his agent in the summer of 1940. Although the lineup at these informal gatherings changed from week to week, regulars included pulp-magazine mainstays such as Kuttner, Otto Binder, Malcolm Jameson, and Manly Wade Wellman, and the topic remained much the same. According to Edmond Hamilton, who stopped in during visits to New York, the lunches invariably turned into lively bull sessions "about new developments in SF."[19]

In his own anecdotes about these chinwags, Bester downplayed his role, describing himself as a newcomer whose greenness showed. He recalled, for instance, saying to Weisinger with a flourish, "I've just finished a wild story that takes place in a spaceless, timeless locale where there's no objective reality. It's awfully long, 20,000 words, but I can cut the first 5,000." Kuttner, sitting nearby, rocked with laughter, probably at the obvious potential for a novice to overwrite such a story and Bester's casual admission of having done exactly that. On another occasion, in an earnest attempt to engage in shoptalk with Jameson, Bester declared, "I've discovered a remarkable thing. If you combine two storylines the result can be tremendously exciting." Reacting with genuine disbelief, the seasoned writer shot back, "Haven't you ever heard of plot and counterplot?" Bester looked back on moments such as these with a degree of embarrassment, calling himself a "dumb kid," but he also felt like an outsider because of his own—then admittedly pretentious—literary ambitions. After attending the gathering a couple of times, he confided to Weisinger that he regarded some of the writers at the table as mere hacks, to which Weisinger responded with editorial acumen, "They may never write a great story but they never write a bad one."[20] Bester later went on to write a story based on his experiences at the luncheon, one that incorporates Weisinger's reply indirectly.

The story's title, "The Unseen Blushers" (1942), alludes to Joyce's *Finnegans Wake* (1939), specifically to the image of Shem the Penman as the "pick of the wasterpaperbaskel" and an "unseen blusher in an obscene coalhole."[21] Joyce portrays the writer Shem as a favorite of the trash bin who labors in squalor, and in the context of his story, Bester links this image of literary obscurity to the pulp writer's probable legacy. Bester perhaps derived the idea of plotting the story around the issue of a writer's legacy from another tale of literary ambition and time travel, Max Beerbohm's "Enoch Soames" (1916), which he would later cite prominently in his novella "Hell Is Forever" (1942); but unlike Beerbohm's Soames, who travels to the future only to learn of his descent into utter oblivion, Bester's unnamed narrator, a "high-class" pulp fictioneer who refuses to do hackwork, finds out that he attains a literary immortality on par with Shakespeare's.[22] This revelation occurs after an outsider named Dugan tags along to the weekly luncheon with one of the regulars, hoping to run a time-travel story idea past the group. Dugan's plot outline involves a researcher who returns to the twentieth century to study a writer who drudged in relative anonymity for the pulps but has been rediscovered in the future. Synthesizing various clues in conjunction with Dugan's peculiar demeanor, the narrator starts to think that Dugan might well be that researcher. Dugan bears all the markers of a time traveler—an odd speech pattern more in line with a future dialect of English than any existing one, symptoms of time disorientation such as speaking of the present in past tense, and an unusual-looking watch, to name a few. And he keeps glancing in the narrator's direction, which gives the narrator the sneaking suspicion that he himself is the writer destined for greatness. As it turns out, the narrator is right in both respects. Within the story's roman-à-clef logic, of course, Bester himself is the narrator, a budding literary genius, while the other writers in the Steuben's group come off in—let us say—a less favorable light.

The tale, which appeared in *Astonishing Stories*, warrants little discussion as a story. It reads very much like yet another of Bester's early efforts for *Thrilling Wonder*, one that he had good reason not to publish earlier given its likelihood of offending the writers caricatured—in particular Wellman, who appears as a pompous blowhard named Belcher. However, the story does offer insight into what Bester took away from the luncheons, if only by negative example. As Dugan recites his story idea, Belcher interrupts him by exclaiming: "Never mind the explanations . . . We've all alibied a Time Machine at one time or another. Land-sakes! You don't even have to anymore. You just write 'Time Machine' and the readers take the rest for granted" (87). As one of Dugan's listeners, the narrator exhibits just the opposite attitude, understanding reading protocols not as givens but as a slippery site of contest between the writer and the reader—in this instance, between Dugan and himself. Paying closer attention to the nuances of the telling than the content of the story, he considers Dugan's sometimes odd demeanor and narrative choices, even subtle omissions, against the available context—for instance, the curious disappearance of one of his own manuscripts—to gain access to a level of meaning not hidden as much as pointed to by extra-coding. This image of the writer as reader—of the writerly reader as the mediator of different narrative strata and vectors of meaning—reveals Bester's early, self-conscious preoccupation with writable fiction, one he carried forward into his later career. This story also represented one of the first indications of his later interest in language change as a plot device.

"The Unseen Blushers" resulted in the first of several off-the-wall episodes in Bester's career occasioned by his sometimes irreverent attitude toward SF. Even if it can be granted that Bester dusted the story off and published it just as he departed the field, it nonetheless produced a considerable backlash. Predictably, it incensed Wellman, but it also elicited an indignant response from several other writers associated with the Steuben's group, particularly Eric Frank Russell. Bester's portrayal of Malcolm Jameson, who appears in the story as Mallison, deeply offended Russell. It went as follows: "He's white-haired, incredibly ancient looking, and he acts half dead. He used to be in the navy so he writes sea stories now. They say that he acquired a particular disease in the tropics that makes him mumble most of the time. He turns out a damned good yarn" (86). Although Bester probably did not know as much at the time he wrote the story, Jameson in fact suffered from very serious condition, namely a case of throat cancer that would end his life within a few short years. As rumor had it, Russell intended to repay Bester's insensitivity by beating him "to a pulp" the next time he saw him. Bester in turn joined a gym, largely as a precautionary measure in the case of such a meeting. Wellman likewise cited Bester's depiction of Jameson as the reason for his outrage, but David Drake, who knew Wellman well, suspected that he in reality found the portrait of himself "unflattering." When Drake compared the original story with Wellman's account, he pointed out that Bester did not engage in a simple character assassination. He complimented Jameson as a writer and portrayed Wellman as not only ostentatious (as he was known to be) but also quite intelligent. Although Drake dismissed the "The Unseen Blushers" as a story, he praised it as a "fair and accurate contemporary picture of the heyday of the pulps," one of some value as a historical document.[23]

Despite getting on the wrong side of the Steuben's group, Bester would leave SF on a personal and professional high note, placing his final and longest effort from his early career, the novella "Hell Is Forever," in Campbell's magazine *Unknown Worlds*. Campbell started *Unknown* as a companion to *Astounding* in 1938 and, in doing so, established a different model within the fantasy market than the shock-and-horror mode characteristic of *Weird Tales*. In particular, he slanted the magazine toward stories that rationalized or ironized fantasy tropes, most commonly through the addition of scientific backgrounds or metatextual reference to science fiction, history, or mythology. More specifically, Campbell's editorial policy favored science fantasy such as Jack Williamson's *Darker Than You Think* (1940), which offers up a scientific rationale for lycanthropy; recursive SF such as L. Ron Hubbard's "Typewriter in the Sky" (1940), which portrays a character aware of his status as a character in a pulp story; and alternate history such as L. Sprague de Camp's *Lest Darkness Fall* (1939), which blends elements of SF, fantasy, and historical fiction.

Bester on several occasions in his career noted his strong distaste for fantasy, which he viewed as "undisciplined and self-indulgent." In his view, fantasy too often amounted to a rigged game, requiring readers to play along *with* writers rather than to match wits *against* them within a clearly defined set of logical parameters.[24] The genre indeterminacy and narrative sophistication of *Unknown*, by contrast, afforded readers a more active role, and Bester came to revere "fantasy in the *Unknown* manner" so much that he felt an urgent need to write one himself, even though he had "no assignment, no encouragement, no approval in advance."[25] He had Schwartz submit his manuscript to Campbell under the working title "The Dead Only Die Once," with little hope of breaking into what he considered the most prestigious genre market of the day, and when Schwartz informed him of its acceptance, Bester was both disbelieving and breathless. According to Schwartz, Bester would some thirty years later talk about April 2, 1942, as "one of the turning points in his life," portraying this particular sale as a boost in confidence that had a lasting impact on his self-image as a writer.[26]

Bester felt less enthusiastic about "Hell Is Forever" when faced with the prospect of considering it for a collection of his short stories published in the seventies. He remembered nothing about the story, no longer owned a copy, and supposed it "just had to be a bomb" given how long ago he had written it, but he needed additional material to fill out the two volumes his publishers wanted, so he asked the staff at *Analog* to dig through their *Unknown* files and make him a copy. When he reread the story—for the first time since its original publication—he noticed signs of overwriting and thin characterization, but against his expectations, he took pride in it all over again. He included it in the first volume of the collection, *The Light Fantastic* (1976), and in the introduction to the story, he said of that young writer he once was: "I feel like a father to that kid and I think he shows promise in 'Hell Is Forever.' . . . I think he ought to stay with it. He might become a pro someday."[27]

Because he recalled almost nothing about the creation of "Hell Is Forever," Bester also used the introduction, one of the lengthiest in either volume, to attempt a "paleontologist's reconstruction" of the story.[28] This reconstruction does not address his specific writing process per se but does piece together some fragments that point toward it. In particular, Bester noted the heavily citational style of the story—its conspicuous references to Huysmans's novel *À Rebours* (1884), Max Beerbohm's story "Enoch Soames" (1916), and George Bernard Shaw's play *The Doctor's Dilemma* (1911), among other texts. If Campbell's editorial policy at *Unknown* called for extra-coding of fantasy, even made it the trademark of the magazine, Bester took up this practice in his own distinctive fashion—through pastiche. He playfully referenced and appropriated various texts to create a saturated intertext, one open to more than just one reading protocol. A reader need not get all the allusions or understand how Bester's approach takes in elements of decadent and modernist aesthetics to enjoy the story or even to feel the effect of narrative oversaturation, but this other level of meaning does produce writable moments capable of enhancing a reader's experience of the text.

Bester often employed a prominent, early allusion to signal his approach in a piece of fiction, and he begins "Hell Is Forever" with a quotation from Beerbohm's "Enoch Soames," a short story defined by its narrative switchbacks and ironic self-echoes, but he does so in a clever manner that calls attention to the playful caginess of Beerbohm's tale. Beerbohm's first-person narrator references several poems by Soames, the story's central character, and Bester uses one of these as an epigraph, attributing it to Soames and indicating that it comes from the larger work *Fungoids*. In other words, he makes no mention of Beerbohm. Bester quotes the fictional poet Soames as though he were a real author, introducing an element of incongruity and metafictional play into the story right off the bat. If this indirect reference to Beerbohm goads the reader to watch out for smoke and mirrors, it also directly foreshadows the story's plot. In Beerbohm's story, Soames is an obscure but original writer, one who feels sure that the future will recognize his genius. Driven by his vanity and his desire to know his literary status a hundred years hence, he makes a Faustian deal with the devil, one that plays out with a notable degree of irony.

The reference to Soames in place, Bester's story gets underway with a sketch of the Society of the Six, a group of jaded English socialites whose relentless search for new sensations leads them to explore the furthest limits of decadence and grotesquerie but always leaves them just where they started: feeling bored. World War II rages outside the walls of Sutton Castle, the site of their revelries, but they pay the war no mind, thinking of themselves as the "last spiritual descendants of Nero."[29] On this night, they plan to amuse themselves with a play about the occult, titled "Astaroth Was a Lady," which five members of the group will stage for Lady Sutton, their host and "Bookkeeper of Disgust" (11). The special-effects coordinator, Robert Peel, lies passed out in a chair, and Lady Sutton heckles the troupe from the divan as she sips champagne laced with opium, but despite this insensate and unruly audience, the play nonetheless builds toward a crescendo: the conjuring of the demon Astaroth, played by a haughty ice queen named Theone Dubedat. This climax delivers much more than expected. On Dubedat's entrance amid smoke and flame, another figure appears on stage alongside her, causing her to exclaim, "The r-ritual—It worked!" The other players back away in terror, and Lady Sutton, who suspects a trick, frantically counts the number of people in the room. The door has been locked all evening, but there are seven. In the ensuing confusion, she suffers a heart attack and dies, and soon after, one of the players, the artist Digby Finchley, blandly declares, "Well . . . That's that" (13).

Little did Lady Sutton know that her companions planned to experience a new sensation without her, that of murder.

Bester perhaps adapted this idea of accidental conjuring from accounts of demons appearing on the Elizabethan stage during the conjuring scene in Christopher Marlowe's *Doctor Faustus* or from the well-known comic allusion to these sightings in *The Puritan*, a play in Bester's day counted among the Shakespeare Apocrypha; but he uses the legend as the basis for a murder-mystery-style plot twist—at least initially. As Peel strips off his costume and admires the realistic dummy of him in the chair, readers learn the truth concerning his responsibility for the special effects—and the full extent of the group's depravity. With Lady Sutton's body not yet cold, they already feel boredom setting in. Peel tries to stave off this undesirable frame of mind by liberating an expensive sapphire ring from Lady Sutton's finger, but the dark comedy of his attempt verges on horror when the finger snaps off and emits a curiously rotten smell, one that Peel passes off with the quip, "She rots fast" (14). Seconds later, an unfamiliar voice addresses the company from thin air and Lady Sutton's black cat begins to purr and arch its back against an invisible figure, a real demon in their midst.

As Bester indicates in his introduction, the luxuriously specific style of the opening section draws on Huysmans—on the deliberately corrupted naturalism of *À Rebours* and the grotesqueness of the black mass scenes in *Là-Bas* (1891). Both this thick description and the murder-mystery plotting serve to rationalize fantasy, but the narrative switchback—the appearance of a genuine demon—fuses realism and fantasy and generates an atmosphere of paradox. Ironically, the five now find themselves in a position not unlike Lady Sutton's, faced with an impossible situation and filled with disbelief, especially after the demon offers each of them a choice that seems too good to be true: the opportunity to fashion a reality based on his or her heart's greatest desire. Bester here again alludes to *À Rebours*, in which the once dissolute antihero Jean des Esseintes withdraws from the world at large in order to shape a private reality in line with his own desires. Faced with the same alluring prospect, the five insist on knowing the proverbial catch, but their cryptic guest reassures them that the price for a demon's services is always "paid in advance" (15). With a somewhat small leap in logic, they take this comment as a reference to their murder of Lady Sutton, thinking they are being repaid for evil services rendered, as it were. Meanwhile, Peel, an engineer, also objects on other grounds, namely that the idea of five realities is a contradiction in terms, but in a strikingly science-fictional manner, the demon introduces him to the notion of probabilistic space-time, the very stuff on offer. Of course, in the end, none of the five is able to resist a chance at unfettered wish fulfillment, at realizing a personalized pocket universe. They begin to edge toward a "glittering veil" the demon has made of an ordinary doorway, drawn like moths toward a flame, but Bester breaks off the frame narrative with a dash that opens out on an episodic structure and five branching storylines (15).

These interior storylines all share a basic structure: one of the five stands before the veil in a probabilistic state, contemplates his or her wish, and passes through the veil to a new beginning. However, each wish brings about a distinctive story logic and narrative mode, so that the story cycles through high fantasy, psychological horror, science fantasy, contemporary fiction, and crime fiction. Though these episodes do not occur in chronological order, the first of them does focus on the first of the five to pass through the veil: Digby Finchley. As an artist, he chooses creative power and an empty canvas. He will mold and shape his universe with his own hand, becoming the god of his world—or so he thinks. Soon after passing through the veil, he learns otherwise. In an unhappy turn of events, his faith in himself as an artist outstrips his actual ability as a creator. For one, he lacks an understanding of physics and mathematics, and the stars and planets in the first cosmos he designs careen out of control, forcing him to unmake it and devote his attention to a single planet circling a single sun. He does manage to keep two moons in orbit around the planet, but this small victory is followed by another striking failure. When he tries to populate his new Eden, the animals and people he molds from the clay run from him in terror, limping and deformed.

Bester's avowed interest in artists and writers associated with the "*Yellow Book* crowd"—Aubrey Beardsley and Oscar Wilde, in particular—here comes to the foreground. Beardsley once commented during an interview, "If I am not grotesque I am nothing,"[30] and an idea along this line becomes a paradox that defines Finchley's reality. Lady Sutton makes a mysterious appearance in Finchley's personal reality, and naturally, he questions her rigorously about the intrusion, which appears inconsistent with the terms offered by the demon. Lady Sutton explains her presence away by saying the dead can enter any reality they want, but she quickly shifts the conversation in another direction, asking him how he likes being a god. A sniveling, self-pitying Finchley replies: "I don't," and he proceeds to explain that all his creations turn out "disgusting and loathsome." Given this cue, Lady Sutton encourages him to create a mirror and look in it. There, he finds the grotesque image of a gargoyle and learns an ironic lesson—namely, "that a god can create only in his own image" (20). If Wilde's Dorian Gray escapes this fate, his corrupted nature displaced onto a painting that he views at his leisure, no such split between representation and reality exists for Finchley. He has no double, and his taint passes straight into all of his creations, placing his horror inescapably before his eyes. He must choose the grotesque or nothing—quite literally.

Each of the interior storylines plays out with similar absurdity. Sidra Peel chooses a reality in which she possesses the strength to murder and thus rid herself of her hated husband, Robert, but she finds herself first stalked by and then wed to her own narcissism, in the form of a male alter ego named Ardis (her name spelled backward).[31] The writer Christian Braugh seeks the truth behind existence and learns of the utter lack of free will. Demiurges run the universe on arbitrary principles yet themselves exist within an infinitely ascending bureaucracy of cosmic puppeteers who pull their strings in exactly the same way. The frigid beauty Dubedat makes the mistake of selecting the reality that most needs her. Finchley has long adored her, and she ends up in her own version of his warped reality, as his brutalized but compliant consort. Peel wishes for his reality to remain exactly the same but, unmindful of the body on the floor in doing so, emerges on the other side of the veil to find himself a scapegoat for his friends and the prime suspect in Lady Sutton's murder.

For each new strand of story, Bester briefly loops back to the frame before changing up the narrative mode, and this loose patchwork results in various forms of juxtaposition and intertextuality. Dubedat's story, for instance, alternates two viewpoints: Dubedat's unfiltered thoughts with passages of scripture quoted from the Book of Maart, a sacred text written by one of Finchley's monstrous children. This combination of interior monologue and mock-biblical style reads like a mashup of Molly Bloom's monologue in *Ulysses* and Friedrich Nietzsche's *Thus Spoke Zarathustra*, and it obviously nods in the direction of modernist fiction. This storyline, the most experimental in terms of technique, transitions into Peel's, which resembles a pursuit scene from crime fiction told from the viewpoint of an overconfident fugitive. Peel believes that cold reasoning and applied science always provide a way out, if not a solution, and his storyline repeatedly slips into indirect discourse that follows his train of thought. Fantasy logic, however, overdetermines Peel's engineering mindset in ways apparent to the reader but not to him. Realizing that the only future awaiting him is a brief, unhappy life on the run, he indifferently settles on suicide as the proper course of escape. His sharp mind knows just how to end his life quickly and painlessly, even how to turn ordinary household goods into foolproof tools of self-obliteration, but his suicide attempts miscarry again and again because he fails to understand that the world he now inhabits exists in violation of the rules of empirical reality. What he needs is to comprehend this unfact, but he cannot, and in the meantime, his rationalism results only in a greater and greater degree of self-mutilation. Even after blowing himself to smithereens, he continues to exist as conscious bits of grit clinging to the rubble of his demolished home. He makes no clever escape from his predicament—or from responsibility for his actions. There is no way out.

Throughout the genre-hybridized interior of "Hell Is Forever," Bester's baroque approach results in the overcoding of conventional genre plots by creating a dense web of crisscrossing techniques, allusions, and internal linkages and asymmetries. Dubedat's name, for instance, contains a complex allusion to Shaw's *The Doctor's Dilemma*. In Shaw's play, Jennifer Dubedat idolizes her artist-husband Louis despite his despicable behavior and self-aggrandizement, and the play as a whole comically examines the narcissistic illusions of all of the main characters, in particular the rational pretensions of a doctor faced with an impossible moral dilemma: two dying patients and the ability to offer only one of them an experimental treatment. Bester's allusion to Shaw not only provides a reference point in interpreting Theone's eventual acceptance of Finchley but also Finchley's faulty self-conception as an artist and Peel's overblown view of himself as a so-called man of science. It links these interior storylines explicitly and all of the five's tales at the level of theme. Bester similarly juxtaposes the Peels' tales through a partly veiled allusion to Horace's Fifth Ode, which is quoted in Latin in Sidra's story and in English translation in Robert's.

Elsewhere, Bester employs a more general but still heavily citational style, largely for the purposes of satire. Perhaps fittingly, this strategy appears most prominently in the storyline of the writer Christian Braugh. After choosing a reality that will reveal ultimate truth, he steps through the veil to find himself in the "Central Administration" offices of the "Universal Control Center." There, he encounters four dwarfish sorcerers, wearing pointy caps and all, and a lengthy episode of "saturnalian slapstick" ensues after they realize that they cannot determine *his* true nature (31). On the face of it, the comedy of this scene arises from physical humor associated with the bumbling of the cartoonish sorcerers, but just beyond this spectacle, it derives from Bester's self-conscious use of fantasy language. The sorcerers attempt every sort of divination they know, and Bester makes a point of mentioning and briefly depicting each of these, including onomancy, genethliacs, sortilege, capnomancy, sideromancy, molybdomancy, and pegomancy. As the sorcerers periodically come to ridiculous conclusions—that Braugh is a porpoise or a salamander, for instance—the lack of meaning piles up. The scene reads as though Bester pulled a grimoire from the shelf and sloppily condensed it with the explicit purpose of producing a nonsense effect. A similar sort of authorial insincerity pervades the overall handling of sorcery. As Bester notes in his introduction, the arcane names employed in fantasy—especially ones drawn from demonology—made him cringe, and his disdain for this common practice visibly emerges here. When one of the little sorcerers calls to the others, each named after a demon, his exaggerated affect is represented in visual terms for the reader with prosodic spellings: "THAMM-uz! DA-gon! RIMM-on!" (28). This stylized presentation of the names, achieved through capitalization and punctuation, stamps the names with the sorcerer's hyperbole, mimicking his comic stress on the first syllable of each name. It also emphasizes the odd spellings and sound of the names themselves. This sort of quasi-typographical play recurs throughout the scene. For instance, the sorcerer's excited chatter appears in jumbled, run-together dialogue that pokes fun at fast-paced mumbo jumbo of chants and spells: "MostastonishingthingDagonthatIeverhespeaksRimmoncoulditbehumanheardwhatitsaidBe lialyou'dthinktheremustbesomeexplanationd'youthinksoThammuzIcan'tsay" (28). Textual effects such as these mesh well with the slapstick comedy of the scene but also reduce the esoteric language of fantasy to absurdity. And significantly, when Bester revised the story for republication in the seventies, he intensified this effect, for instance, by altering the sorcerer's filing system so that it includes not only alphabetical ranges such as "A–AB" but also enigmatic designations such as "#–, &–1/4, [and] *–c."[32]

Together, the interior storylines of "Hell Is Forever" function as a kind of narrative funhouse, one that presents the reader with new distortions and mirrorings at every turn, but a final twist in terms of technique even further underscores the no-exit theme. Bester never returns to the frame narrative proper. Rather, in the final storyline, elements of the original frame slowly bleed through into Robert Peel's reality, forcing a synthesis of clues planted throughout the wider narrative. The first of these narrative "tells," if they may be called such, was Lady Sutton's curiously rotten body, which suggested that she had died well before the five killed her. Such uncertainty about the boundary between life and death, and about Lady Sutton's status as a character, echoes through the subsequent storylines. Sidra, for instance, senses an "alien and distorted" quality in the landscape of her world, that the vegetation is not really "alive" (23), and the little sorcerers greet Braugh with the observation, "It's not dead because it don't smell. It's not alive because only the dead ones come here" (29). Lady Sutton appears where she should not—in Finchley's reality—seeming to know more than she should about the afterlife. Now, she comes to Peel in a similar fashion. Her appearance—and the revelation that follows it—makes sense of these lingering traces of meaning. She is Astaroth, the demon assigned to arrange "hells for the damned." Amused by the novelty of the five's plan to murder Lady Sutton, she could not resist assuming the Lady's identity, playing along, and turning the tables on them, namely for a bit of amusement that would alleviate the "boredom" of her job (45). This admission brings the circumstances of the play back to mind, along with a host of now apparent double meanings. Its title, "Astaroth Is a Lady," expressed a literal truth and might even be thought to serve as the first and most prominent cast listing. In the guise of Lady Sutton, Astaroth did not heckle the players but toyed with them when she asked questions such as "What's a Necromancer?" and "Who's this Astaroth?" (10). She acted her role brilliantly to an unwitting audience. Lady Sutton's black cat Merlin, in cozying up to the invisible demon, foreshadowed the actual course of events: that Astaroth would for a short time keep the five much like pets or, more properly, as her familiars. The price the five had already paid was death—they were dead all along, killed in an air raid before the story even began. Like the play within the story, the frame narrative itself is illusory, and like the characters, the reader is now left no way out. This unexpected narrative dead end is underscored by Astaroth's final declaration that "each living creature creates its own hell forevermore"—that *all* are damned, and all "the damned of all eternity in an infinity of self-made hells" will hear her and make "no answer" to her justice (45).

Not long after the publication of "Hell Is Forever," Bester wrote a letter to Anthony Boucher about his purpose in the story, saying, "The most hypnotic thing about magic is not its plausibility, but an instinctive gullibility in every human."[33] The stories of the five all illustrate this point, reversing the poles of Freudian wish-fulfillment in the process. The five do not realize their wishes in dreams. Their dreams reveal the latent, narcissistic content of their wishes, forcing them to face for eternity what they most wish to disown. For them, wish fulfillment is not compensatory, as Astaroth lets them believe; it instead shatters their false self-images. Considered in a wider purview, it demonstrates the inevitability of human egotism—that every human possesses a partial understanding of the world and his or her place in it. One critic has compared Bester's theme to that of Jean-Paul Sartre's *No Exit* (1944), in which three damned individuals find their punishment in one another's judging gazes, but Sartre's play ends with the famous line, "Hell is other people."[34] In Bester's story, hell is unmediated self-knowledge, truly knowing and being forced to live with one's self—including one's disavowals and unconscious desires. Darrell Schweitzer has eloquently described the most important goal of horror fiction as the creation of a "convincing sense of unreality, of our conceptual universe coming apart at the seams."[35] Even if the young Bester did overwrite "Hell Is Forever," his maximalist approach—to plotting, intertextuality, and style—results in exactly such excess. It courts that elusive uncertainty and dread that comes when all of one's rationalizations of self fall away, leaving one face to face with the apparent absurdity of existence.

Bester might easily have written "Hell Is Forever" and other of his more complex pulp stories in a conventional manner—he clearly knew the formulas—but he chose instead to experiment with writing and reading protocols in a self-referential way. These stories not only show Bester's writable approach in the making but also reveal that his aesthetic had its roots in bricolage, or the practice of drawing on heterogeneous sources and writing styles to create unexpected narrative tensions and unities. Bricolage works by a logic of excess and encompasses more local strategies such as extra-coding, pastiche, intertextuality, and allusion. By definition, it re-orders reading protocols, requiring the reader to switch codes and synthesize incongruities. The writer need not even understand all the levels of meaning bricolage creates, and as such, the practice affords the reader not only an active but a somewhat open imaginative role in the production of the text. Late in his career, Bester addressed this concern with the reader's agency by saying: "There's nothing you can impose on the reader. The reader owes you nothing. You owe everything to the reader," and that attitude is already present in the best of his pulp stories.[36] It is especially visible in his tendency to write to all levels of his possible audience, building multiple paths into his stories, paths capable of satisfying various types of readers.

CHAPTER 3

COMICS, RADIO, AND THE RETURN TO SF

"Hell Is Forever" marked Bester's last publication in the SF field for eight years, but the next part of his career, during which he switched his focus to comics and progressively branched out from there into radio and television, deserves more than the passing attention it usually receives. Frederik Pohl, for instance, has more than once glossed over this portion of Bester's career by characterizing him as a "money writer." By Pohl's account, when comics boomed, Bester followed the money trail there and then graduated to radio and television, where the pay was even better. When the financial incentives to write SF increased after World War II, with magazine word rates having "tripled," Bester returned to the field, with a little coaxing from editor Horace L. Gold.[1] Certainly, economic motives played a role in Bester's movements in and out of the field, but as he himself once noted, he gave up two lucrative shows and "lost money" to return to SF in the fifties.[2] During the forties, Bester had grown discontented with the pressures—and especially the creative limitations—of narrowly commercial writing. Bester's image of himself as a writer changed significantly during this period, and it was this changing self-concept and a need for fresh challenges, as much as anything else, that eventually led him back to SF.

Bester's opportunity to move into the field of comics stemmed from his relationship with Weisinger and Schiff. In March 1941, his mentors at *Thrilling* left Standard Magazines to edit *Superman* and a range of other comics for National Allied Publications, and soon after, they invited Bester to follow them. Bester joked that the three of them "hadn't finished with *Ulysses* yet," but in truth, the booming comics industry was urgently in need of writers.[3] Bester initially scripted comics on the side, doing uncredited work for *Superman*, but his stint writing for both mediums did not last long. The financial incentives to devote his time to comics were in fact great, given Bester's circumstances at the time. Bester had married eighteen-year-old aspiring actress Rosalind "Rolly" Goulko in 1936 while studying law at New York University, and five years later they still lived a "make-ends-meet" lifestyle, managing that only with the help of their parents. The regular wages Bester could earn promised a new stability and independence, and he remembered that after making the move to comics, he said to Rolly—just before taking her and her mother out to dinner at a nice restaurant—"Darling, do you realize from now on I can make . . . I can make *eighty dollars* a week?"[4] When he later recounted the incident, Bester laughed at his grandiose notion of his new salary, but at the time, $80 a week almost certainly transformed his and Rolly's lives. 1940 U.S Census data indicates that in 1939 Rolly had earned their entire income of $600, an average of only $50 a *month*.[5] Even a generous estimate of Bester's total income from his pulp stories would place his earnings over approximately three years at about $1200. What is more, after Bester worked his way up through the ranks, he eventually earned as much as $13.50 per page of script, becoming one of the best-paid writers in the business.[6]

Bester, of course, faced a serious quandary when he changed focus, namely that he did not have the remotest idea of how to write a comic. With Weisinger's help, he received his first lesson from Bill Finger, the legendary co-creator of Batman. One Saturday morning, during a meeting that lasted about two hours, Finger walked Bester through a thirteen-page story, going panel by panel as he explained pacing, visualization, and layout, among other

Rolly Bester, publicity photo for *The Fat Man*, ABC Radio, 1948.

matters.[7] Bester never forgot this lesson in the craft—or Finger's patience and generosity. During the grueling apprenticeship that followed, Weisinger and Schiff used him far less gently. As he put it, "they . . . hammered me, bullied me unmercifully. But I became a writer, by God!"[8]

Bester's tenure in comics appears to have lasted for four or five years. By the fall of 1941, Bester had begun to earn story credits, penning a Starman tale in the October 1941 issue of *Adventure Comics*, and from there, he went on to contribute regularly to *Captain Marvel* and *Green Lantern*, among other series; to co-create the original character Genius Jones with Stan Kaye in 1942; and to ghost Lee Falk's *Mandrake the Magician* and *The Phantom* for King Features during World War II. In interviews, Bester cited various end dates for his work in comics that ranged anywhere from 1942 to 1947;[9] but the regular appearance of his stories in *Green Lantern* up to the June-July 1947 issue suggests that he remained active in the field until closer to that date and that his work in comics overlapped significantly with the next stage of his career in radio.

George Burns once said of the demise of vaudeville, "There just ain't no place for the kids to be lousy anymore," and Bester quoted that quip by way of portraying his work in comics as an apprenticeship with a twofold effect. On the one hand, comics helped him get a "lot of lousy writing" out of his system; on the other, it gave him "splendid training . . . in visualization, attack, dialogue and economy" that served him well later on in his career. In assessing the comics field in general, Bester noted that he disliked the limits that comics scripting placed on character development and story—that is, the necessity for clear-cut heroes and villains and strictures against the depiction of sex and violence—but he did enjoy the looseness of the medium, which was still in its youth and essentially being invented not only by editors and artists but also by writers such as himself.[10]

During his stint in comics, Bester had made inroads into the entertainment industry, largely through Rolly, who occasionally landed roles on Broadway and worked regularly as a radio actress. Initially, he steered in the direction of Broadway, readapting the English libretto for Modest Mussorgsky's opera *The Fair at Sorochyntsi* in 1942 and writing an original libretto based on "Cinderella" for a play-ballet starring Maria Gambarelli the following year. However, a real breakthrough occurred when Rolly told Bester that the radio mystery *The Return of Nick Carter* desperately needed scripts. Engaging in a kind of self-pastiche that remained central to his writing process ever after, Bester turned two of his better comic book stories into radio scripts, and the show's producer not only accepted them but "*loved*" them.[11] After "The Horoscope Murders; or, Nick Carter and the Mystery of the Avenging Astrologer" and "The Drums of Death; or, Nick Carter and the Mystery of the White Witch Doctor" aired in March 1944, Bester became a regular writer for the show and branched out from there, contributing to *The Shadow*, *Charlie Chan*, *Hercule Poirot*, *Nero Wolfe*, *Treasury Agent*, *The Falcon*, and several other radio mysteries over the next eight years. During this period, he adapted his earlier work on a regular basis. According to Schwartz, his former agent who later followed *him* into comics, Bester regularly stopped by the DC library to "swipe from" his own comic scripts, even after having left the field entirely.[12]

Bester also formed another habit in response to the pressures of writing for radio. He regularly spent time in the reading rooms at the main branch of the New York Public Library, speed-reading all manner of books as he looked for fresh ideas, or "gimmicks," as he called them. Using a technique he had developed in law school, he skimmed an average of twelve or so books per session, searching for unusual information about art fraud, police procedures, and trafficking, and randomly cycling through material concerned with "psychiatry, scientific research, color dictionaries, music, demography, biography, plays," and an "endless" array of other topics. He copied interesting quotations, anecdotes, or ideas into a commonplace book that he called a "gimmick book."[13] This diary of sorts, which Bester maintained religiously, grew to several volumes by the time of his death. Throughout his career, it served not only as a repository for his research but also as a place for ideas to mix, recombine, and develop, often over long stretches of time. When confronted with that trite question that so many writers abhor—"Where do you get your ideas?"—Bester always had an easy answer: his gimmick book, which he said contained more ideas than he could "write in a lifetime."[14]

Inevitably perhaps, as the newer medium of television overtook radio, Bester also tried his hand at teleplays. He began writing for television as early as 1949. "The Lost Child," an original short-form drama that aired in August of that year, suggests that he struggled with the transition. The plot of Bester's teleplay involves a mother searching frantically for her lost child, largely by way of telephone calls that build up to a revelation: her son died a year ago, and unable to accept his death, she relives the traumatic experience of his loss over and over, caught in a loop of post-traumatic stress. A *Variety* review of the program suggests that although Bester's use of dramatic monologue and limited point of view served as an excellent showcase for actress Luise Rainer's acting "pyrotechnics," the story fell flat as visual narrative due to its psychological premise.[15] Later in his career, Bester would say that the television medium did not suit him as a writer. In his view, many of the psychological facets of human experience that he most wished to explore were out of bounds in television, in part due to the added expense of shooting a script containing, say, synesthesia sequences but also because producers had a condescending attitude toward viewers and turned down story ideas that expected much, if anything, of them.[16] Bester wrote unhappily for the medium for about three years, scripting episodes for *Tom Corbett, Space Cadet* and *The Doctor*, among other series, and serving as the head writer for Paul Winchell's eponymous variety show, which featured music, skits, and a quiz segment called "What's My Name?" He probably landed this last job based on his experience writing for radio programs with similar formats, particularly the quiz show *Forty-Five Questions from Broadway* and the musical variety show *Harvest of Stars*, but he became so disgruntled working on *The Paul Winchell Show* that he quit television sometime in 1951 and wrote the caustic mainstream novel *Who He?* (1953), which pilloried the TV industry in general and *The Paul Winchell Show* in particular. (The novel's title alludes to the show's quiz segment.) Although Bester later wrote TV specials and showcases, he refused to write standard shows from then on, citing a lack of creative freedom. He illustrated this choice with a joke: "What is a camel? A camel is a horse designed by a committee." Scripting for weekly TV was, in Bester's opinion, not writing but "committee work."[17]

Bester continued to write regularly for radio during his years in television, especially for *Nick Carter* and *The Shadow*, which aired episodes that he had penned until the end of 1952. During this period, he contributed some of his *Shadow* scripts under the byline John Lennox, possibly for a very practical reason. Because of his heavy workload, he sometimes adapted a script sold to one show for the other.[18] Nonetheless, this pseudonym perhaps also manifested his growing discontent with commercial writing in general. Considered in the context of advertising for the show, it takes on the hues of a personal joke and a pun. Lin-X Home Brighteners sponsored both *Nick Carter* and *The Shadow* during the period Bester wrote for them, and his pen name can be read as a comical equivalent of "John Doe," one in which the writer's name becomes little more than a placeholder for a company's name and advertising interests.

In a 1951 column for the trade magazine *The Writer*, Bester addressed the topic of "Writing the Radio Mystery" and made his growing dissatisfaction with commercial writing clear, tossing out the bald statement: "I hate radio but I love the money." To confront his own boredom with the medium, he had homed in on the "difficult and fascinating problem of technique" and shopped around scripts to shows willing to handle offbeat themes.[19] Meanwhile, writing for television did not even afford him these consolations. As he noted later in his career, he felt bogged down and insecure at this moment, as though he had begun to write at a much slower pace and perhaps lost his touch, but as he dug deeper into his files looking for source material, he learned an important lesson about himself as a writer: he had not fallen off form but had become more "discriminating" and "self-critical," and now produced "less schlock." He took more time to write because he aimed for higher-quality scripts and wanted to produce better ones still. In the wake of this self-realization, he felt even less inclined to do journeyman's work, but he found no outlet to express his ripening creativity. In fact, his producers seemed to prefer for him to submit what he considered "second-rate" scripts.[20]

Although by his own account he had read little SF during the bulk of his years in radio and television and written none, Bester would now turn to SF as "therapy," as an escape valve for his pent-up creativity.[21] According to Pohl, who occasionally bumped into him in the CBS building cafeteria at this time, Bester began during the late forties to tinker with the idea of writing an occasional SF story, "just for the fun of it."[22] In 1949, a philosophical disagreement with a friend provided him a perfect opportunity to act on that impulse. His friend insisted that intelligence went hand in hand with moral accountability—that rational people had no excuse for doing wrong. Following Freud, Bester countered that unconscious desires often compelled bad behavior, finding their way around good intentions and rational thinking alike. Though the argument ended in a stalemate, Bester set out to illustrate the Freudian point of view in his fiction.[23] He had been interested in compulsives for some time and used them regularly in his radio scripts, usually as villains or minor characters, but he had largely been confined to engaging with compulsion as a behavioral gimmick. Now, he would treat it as a central theme in his story "Oddy and Id." At this point, the stage was set for his ill-fated first meeting with John W. Campbell.

In terms of technique, Bester more or less picked up where he left off with Campbell and the *Astounding* market eight years earlier. "The Devil's Invention"—as Campbell retitled the story, after insisting that Bester drop all the overt references to Freud—nests a science-packed interior plot within a wider psychological one, teasing out satirical implications by way of the juxtaposition; however, in contrast to his stories from the early forties, Bester here achieves tension between these doubled levels of meaning without recourse to a frame story proper. Instead, an omniscient narrator hints at but withholds key information from the reader, forcing the reader to guess at the psychological import of the plot on the basis of objective descriptions of events.

The psychological plot is introduced in the very first line, with a moment of explicit metanarration that seems to lay all the cards on the table: "This is the story of a monster."[24] This assertion, however, goes unexplained. The narrator instead recounts young Odysseus "Oddy" Gaul's life to date in a series of rapid-fire episodes. In presenting this backstory, the narrator periodically repeats the word "monster," transforming the opening line into an enigmatic leitmotif—enigmatic because although readers later learn that Oddy is a rare creature, a "Fortune Prone" who always gets his heart's desire, he hardly seems monstrous at all (137). He craves ordinary comforts that any child would desire: the love of his parents, safety from harm, the admiration of his peers, and loads of candy. What is bizarre is that even with the odds stacked against him, he manages to get these things, often through fluke circumstances that his family and friends rationalize as extraordinary good luck. And therein lies the rub. Much like the nature of his monstrosity, the specific mechanism of Oddy's singular good fortune goes unexplained. Bester also adds a second barb to the narrative hook: these troubling unknowns are carried over into the next part of the story with particular emphasis after the narrator hints that the local effects of Oddy's "monstrous evil" will infect the world at large once he leaves his small hometown for college (134).

With the mystery of Oddy's freakish good fortune established, the rhythmic repetition of the leitmotif ceases, the tempo of the story slows down, and an overall shift in narrative mode occurs. The narrator lingers on a defining period in Oddy's college career and introduces the reader to the story's actual protagonist, a Harvard professor named Jesse Migg. It is important that, from this point forward, the story proceeds largely within the confines of Migg's limited viewpoint. Migg teaches a range of courses associated with the physical sciences and notices that Oddy never fails to complete a lab assignment, even when issued broken equipment or faulty materials. A brilliant problem solver, Migg sets out to determine the chain of causation behind Oddy's peculiar successes and slowly figures out that each depends on a nearly impossible string of coincidences. Having gathered this evidence, he formulates a theory of the "Compulsion of Probability" to account for Oddy's strange powers and seeks out a select group of his colleagues at the university as a sounding board for his ideas (137).

The story's internal plot is dominated by exposition that results from Migg's step-by-step reasoning, which brims with applied and speculative science amenable to Campbell's approach. It also sets up Migg as a fact-chewing scientist-hero. Wary but optimistic, he considers Oddy an "angel" of sorts and comes up with a strategy to steer Oddy's powers toward the greater good, in particular the prevention of an impending war over a diminishing resource: fissionable ore, which the narrator describes as the thirtieth-century equivalent of oil. Meanwhile, Migg's colleagues come around and, not without a little grandiosity, appoint themselves the "executive committee for Fate" (140). Their mindset, as a group, soon comes to the foreground of the story.

Migg's plan involves taking advantage of Oddy's youth and predisposition to "hero-worship." Specifically, Migg asks his peers to charm and bedazzle Oddy, to instill their ethics and idealism in him by setting themselves up as idols. Migg's plan clearly enflames the vanity of his companions, who not only feel "flattered" but also take turns playing the Great Man with over-the-top relish (142). Though less comfortable in his role, Migg pictures himself as the final object of Oddy's adulation, as the best among his peers—a viewpoint the narrator describes as "frightfully conceited but true" (143). If the self-pride of these would-be heroes makes the reader suspicious of their motives, Bester's delicate shading of specific characters likewise hints at a larger satirical purpose in handling the scientist-hero. For instance, the mathematician Hrrdnikkisch sports a fantasy name of the sort Bester loathed, and his apparently intimate knowledge of "Stone Age fiction" raises a red flag—that is, he knows just a little too much about Ruritanian romance, a type of fiction noted for its involvement of readers in unbridled wish fulfillment. The narrator also likens Hrrdnikkisch to a "flamboyant character out of Rabelais," and though subtle, this allusion proves significant (143). Bester deeply admired Rabelais, having first read him at age ten after sneaking a copy of his works from his "father's locked closet."[25] The fourth book of Rabelais's *Gargantua and Pantagruel* parodies the *Odyssey* and epic heroism, and contains a famous scene in which a conceited and conniving shepherd falls prey to his own profiteering scheme and his own flock of sheep. Specifically, the shepherd tries to con the Odysseus-figure Panurge, who brings about a striking reversal by buying a ram—the leader of the flock—at a ridiculously high price and throwing it overboard. The rest of the sheep naturally follow and, in the process, drag the frantic shepherd into the sea. Oddy Gaul's name, which suggests "French Odysseus" or "Odysseus of France," arguably aligns him with the trickster Panurge. At the same time, the satirical extra-coding of Hrrdnikkisch implies not only that Migg and his ad hoc committee for fate harbor some wish-fulfillment fantasies of their own but also that they may well become unwitting victims of their own plan—*moutons de Panurge*, as it were.

That is, of course, how it turns out. Pressed for time as war looms ever larger on the horizon, Migg and his team decide to bring Oddy's education to an end by making him aware of his extraordinary powers. They do so by way of a question, asking if he has ever indulged the common fantasy of suddenly discovering that he is not an ordinary person but a powerful "king" (143). When he quietly admits that he has, they tell him that in his case, the fantasy is fact, a cold reality. Oddy at first reacts with disbelief, suspecting a joke on the part of his mentors, but when he finally comes around, he reveals that he has often dreamt a far greater dream: that of being the "one man who could run the world" in just the right way (144). A little disconcerted, Migg encourages him to start with a smaller ambition: preventing the war. Needless to say, Oddy agrees, with promises of admiration and fidelity, but a clear sign of trouble soon emerges—the war breaks out in a matter of days. Shortly thereafter, Oddy is commissioned as a foot soldier and singlehandedly brings about a key victory. As he performs similar feats of heroism again and again, he rapidly ascends through the ranks, and within six months, he personally negotiates a peace accord and is named Grand Solon of the new Solar Society formed from the remains of the warring states. Only then does Migg understand the extent of his own tunnel vision and the mechanism of Oddy's gift. Oddy does not control his powers: they stem from "the primitive impulses of his subconscious mind," or his Id (145). By making Oddy conscious of the reach of his powers and involving him in a matter of such grand import as the war, Migg's scheme has actually enabled Oddy's Id, made the entire world its stage. After Migg comes to this realization, he flatly declares: "We were fools . . . We should have killed him. He isn't an angel. He's a monster" (145).

In a superficial way, Oddy's character functions as a postwar satire of the cults of personality associated with European fascism, but within the story,

Oddy's mentality directly satirizes the intellectual egotism of the problem-solving hero. Overconfident in their abilities and quietly seduced by their own sense of self-importance, Migg and his companions manage little more than a perverse implantation of their paternalistic attitude in Oddy, who desires nothing as much as the sort of hero-worship he has shown them. Bester once again takes up a common power-fantasy formula of genre SF, the one-man-to-save-the-world plot, but he here overdetermines it through self-conscious doubling. For the reader who seizes on this writable moment at the end of the story, Oddy reflects back the values of his mentors as an image of bad faith. He is "sincere, idealistic, charitable, kindly and sympathetic" but also the "feudal overlord of a Family of Planets that suffers misgovernment, oppression, poverty, and confusion" (144–45). He embodies a return of primitive violence in a bourgeois form—becomes a double image of civilization and its discontents. Bester postulates a logical extreme, the Midas touch of Oddy's Id, as a cynical counterpoint to the belief in progress. This point is underscored by the fact that because of Oddy's unstoppable charisma, his mentors fall into his neurotic pattern of arrested development. The story fades out with a circular return to the "egotistic craving" of the infant Oddy and the inexorable—but now substantiated—logic of the story's opening (133). The monstrous Oddy will have his way forever: "That was Jesse Migg's last sane statement. Now, of course, he adores Gaul the Glorious, Gaul the Gauleiter, Gaul the God Eternal who has achieved the savage, selfish satisfaction for which many of us yearn from birth, but which only Oddy Gaul has won" (145). The scientist-hero does not solve the problem at hand. To the contrary, through his own hubris, he meddles with powers beyond his control and falls prey to them, losing both his rationality and individuality in the process. The final image shows Migg following all of humanity into a state of oblivion, drowning in the swelling sea of Oddy Gaul's ecumenical desire; and once again, Bester questions the assumptions of science fiction as a category, leaving the reader to contemplate the human psyche, at least as Freud imagined it, as a dangerous chink in the armor of scientific endeavor.

Like "The Push of a Finger," "The Devil's Invention" gently ironized the *Astounding* ethos even as it appeared in the magazine's pages, but it is noteworthy that Campbell's cuts, which consisted mainly of removing terms such as "Id" and "unconscious," left the structural irony of the story intact. Even so, after Bester reverted the changes for a reprint that appeared the following year in Bleiler and Dikty's *Best Science-Fiction Stories: 1951*, the story's ending popped stylistically and thematically in ways that it did not in *Astounding*. For instance, the version edited by Campbell offered this bland explanation of Oddy's powers: "In many men, conscious desire and subconscious desire do not correspond. They do not in Oddy" (145). Bester's preferred text read: "The control lies in Oddy's Id . . . in that deep, unconscious reservoir of primordial selfishness that lies within every man."[26] This latter version not only offers up a sonorous repetition of "lies" and a prosodic use of the ellipsis, it also gives "lie" a double meaning, suggesting the Id as a wellspring of self-deception. Unlike Campbell's version, Bester's is not earnest but satirical and self-aware—and more clearly implicates Migg and his cohort in the common fate their world.

Bester made no special claims for "Oddy and Id" as a story, depicting it simply as a transitional piece in which psychology had taken on a new prominence in his work, but he would reflect on the significance of his encounter with Campbell time and again when commenting on this juncture in his career.[27] He had returned to SF in search of creative freedom, and the editor had greeted him with a heavy-handed attitude that reminded him of his discouraging experiences with radio and television producers. However, Campbell should probably be thanked for rubbing him the wrong way at precisely the wrong moment. Bester reacted by seeking out an edgier market for his work, and luckily, such a market had just emerged: *The Magazine of Fantasy and Science Fiction*, which first appeared on newsstands in October 1949. In fact, in the second issue of *Fantasy and Science Fiction*, Tony Boucher and J. Francis "Mick" McComas had practically sent Bester an embossed invitation to contribute to the pages of their fledgling magazine. Their introduction to Damon Knight's "Not with a Bang" placed Bester in esteemed company, comparing his "Adam and No Eve" to Mary Shelley's *The Last Man* (1826) and M. P. Shiel's *The Purple Cloud* (1901), and it positioned Bester's story as the pinnacle of "modern" handlings of the classic "Last Man on Earth" theme.[28] Relatively little known in SF circles at the time, Bester welcomed this highly favorable notice and promptly sent Boucher a note of thanks, along with a manuscript to consider.[29]

Much like "Oddy and Id," the story Bester eventually fashioned from that manuscript, "Of Time and Third Avenue" (1951), would prove transitional.

Bester was still attempting to find his bearings—and his voice—in a field that had been on the periphery of his vision for nearly a decade. In part, he wrote the story out of a simple desire to portray a familiar locale, P. J. Clarke's on Third Avenue in midtown Manhattan, where he often socialized with the network-television crowd after live shows; but he also hoped to dismantle the "exhausted" plot scenario in which an almanac or newspaper from the future ends up in the past, bringing with it unlimited opportunity or grim news, or sometimes both at once. The story began as the first act of a play set in P. J. Clarke's, which Bester wrote and then set aside until an irksome variation on the newspaper-from-the-future plot prompted him to pick it back up and turn it into an SF story.[30] Although Bester did not recall the exact source of his irritation, he likely had plenty of variants to choose from: this type of plot had already crossed over into mainstream media in the mid-forties. *It Happened Tomorrow* (1944), a fantasy film loosely based on Lord Dunsany's one-act supernatural play "The Jest of Hahalaba" (1928), had employed the newspaper-from-the-future gimmick to notable box-office success, and several radio adaptations followed, the first of them for CBS New York's Lux Radio Theatre. Even as Bester prepared his story for publication, a new adaptation of the plot was in the works for CBS's Lux Video Theatre, which continued the long-running radio series on television. The episode would air as "The Jest of Hahalaba," just after Bester's story came out in the fall of 1951.

It is important to mention that although Bester would carry forward some elements of his early approach throughout his career, his foofaraw with Campbell clearly inflected his line of attack at this moment. Most notably, he put aside the plot type he had developed for the *Astounding* market, which involved nesting a scientific storyline within a wider philosophical or psychological frame, and experimented with language itself as a plot device. The idea that language might function as a driver of plot perhaps seems slippery, a problematic conflation of plot with story, but this strategy had been common in SF since its pulp days and accounted in part for SF's ability to borrow and hybridize all sorts of plots. Conceptually rich neologisms, in particular, had long been used to paper over gaps in scientific plausibility, foster the suspension of disbelief, and propel plots forward. A term such as "hyperdrive," shorthand for an engine capable of faster-than-light travel, provides a ready example of this practice and its ability to open up wide possibilities for incident in an equally wide range of settings. According to Peter Stockwell, such neologisms tended to work primarily within the register of hard sciences such as physics and engineering, especially in pulp SF.[31] In "Of Time and Third Avenue," Bester would employ neologisms extensively, but with a difference. He would bring about a shift in register, extrapolating primarily on psychological and sociolinguistic grounds, with the latter of the two taking precedence.

Considered solely in terms of plot points, very little physical action occurs in "Of Time and Third Avenue": a stranger negotiates the rental of an Irish tavern's back room for $100 and then makes peculiar use of a pay phone; a couple, regulars at the tavern, stop in for an afternoon soft drink; to their surprise, the stranger invites them to share the back room, and they talk. What incites the plot and moves it along is the stranger's odd demeanor, especially his speech. Admittedly, he looks unusual—young but very pale and hairless—and his clothes squeak unaccountably, but his otherness shows most in his language. He says, "MQ" for "yes" and "chronos" for "hour," and in the opening scene, the tavern's barkeep takes him for a "foreigner," probably a "Russian."[32] The stranger denies that he comes from outside the United States but also seems to be hiding his true identity. When asked his name, he identifies himself as "Boyne," by all appearances choosing the name on the spot from a poster on the wall that reads, "WHO FEARS MENTION THE BATTLE OF BOYNE?" (3). His behavior is similarly suspicious. He clips a cryptic device to the pay phone before placing his call and appears to conduct his conversation in code. Once again, his use of language—here a disorienting jumble of coordinates and talk of probabilities—comes to the foreground. By the time he ends the call with the farewell "Luck my Para," which reads in context like a condensed form of "Wish me luck, my friend," his inscrutable manner of speech perhaps weighs more heavily on the reader's mind than the question of his identity (4).

The opening of the story hints that Boyne is a spy, but the mystery of his identity is not drawn out much longer, at least not as a means of keeping the reader guessing at possibilities. Oliver Wilson Knight and his girlfriend Jane Clinton arrive at the tavern, and Boyne—after surprising them with his knowledge of their names and the details of their day—proceeds to lay bare his purpose. The year is 1950, but Knight has just purchased a 1990 almanac from a bookseller, and Boyne wants him to hand it over unopened. By his own account, he is an adjuster sent from the future to right a "mistake" that poses a grave threat not only to the existing timeline but also to Knight's personal well-being (5).

From this point on, the plot hinges less on who Boyne is than on whether or not Knight will believe him. In this respect, "Of Time and Third Avenue" resembles Bester's 1942 story "The Push of a Finger." Bester places his characters—and by extension, the reader—in a rhetorical situation, faced with the prospect of being duped by unreliable narration. Knight's response to Boyne underscores this narrative strategy. As Boyne attempts to persuade him to give up the almanac, Knight cycles through forms of disbelief. Is Boyne mentally unbalanced and dangerous? Is he one of those proverbial oddballs with a story to tell, the type one sometimes meets in a bar? Is he in on an elaborate practical joke? Much of the suspense in the story derives from this play of possibilities and from the way Bester captures the weird psychological atmosphere of a surprising encounter in a mundane setting. However, it is Boyne's unusual language that thickens the plot and moves it toward resolution.

Boyne's speech bears various markers of language change, of an English language that has drifted morphologically and lexically over time. For instance, he refers to the card game "Solitaire" as "Solhand," which suggests a syntactical inversion and blending of "a hand of solitaire" to form the latter word, and he employs neologisms such as "thisney" (7), "vorloss," "verdash" (8), and "null-coordinated" (7). The first of these, possibly a play on "Disney," means "boring" in the context of the story. The second and third sound German and are perhaps derived from that language, which Bester studied in college, but they do not appear to be identifiable transliterations of specific German words. Boyne's use of "vorloss" suggests "without" as a probable meaning, and Boyne himself translates "verdash" as "regret." In linguistic terms, these neologisms resemble loanwords borrowed from another language and used colloquially in English, words such as "hamburger" (German) and "graffiti" (Italian). The final term, "null-coordinated," which means "pointless" in the story, indicates a larger shift, one in cultural context. It suggests that Boyne comes from a future society that assigns high importance to coordinates—probably space-time coordinates of the sort used to locate Knight—and employs them as a fundamental way of understanding reality, so much so that reference to them has come to permeate language at the conceptual level.

Of course, a reader need not be a linguist to understand how these neologisms work in the story. Even if Bester invokes the complexities of language change, the point is that Boyne's speech represents an unsettling intrusion of an unknown future on the present. His words resist and elicit interpretation all at once. They are defined in context under the pretense of Boyne searching for the right word—the twentieth-century word—that Knight will understand, but not before they introduce a sense of otherness that slowly builds in significance and ultimately sways Knight. On the whole, Boyne's linguistic difference appears too unaffected and logically consistent to be an act. At the level of story, it points realistically to another reality; and for the reader, this ambiguous but open layer of meaning offers up a series of writable moments—junctures at which to pause and puzzle out any of a variety of implications that lend credibility to Boyne's fantastic claims and depth to his character. Certainly, it is important that Knight comes around to Boyne's point of view and gives up the opportunity to look into the future. In doing so, he puts the "dreams of childhood"—or wish fulfillment—behind him, choosing instead the adult world of uncertainty and responsibility (6). (In this respect, he offers an exact counterpoint to Oddy Gaul in "Oddy and Id.") But what matters most in narrative terms is *why* Knight believes Boyne and surrenders the almanac. Though Bester plants some meaty clues in Boyne's words, he largely leaves the work of answering this question to the reader's imagination.

This appeal to the imagination is, in a way, the crux of the story. In his attempts to dissuade Knight from using the almanac, Boyne compares doing so to the futility of cheating at solitaire. Knight must decide whether to seek "security" in stacking the deck and knowing what to expect or to play the game, with all the risks and surprises that that entails (7). In other words, he must decide whether to read his life in the pages of the book or to write his own story in earnest. It is worth noting that Knight is a decentered protagonist—Boyne's intense presence in fact overshadows him throughout the story—and that the reader's focus is channeled toward Knight's quandary more so than his qualities as a character. In a sense, his dilemma becomes the reader's dilemma, even a playful metacommentary on what it means to be a reader. Will the reader write the story, imaginatively speaking, or merely read it?

Initially, Bester perhaps expected too much of the reader. Boucher and McComas thought so, at any rate. In their view, Boyne's future-speak was overwhelming in the original draft, and they asked Bester to have Boyne "talk 1950 . . . until he loses himself in the passion of his arguments."[33] On similar grounds, they also rejected one of Bester's many proposed titles for the story, "The Future Is Tekon," characterizing it as "meaningless & even irritating" to prospective readers.[34] It is important to note, however, that their objections related primarily to Bester's use of language. Even though there was quite a bit of back-and-forth about the resolution of the story between author and editors, Bester made some concessions to the reader from the start. He did not, for instance, deny wish fulfillment altogether. After Knight returns the almanac, Boyne promises him a token of the future, one that will not disrupt the existing timeline, but says only that the barkeep Macy will deliver it. Just after Boyne leaves, Macy rushes in, claiming that Boyne paid him with counterfeit money, and shows Knight the 1980 date on the $100 bill he received. This revelation sets Knight guessing at Boyne's identity all over again—until he notices another detail on the bill: his own signature alongside the title of Secretary of the Treasury. This entertaining twist both underscores Bester's point—Knight holds himself accountable for the unpaid debt—and allows for a less grandiose form of wish fulfillment. Knight's future job title signals not easy wealth and power but hard work and somber responsibility. To be sure, Bester understood wish fulfillment as an important part of the science fiction imagination—and of SF's capacity to entertain—but he here insisted that this impulse be tempered by mature reflection rather than become a ritualized, readerly experience.

If Boucher and McComas judged the manuscript correctly and Bester did initially overwrite the story, it is interesting to speculate as to why. Did his bad experience with Campbell spur him to experiment even more aggressively? Did his view of SF as a vehicle for creative release make him somewhat self-indulgent? Whatever the case, Boucher and McComas, who were widely known for their encouraging and judicious correspondence with writers, reined Bester in gently. Bester's letter in response to their request for revisions thanked them effusively for their praise and assistance, showing how much he appreciated their soft touch. It also asked them for a further piece of advice, about an idea for a story to be titled "Sardine."[35]

Those familiar with Bester's *The Demolished Man* will know that a game called Sardine plays a central role in its plot, and remarkably, the synopsis of "Sardine" included in Bester's letter is none other than an early outline of sections of that novel. Primarily, Bester wanted to know if Boucher and McComas thought the plot worth pursuing and whether they would consider it for *Fantasy and Science Fiction*. Although they liked the plot immensely, they balked at a storyline of such exceptional complexity being written to their magazine's twelve-thousand-word maximum. Other magazines, including *Astounding*, *Amazing*, and *Startling*, might consider it at a somewhat longer length, they said, but they recommended turning it into a novel and submitting it to Doubleday or a similar publishing house for hardcover publication.[36] Bester often credited Horace L. Gold, *Galaxy*'s editor, with urging him to write *The Demolished Man*, but his response to this piece of encouragement and advice from Boucher and McComas perhaps reveals a more complex backstory for his decision to write the novel. Sounding as though the thought of a novel had yet to cross his mind, Bester replied that as a writer specializing in half-hour scripts, the "prospect of doing 60,000 words" filled him with a terror akin to "stage fright," but he also indicated that he intended to follow their advice and take the leap, attempting the longer form.[37]

Despite his anxieties, the stage was set for Bester's most unique performance to date. His encounter with Campbell had solidified his conception of himself as a writer standing "outside" the SF world, looking in;[38] his experiment with language in "Of Time and Third Avenue" had set out a new course for his fiction; and the editorial guidance of Boucher and McComas had helped him gauge the boundaries of the SF marketplace and begin to find his own voice. As he attempted the longer form, these factors would combine with Bester's restless inventiveness to explosive effect.

CHAPTER 4

THE EUREKA YEARS

Bester first told Boucher and McComas of his intention to write an SF novel in early May 1950, and afterward, aside from a few telegrams concerning the publication of "Of Time and Third Avenue," his correspondence with them more or less ceased until the fall of 1951, when he again mentioned the novel and asked them for further advice concerning hardcover publication. During this period, he planned and drafted *The Demolished Man*, mostly in consultation with Horace L. Gold, an old acquaintance who was in the process of launching another new SF magazine, *Galaxy Science Fiction*. Although Bester and Gold had followed similar career paths, starting in the pulps and moving on to comics and radio, they first met each other through Bester's wife, Rolly, who had appeared in several of Gold's radio scripts.[1] By Bester's account, he and Gold had been out of touch for some time when they resumed their acquaintance. Gold had served in the Pacific theater during World War II and returned from combat with an acute case of agoraphobia that left him largely housebound. He was essentially getting *Galaxy* off the ground from his apartment, conducting as much business as possible by telephone; and one day, he called Bester "out of the blue" to ask him to contribute to the magazine, probably as part of a larger effort to develop a list of writers before the magazine's official launch in October 1950. Bester initially responded to the request with reticence, citing his busy schedule as a script writer and saying that he "wasn't much of an SF author anyway," but Gold persisted, and Bester enjoyed talking shop with him so much that he warmed to the idea of becoming a *Galaxy* author.[2]

The timeline for Bester and Gold's early conversations remains uncertain, but the two very likely began discussing *The Demolished Man* in a serious way around the same time Boucher and McComas suggested to Bester that he expand his story idea for "Sardine" into a novel. On the one hand, Gold indicated that although he and Bester had talked about the novel an average of four hours a week for well over a year, Bester actually wrote *The Demolished Man* in less than three months.[3] On the other hand, Bester noted that he finished a draft of the novel at "end of the summer" in 1951.[4] As such, the period extending from the spring of 1950 to September 1951 fits both of their suggested timelines fairly well, especially given Gold's notoriously short production schedule for *Galaxy* in its early days.

Bester and Gold's conversations initially focused on "perhaps a dozen" story synopses the author had sent to the editor.[5] Gold rejected one of these outright but liked two others particularly and suggested combining them as the premise of a novel. According to Bester, the first of these focused on a future in which the development of "time-scanners" has made getting away with a crime a near impossibility—the police simply scan the past to identify the culprit. The second centered on a future in which advanced psychology or even telepathy has become a means of bridging social and cultural divides. Gold plucked the mystery and suspense element out of the first storyline, focusing on the question of how a criminal would plan and execute a crime in a future society with highly advanced policing methods. In regard to the second, it was the idea of telepathy as a source of epochal social change that grabbed him. After blending the two ideas, Gold proposed that Bester write about a crime committed in a society with a telepathic police force. How would telepathy change law enforcement? How would a criminal evade detection with the odds stacked against him?[6]

If Bester at first felt "quasi-interested" in writing an SF novel, Gold's suggestion intrigued him, especially the part about reimagining crime and policing through the lens of telepathy. According to Bester, nearly all of the story outlines he sent Gold engaged in some way with the notion of social and cultural change at the psychological level, and Gold's emphasis on telepathic policing opened up immense possibilities for world-building along those lines—for imagining how the advent of telepathy would influence not only a specific institution but also the very fabric of "life as we know it." The prospect of treating telepathy as a point of radical rupture in the understanding of social reality—or as a novum, to borrow Darko Suvin's later term for such conceptual dislocation—excited Bester so much that he drafted a "bubble" for the novel, one resembling the high-pitched prologues used to introduce radio shows. However, by his own admission, he "had not yet fallen in love with the book."[7]

That happened when he began to wrestle with the question of how to extrapolate psychological change convincingly. As he often did, Bester starting by working backward from ordinary experiences. In the evenings, he regularly attended or hosted social gatherings for "very quick and very hip" entertainment insiders who shared the same slang, jokes, and up-to-the-minute attitude; and sometimes, a "square" turned up at one of these events, appearing "completely out of place," lost in a world of unfamiliar codes and connotations. As an exercise, Bester tried to imagine a group of telepaths at a soiree of this sort. How would telepaths make conversation? What party games would they play? How would in-group and out-group dynamics work? These questions brought on an epiphany: a focus on language could not only convey the psychological subtleties of a future in which telepathy complicated social identity but also open up a wide avenue for stylistic experimentation. Telepaths, or "espers," would still employ language but communicate differently from "normals," especially among themselves. In fact, they would possess telepathic ability in differing degrees and develop their own social hierarchy on that basis. At an all-esper gathering, telepaths would favor a visually rich, mentally transmitted mixture of words and images rather than speech. Speech would appear gauche, a mark of lower-level ability and lower group status.

Along the same lines, telepaths would develop their own idioms, metaphors, and in-jokes—their own evolving linguistic culture defined over and against that of normals—but they would need to constantly code-switch between telepathic and spoken language, to accommodate not only normals but also other, less-advanced espers. Bester once again turned to language change as a form of extra-coding, as a way of layering meaning, and after he spent a couple of days in his workshop sketching out what were essentially highly patterned word clouds representing rapid-fire, group telepathic speech, he "fell in love" with the book for real.[8]

Bester's conversations with Gold soon increased in frequency and intensity but grew narrower in focus, returning time and again to a key issue: how to hybridize detective fiction and SF. This question had been in the air since the late forties, and John W. Campbell had expressed doubt that a true fusion of the two genres could occur. According to Isaac Asimov, Campbell had suggested to him that SF writers would find it too easy to cheat the discovery process. A writer could simply have a science-fictional detective whip out a gadget and say, "As you know, Watson, my pocket-frannistan is perfectly capable of detecting the hidden jewel."[9] Such a bait and switch would not only deflate any and all suspense but also squander the reader's willing suspension of disbelief; and to complicate matters even further, a writer portraying a technologically advanced society might even find it necessary to presume that such a device could or would exist.

Skepticism such as Campbell's did not, of course, prevent writers from attempting to combine the virtues of the two genres—Asimov reportedly began writing *The Caves of Steel* (1954) in an effort to prove Campbell wrong. However, Campbell's concerns were well founded. An admirable but failed attempt at cross-pollination between SF and mystery appeared in print just as Bester wrote *The Demolished Man*. Kenneth Fearing's 1951 novel *Loneliest Girl in the World* featured a researcher-cum-detective trying to solve a longstanding family mystery through the use of a massive and borderline sentient audio library named Mikki, but its climax rang hollow because the finely shaded characterization and suspenseful psychological plot ultimately gave way to a thin and unsatisfactory revelation: Mikki has possessed real-time recordings of the events in question all along. The protagonist just needed to figure out how to call them up. Although rather more sophisticated in conception than

Campbell's "pocket-frannistan," Fearing's futuristic audio library demonstrated the editor's point perfectly. It resulted in a heavy-handed infodump and attendant sense of letdown, failing to deliver on the reading protocols established earlier in the novel.

As Bester considered how to combine mystery-and-detection with SF, his knowledge of various plot types guided his thinking. For him, the problem lay not in a fundamental disconnect between SF and detective fiction but in the use of the closed-mystery format. Closed mysteries, sometimes referred to as whodunits, concealed the identity of the killer or thief until late in the story and as a result often required heavy exposition to unravel a tangled skein of plot. Bester thought that the open-mystery format, which identified the murderer or thief from the outset but withheld details about motive or the method of the crime, promised greater opportunity for synthesizing the two genres. The possible emphasis on motive, in particular, could shift the narrative pivot point from evidence collection, or the means thereof, to the greyer area of human psychology. His conversations with Gold began to turn invariably in this direction and again led to an aha moment: what if, for psychological reasons, not even the criminal fully understood his motive? In Bester's view, this premise would not only allow for a "new form of open mystery," one rooted in depth psychology, but also admirably complicate the discovery process.[10] After all, even a talented telepathic detective would struggle to extract information from the darkest regions of the unconscious, especially when the suspect's own self-rationalizations and involuntary mental blocks stood in the way. Likewise, the apparent openness of the mystery would be a facade and gradually erode as the reliability of both the suspect's viewpoint and the detective's conclusions came into question, principally on the basis of contextual clues relating to matters beyond the logistics of the crime itself. In this respect, Bester also carried forward a strategy from his early career. He hoped to create a slow-burning psychological plot that troubled the background of the story before igniting in full at the climax.

Bester and Gold shared several key attitudes about writing—not the least of which was the idea that a good writer would engage in "tremendous attack on a story," starting it at a level of complexity that a weaker writer would end it.[11] To that end, Bester decided to develop the hidden-motive premise from the opposing viewpoints of dual protagonists, both of them antiheroes. In the novel, business magnate Ben Reich faces off with esper detective Lincoln Powell. (Bester actually changed the latter's name from serial to book publication. Powell's first name was originally Preston). In a society practically free of murder and other serious crimes due to a telepathic police force, the two engage in a deadly, high-stakes struggle. Reich risks the ultimate punishment, Demolition, to kill his chief rival Craye D'Courtney and pave the way to a solar-system-wide corporate empire; but he suffers from recurrent nightmares about The Man With No Face, and from the outset, his anxiety dreams suggest that his compulsive drive to kill D'Courtney relates to a psychological mystery far more complex than a matter-of-fact profit motive. Powell, on the other hand, knows Reich did it but not how he did it. That is, his dilemma arises less from an internal conflict than from external circumstances. He must build his case in the face of ethical and legal constraints, particularly those stemming from The Esper Pledge. This oath does not necessarily protect normals from invasive "peeping," as mind reading is colloquially known, but it does discourage espers from invading normals' privacy.[12] That is, it serves as an ethical guideline for the use of telepathic powers, enlisting espers to "keep silence" on thoughts that "ought not" be revealed (98). In general, the Pledge resembles doctor-patient privilege in its logic, but in matters of law enforcement, it takes on an added dimension, serving as the basis for a suspect's right to silence. During interrogation, a suspect may refuse telepathic examination, and in any event, telepathic evidence is not admissible in court. Even if Powell cheats the discovery process by illicitly peeping Reich—which he does repeatedly—he must produce objective evidence of Reich's guilt, and it becomes increasingly apparent as the plot progresses that his promising career is on the line if he fails to do so.

However much Gold helped Bester to develop this line of attack on the story, Bester had his own longstanding reason for pursuing it. Writing for comics and radio, he had grown "sick and tired of the good-guy–bad-guy cliché," so much so that he often found himself siding with villains and against heroes. In fact, by his own admission, his soft spot for bad guys posed a problem in the writing of *The Demolished Man*. He found it easy to round out Reich's character, but he labored to give Powell any sympathetic qualities at all, especially in the *Galaxy* serial, which he later revised extensively to address the issue.[13]

Clear precedent for Reich's character appears in Bester's earlier work, indicating that in addition to brainstorming with Gold, he engaged in self-pastiche, or adaptive borrowing of older material. Bester once indicated that he developed the open mystery format of *The Demolished Man* in response to one of his own radio scripts. While mining his files for story ideas, he came across the script and realized that he "had written all the wrong scenes. It was a solid story but in the attempt to keep it a closed puzzle [he] had been forced to omit the real drama in order to present the perplexing results of the behind-the-scenes action."[14] Arguably, this comment refers to "The Man with No Face," a *Shadow* script from 1949 in which the real drama centers on an unusual criminal and pattern of crime but, for the most part, gets lost in the background of the story. The script features Cheater Slade, a career criminal horribly disfigured in a fire while escaping the police. In the aftermath of the incident, he becomes a drifter and wanders for some twenty years without a face or a memory—until he happens on his old neighborhood. These familiar surroundings trigger an episode of traumatic recall, and he begins to relive a brutal killing spree from his past, taking random victims in the same locations as the earlier murders. In keeping with the closed mystery, listeners experience only bits and snatches of this action directly. For instance, in a fragmentary and enigmatic scene, they hear the killer calling one his victims by the wrong name as he approaches and the victim muttering in terror about the killer's lack of a face. Likewise, listeners know almost nothing of Slade's backstory until the big reveal at the end of the episode, when the detective connects the puzzle pieces for them.

Even if Bester did not refer to this script specifically, it nonetheless illustrates his point and provides an instructive example of how he adapted his own material. Outwardly, Slade resembles Ben Reich very little as a character—he is a common street tough through and through—but inwardly, the two suffer from the same psychotic mindset, committing their crimes on the basis of repressed memories and projecting their delusions onto the world around them. In other words, Bester borrowed not the character but the technique—the device of unconscious motive—and transferred it to an open mystery format that would bring the hidden psychological drama and accompanying action into to the foreground. To boot, he reimagined Slade's physical disfigurement as a metaphor for dissociative identity. Reich repeatedly encounters "The Man With No Face" in his nightmares, and this haunting symbol functions as a screen or veil hiding a shadow aspect of his own identity, one related to D'Courtney.

Bester in some ways simply revived strategies dating back to his days as a pulp writer in setting up the conflict between Reich and Powell. As he had in early stories such as "The Probable Man" and "Hell Is Forever," he employed early instances of metanarration and narrative incongruity to draw attention to SF reading protocols and shift the focus from hard science to psychology. The *Galaxy* serial included a prologue, one very likely based on Bester's initial introductory "bubble" for the novel; and it not only detailed social and economic changes resulting from the advent of antigravity generators, space exploration, and telepathy, thereby fleshing out the novel's background, it also introduced a key moment of metanarration that alerted the reader to approach the story—especially the question of the true protagonist—with caution. This prologue opens with an account of Edward Turnbul, who conducts the first successful null-gee experiment with the "dashing insouciance" of a "fictional hero," but the narrator dismisses him—and the very idea of the scientist-hero—in the span of a few sentences. "Forget Turnbul," the narrator instructs the reader. "He is not your protagonist. If you identify with him, you will be lost in this story, as Turnbul himself is lost in the shifting pattern that produced the Demolished Man."[15] This comment all but declared to readers of the day that Bester meant to write against the grain of techno-adventure, especially the type that established a clear line of identification with a scientist-hero and then allowed the reader to sit back and enjoy the ride. In effect, the narrator positions readers themselves as problem-solvers, charged with the task of sorting through and rearranging bits and pieces of an unstable "pattern" in order to create meaning. This instance of metanarration, in other words, cultivates a writerly reader. It also unsettles rather than determines the reader's line of identification, foreshadowing Bester's use of dueling protagonists.

Although the prologue would eventually get cut from the novel, Bester opposed the change every step of the way, showing how much he valued it as a framework for the narrative. When Gold tried to drop it, Bester tried but failed to convince him of its importance, so he switched tactics, citing the short production schedule (which left less than twenty-four hours to adjust the manuscript before it went to the printer!), and eventually won out. Later, Bester's book publishers asked him to delete the prologue, and he again protested. This time, however, he came up against New American Library's hard seventy-thousand-word limit for paperbacks. The editors there informed him that they could drop the prologue and bring the book to length without labeling it "abridged," a designation that usually hurt sales. On that basis, NAL more or less mandated the change.[16]

The text proper also instigates a narrative side game but introduces it on different terms: Bester includes an early and thinly veiled clue that reads almost like an unintentional error. Against the ropes in his corporate battle with the D'Courtney cartel and before he settles on such a drastic measure as murder, Reich sends D'Courtney a coded message proposing an alliance. It reads "YYJI TTED RRCB UUFE AALK QQBA," or "SUGGEST MERGER BOTH OUR INTERESTS EQUAL PARTNERSHIP" (18). As Reich composes the message, the reader gets a direct glimpse of the secret code that cartels use to communicate, namely a two-column list that includes a sampling of ciphers beyond those that the message requires. Several pages later, Reich receives the reply "WWHG" and flies into a rage, screaming "Offer refused! Refused! REFUSED!" (25). In that instant, he makes up his mind to kill D'Courtney. What is more, readers who fail to consider Reich's dialogue against the available background information are misled, not necessarily by the narrative itself but by their own passive reading. A quick flip back to the codes, which stand out prominently against the regular text, reveals that "WWHG" actually means "ACCEPT OFFER" (17). A cipher for refusal does not even appear in the list.

In the novel as a whole, narrative tells and purposeful omissions tend to linger ambiguously in the background, playing off of one another in a fluctuating pattern. They gain significance by virtue of accrual and juxtaposition. By comparison, this early clue is a blunt instrument. It is flatly empirical, resolved into an apparent fact through a slight inference on the reader's part or, failing that, through a trivial bit of rereading. In all likelihood, Bester banked on readers catching it. But to what end? At first, the clue appears almost hamfisted, a sign either of Bester's underestimation of readers or of his ungainly handling of the plot—perhaps even of an editing or printing gaffe—but this impression changes as one tries to pin it down. Why does Reich misread the reply? Has he confused the codes? Cracked due to mental strain? Become so fixated on the idea of killing D'Courtney that he suffers from tunnel vision? Even if Reich's misapprehension hints at a psychological cause—a festering compulsion or a broken mind—this clue is most significant as a reading cue. The tangible evidence of the cipher in the Executive Code Book, which the reader has seen along with Reich, gives way to a psychological quandary. In other words, this odd moment signals how to read the novel rather than conveying specific content. It suggests that the reader look beyond the physical evidence and fast-paced action to the psychological layer of the plot. As such, it offers direction just as much as the possibility of misdirection, even gesturing toward motive as the narrative's central concern. Bester plays fair with the reader, offering up a crucial clue to the reading protocol necessary to solve the mystery, and the side game is on for real.

If Bester continued to make use of narrative strategies in place since his early career as he wrote *The Demolished Man*, he also developed his newfound interest in language change as a thematic device and tool for world-building. Discussions of Bester's fiction often point toward this facet of his work by way of critical catchphrases such as "typographical tricks" and "pyrotechnic" style but rarely do it justice. Arguably, the latter description, though it varies in meaning from critic to critic, even puts Bester's use of language on par with lightweight special effects.[17] To the contrary, Bester's play with language involves a range of specific techniques from nonstandard orthography to stream-of-consciousness narration, and his style not only serves to dazzle and entertain—it opens up metalinguistic terrain for the reader, particularly with regard to esper psychology and culture.

For those who might not be familiar with the term "orthography," it refers to the rules for writing a language—with respect to spelling, capitalization, punctuation, and so on. Nonstandard orthography deviates from or bends the rules, sometimes purposefully. As an example, SMS language or text-speak—which employs abbreviations, stylization of words, paralinguistic features such as emoticons, and other devices—often flouts the rules of standard written English, largely for the sake of brevity or personal style. In *The Demolished Man*, Bester turns to nonstandard orthography as a means of portraying the ins and outs of telepathy as a mode of communication. As imagined by Bester, telepathy resembles writing. Espers transmit not just impressions but formed speech in a visual medium. They send these thoughts almost instantaneously—whole conversations occur in the span of seconds—and they often make use of either shorthand or extra-coded language to convey maximal meaning in the most condensed form possible. Espers commonly substitute symbols for words or expressions, as in the use of "&" for "and" and "?" for interjections indicating surprise or confusion, and in at least one instance, two characters are described as conducting an entire argument in "sine curves" (40). Espers also visually overcode words to embed the speaker's attitude in the word itself, as when Powell sends an Old-English "**Blessings!**" to his friend and would-be girlfriend Mary Noyes to express his over-the-top gratitude for her help, or when Noyes sends "*$N̸ØW̸*" with italics and vertical strikethroughs to Powell in an effort to censure him for his aloof attitude toward her (32–33). Needless to say, this practice extends to esper-style humor. In mock distress, Powell asks Noyes to help him throw together appetizers for his party by pleading for "Canapés$^{\text{S.O.S.}}$?" (33). Later, he points out Wally Chervil's excessive girth by referring to his guest's "(lap)^2," using parentheses to visually represent Chervil's bulging belly, and adding a mathematical notation to stress its size (37). In other instances that Bester does not attempt to represent orthographically, espers forego the use of language altogether, relying entirely on idiomatic images that communicate common ideas in a distinctive but immediate way. For example, the image of a "horse laughing" is more or less equivalent to "laughing my head off" or, in the parlance of contemporary texting, "LMAO" (89). The image of a "cat smiling" means "the cat that ate the mouse" (152). Both images express context-specific meaning paralinguistically, much like emoticons that convey tone or attitude without words. Certainly, Bester's development of a nonstandard orthography to represent telepathy facilitates flashy, idiosyncratic style, but it amounts to rather more than the "amusing use of typographic patterns."[18] It also serves a larger thematic purpose, drawing attention to esper language practices as a window on esper social identity. Espers share a common language with normals, but they code that language differently, not only to adapt it to the medium of telepathic communication but also to mark out their difference.

This connection of language and social identity comes to the foreground most particularly in the esper practice of "weaving," which Bester portrays through stream-of-consciousness narration. Shortly after guests arrive for the all-esper party at Powell's house, Powell exclaims, "*@tkins! Chervil! Tate! Have a heart! Will you people look at the pattern (?) we've been weaving . . .*" Of course, what Powell means is that the zigzagging "TP chatter" in the room forms no pattern at all, and on his prompt, his guests begin to piece together a conversation that, as Bester represents it, reads in multiple directions at once, with some senders' words being incorporated or reticulated into others' statements in an expanding network (35). (By Bester's account, making this conversation "interlock completely" took him no less than "*four days.*"[19]) Another type of weaving occurs at the party when the espers play a telepathic version of Rebus. Generally, "Rebus" refers to a puzzle in which a combination of letters, images, numbers, or symbols cleverly conceal a word or phrase. Thus, in a very basic example, the letter "a" plus a picture of a door equals "adore." Espers have turned this type of puzzle into a party game, adding new layers to it along the way. Text, for instance, now becomes a way of camouflaging the images that spell out a word or phrase. One of the players weaves an "old poem"—actually the opening of Matthew Arnold's "Dover Beach"—into the image of an eye in a beer stein, apparently hoping that the incongruity of the poem's content with the sight pun will misdirect others from the correct answer: Einstein (38–39). As a conversational art and an entertainment, weaving cements social bonds, but it also reflects an essential aspect of esper psychology. Awash in others' thoughts, espers crave the society of others of their kind—of those able to give pattern to the chaos—and they derive their sense of belonging from the very act of weaving. Jerry Church, an esper banished for violating the Pledge, illustrates this point well. An "Esper ~~2~~" whose very classification puts him under erasure, Church lingers outside Powell's house during the party, eavesdropping as an "ever-changing, exhilarating design" ebbs and flows inside. He feels utterly "starved" for "his own people" and the social pleasures of weaving after ten years in exile, living on a "sub-marginal diet of words" alone (38).

The vibrancy of language and identity in the emergent esper culture, by all appearances, runs counter to the wider social reality of the twenty-fourth century. Though the reader catches only glimpses of society at large, in those instances commercialism and decadence go hand in hand. Spaceland, a vast, piecemeal assembly of resorts and amusement parks in the dead of space, panders to the whims of the moneyed elite, and closer to home, Chooka

Frood's Rainbow House, a gaudy "Frab Joint" specializing in fortune telling and sensual "vices" of any and all varieties, does much the same for a much broader—and seedier—clientele (116–17). In both of these settings, identity is a commodity, a thing to be bought and sold rather than an aspect of selfhood or of social bonding, a point Bester underscores by drawing attention to the appropriation of traditional identities for commercial purposes. For instance, when Powell visits Spaceland, he happens across a replica of Notre Dame Cathedral with a sign identifying it as "Ye Wee Kirk O Th' Glen." A canned voice booming from speakers built into the mouths of the gargoyles on the towers baits tourists with promises of robotic recreations of events in the lives of Moses, Christ, Mohammed, Lao Tse, Buddha, and Mary Baker Eddy, among others, but also cautions those who enter to refrain from "LOUD TALKING OR LAUGHTER" due to the "SACRED NATURE" of the attraction. As the message begins to cycle in different languages, to reach the widest possible range of "WORSHIPERS," Powell bursts out in laughter at its absurdity—its superficial seriousness, its flattening of diverse religious identities, and its own profane blaring (163).

Bester also presents such cultural decay in individual terms, laying particular emphasis on language. In his portrayal of Maria Beaumont, a dissipated socialite of a less-sophisticated sort than Lady Sutton from "Hell Is Forever," he again employs nonstandard orthography, but with a satirical edge that contrasts sharply with his handling of esper language. When Beaumont invites Reich to a party at her home, she writes him a note reading: "Darling! Darling! Darling! I thot you'd forgoten . . . little ol sexy mė. How 2 divine. Come to Beaumont House tonite. Were haveing a party" (45). Beaumont's unintentional misspellings lay at the exact opposite end of the communication spectrum from conscious language play, showing an utter lack of rhetorical awareness and control, and her fatuous use of "2" serves no stylistic purpose, though it perhaps helps her avoid the difficult choice between "to" and "too." She also engages in paralinguistic communication, enclosing a nude self-portrait inlaid in an imitation jewel along with the note, but this crude self-advertisement positions Reich as a spectator rather than an interlocutor. Compared to espers' language play and weaving, which aims to produce cultural common ground, Beaumont's use of language signals a narcissistic rather than socially oriented identity, a relative absence of culture in the sense of a shared, actively evolving literacy practice. As her nickname—"The Gilt Corpse"—suggests, she represents a dominant but deteriorating order, one rife with signs of decay (55).

Bester's focus on language change as a means of world-building at the psychological level deepens the conflict between Reich and Powell even as it illuminates the impact of telepathy on twenty-fourth-century crime and policing. It sets in motion a dialectic of character and context that adds depth to both. In a future where telepaths routinely peep either criminal intent before a crime or evidence of guilt after, strategies of evasion prove limited, at least for normals. Reich, however, proves adept at psychological warfare, seizing on language as a key weapon. For instance, he develops an ingenious means of mimicking the mental blocks that espers use to mask private thoughts and other confidential information. As a matter of course, Reich's corporation attempts to curb undesirable behavior in employees through subliminal "conditioning," and by way of requesting a catchy song for that purpose, he casually asks spunky songwriter Duffy Wyg& to perform her most "persistent" jingle to date, one that lodged in listeners' minds with absolute tenacity (47). She demurs, warning him of the dire aftereffects, but eventually gives in and plays him a monotonous little earworm called "Tenser, Said the Tensor." Overcoded on purpose and in the extreme, the song contains, in Wyg&'s words, "some real gone tricks" (49). It incorporates a host of melodic clichés, and the lyrics combine irregular meter with frequent, misplaced internal rhymes such as the ones evident in the phrase "Tension, apprehension / and dissention have begun" (48). It also halts on a "semi-cadence," or hanging beat, that loops back to the first note and, in effect, starts the song again (49). Not unlike Joyce's *Finnegans Wake*, which breaks off in the middle of a sentence completed by the fragmentary first line of the book, the song never actually ends. In accordance with Reich's plan, "Tenser" establishes itself firmly in his mind, and when he needs to block peeping, he simply focuses on it to generate an intense interference pattern.

In a similarly clever psychological maneuver, Reich also provides himself with an alibied opportunity to commit the murder. Knowing that the gravely ill D'Courtney will spend a single night at Maria Beaumont's and that she will throw herself a birthday party on the same evening, Reich finagles an invitation and buys her a distinctive present, an "obsolete printed" book of "ancient" party games (44). Of course, he does so only after wandering conspicuously through a store, muttering about being at an utter loss for a gift idea, and when he does finally pick up the book, almost as if by accident, he plays up its poor condition in front of the growing hoard of salespeople assisting him. Afterward, he expertly defaces the book further, so that only the game Sardine remains legible. Then, according to the ostentatious gift-giving customs of the day, which dictate that a present arrive with a price tag attached, he sends it out to an antiquarian, who verifies its authenticity, condition, and value. Basically, Reich overcodes the book to make it signify only in ways that serve his purposes. He damages it in a fashion consistent with its age to deceive the appraiser, but at the same time, he leaves only one game for Beaumont to choose, thereby giving the text a highly restricted, even redundant, meaning. Admittedly, Reich takes a risk in presuming that Beaumont will ask her guests to play the game, but given that Sardine is a version of Hide-and-Seek played in the dark, he banks on her decadence—on her seeing the game as a way to spice up the party for her novelty-hungry guests. With any luck, the game itself will afford him enough time to sneak away to D'Courtney's quarters in the darkness, commit the murder, and return unnoticed. (In the end, Beaumont's response far exceeds Reich's expectations. She suggests, much to her licentious guests' delight, that they play Sardine in the nude.) Of course, in the wake of the murder, another audience for the book emerges: police investigators. Predictably, they find it difficult, even by way of peeping, to hold Reich accountable for the book's limited content or for Beaumont's decision to include the game among her birthday entertainments. Reich has manipulated not only the physical evidence but also the psychological footprint of the crime, alibiing his opportunity in the minds of the salespeople, the appraiser, the guests, and Beaumont. He manufactures reasonable doubt, imbuing both his selection of the book as a gift and its suspiciously narrow message with the troubling hues of coincidence.

Such recoding, it is worth pausing to note, also occurs at the level of plotting. Whodunits from the Golden Age of detective fiction such as Ngaio Marsh's *A Man Lay Dead* (1934) regularly featured murders committed at social gatherings under cover of darkness, utilizing the lights-out trope as a way to initiate a Clue-like guessing game focused on the question of who has committed the murder. Bester switches up the usual reading protocol, making the backstory of Reich's opportunity—that is, how he gets the lights out in the first place—more important than the event itself. He appropriates the machinery of mystery plotting and puts it in the service of science-fictional world-building, producing a hybrid plot device in the process.

Bester brings the concept of language change to bear on policing in a more disturbing manner, raising specters of the abuse of power. High-grade espers such as Powell live and work in a predominantly normal society, and as a matter of routine, they code-switch between speech and telepathy or even carry on divergent conversations in both mediums simultaneously, engaging in what might be termed multiplex communication. In his detective work, Powell turns these everyday practices to the ends of interrogation, arguably in a manner that skirts the boundaries of ethics and procedure. That is, when dealing with normals, he needs aboveboard statements, volunteered rather than peeped, but he often employs his telepathic abilities in a questionable manner to secure admissible evidence. Take, for instance, his attempt to discover how Reich incapacitated D'Courtney's bodyguards and gained entry to the room where he committed the murder. As the reader knows, Reich has used a Rhodopsin Ionizer—a type of knock-out drop deployed visually through an intense flash of light—and covered his tracks very carefully. His R&D labs developed the device in secret, and after stealing a prototype, Reich arranged an accident to destroy all the related research and materials. Powell's forensics team is able to make an educated guess as to Reich's method but not to uncover evidence that a gadget such as a Rhodopsin Ionizer actually exists. As a result, Powell needs the scientist who invented it to reveal the design. That way, his experts will be able to reproduce the prototype as an objective link in the chain of evidence.

Powell does not bring the scientist, a normal named Dr. Wilson Jordan, in for questioning. Instead, he invites him to tour the Guild Laboratory and enlists the esper researchers working there to wheedle the information out of him. The interrogation does not occur in the box, as in a police procedural, but it does involve a psychological game. Powell reassures Jordan that his visit has absolutely nothing to do with the investigation and remains all charm and deference with him verbally, but on the telepathic level, he cynically instructs his esper colleagues to conspire with him in "*pulling a fast one.*" Powell knows just the right pressure points in Jordan's psychology, and he asks them in particular to make the scientist *"feel paternal,"* to appeal to his professional vanity (140). With no apparent qualms, they fabricate phony, even absurd, visual research problems as a pretext for fawning over Jordan and begging him for advice. Seduced by nothing less than several hours of contrived hero worship, Jordan freely offers all of the information Powell requires and leaves none the wiser of the deception. In fact, he feels sure that he has "materially benefited science and never betrayed that fine and generous patron, Mr. Benjamin Reich" (142). Even if Jordan represents yet another of Bester's caricatures of an egotistical scientist, this scene portrays a dangerously uneven power dynamic at work in the context of law enforcement, one that Powell and his esper associates exploit without a second thought. They feel no scruples about psychological duplicity, even appear to revel in it, and the line between telepathy as a heroic attribute and a tool for callous manipulation grows paper thin, leaving the reader to decide if the end justifies the means.

Late Australian critic and novelist George Turner once characterized *The Demolished Man* as a "triumph of style over content," asserting that Bester "faked" telepathy, using slick verbal tricks to gloss over related "mechanical problems" and thus sidestep the "science" in science fiction.[20] In his view, Bester failed to extrapolate in a science-fictional manner, neglecting to explain with precision how telepathy works and why it exists; but to accept Turner's reading, one must collapse style and language, ignoring the latter as a basis for extrapolation. Bester does deemphasize the hows and whys of telepathy in terms of presenting it in pseudoscientific terms—the only possible "scientific" terms—but he captures its social dimensions in a highly realistic manner, presenting it as a likely source of language change, perceptual evolution, and psychosocial division. This technique was no accidental side effect of superficial stylistic choices. As Bester himself explained, he understood style as a basis for linguistic extrapolation. Once, when asked about the role of typographical play in his fiction, he testily responded that it was not merely a stylistic "trick" and underscored its importance to world-building. Specifically, he connected it to his desire to "create an entire milieu," one with hyperrealistic touches of "color" and texture.[21]

If Bester turned to language to dramatize psychological change, he also paid heed to the wider social climate sure to surround such change. As one would expect, with the rise of telepathy, some normals have come to fear or resent espers, thinking of extrasensory perception as a threat not only to privacy but also to the structure of society as they know it. They view telepaths as a powerful social in-group, as an elite minority that is changing society from the inside, perhaps even becoming a master class—and their concerns are hardly unfounded. The Esper Pledge encourages telepaths to think of membership in the esper community as a familial relation superseding all other social ties. The laws of the Esper Guild, independent of the legal system at large, require telepaths to marry other telepaths as part of a eugenic plan designed to preserve and refine the trait. Telepathic ability confers immense social advantages on those who possess it, including ready access to educational, employment, and networking opportunities available through the Guild. More disturbingly, a splinter group known as the League of Esper Patriots agitates against the Guild and borders on "fascism" in its promotion of the view that espers are a natural-born "aristocracy" fitted to rule over normals (99). Even espers of a more democratic stripe condescend to normals, matter-of-factly characterizing them as "deaf-mutes" (23). In general, espers understand themselves as the pinnacle of evolution, but Reich—who counts himself among the skeptics—responds to that idea with disdain, saying: "Those damned mind readers are supposed to be the greatest advance since Homo sapiens evolved. E for Evolution. Bastards! E for Exploitation!" (13).

Naturally, some normals also regard telepaths highly. A good number even envy espers, harboring false hopes that they themselves possess latent ability. Every day, normals who want testing or training line up in the Guild lobby, and a receptionist handles their insistent inquiries, all the while secretly conducting the basic guild test. That is, as she answers questions verbally, the receptionist simultaneously broadcasts, *"If you can hear me, please go through the door on left marked EMPLOYEES ONLY"* (97). Unfortunately, this simple ruse for identifying latent espers rarely yields results because most of the hopefuls prove "deaf" to her announcement (97). Powell's attitude toward such want-to-be espers is instructive. He describes their mindset in terms of wish-fulfillment fantasy. From his perspective, they romanticize telepathic ability as a "magic quality" that will transform their lives, allowing them to stage-manage other people and game the system for personal gain. By contrast, Powell understands the pressures of the esper world from the inside, citing in particular the stringency of Guild laws that govern the use of telepathy and the "heavy" ethical responsibility that comes with esper powers (96). Though he sometimes bends the rules, he takes Guild Law and the Esper Pledge seriously, seeing them as necessary but imperfect instruments of the greater social good. Powell's notion of social change as a difficult process requiring checks and balances offsets Reich's picture of espers as exploitative, and considered side by side, their viewpoints dramatize a society in a state of uneven development, afflicted with a divided consciousness of itself.

Competing perspectives such as Reich's and Powell's ensure that the novel never slips into a simple us-versus-them mentality. Bester's espers comprise neither a Van Vogtian pariah elite nor a corps of Orwellian thought police; and Bester's image of a hybrid society at odds with itself results in a rich interplay of character and context, especially with regard to Powell. If normals fear psychological manipulation at the hands of espers, Bester nonetheless writes Powell as a character prone to duplicity. In general, telepaths exhibit a heightened "responsiveness" to their surroundings, and because of his "enlarged sense of humor," Powell often responds to amusing or tense rhetorical situations with lies on the scale of tall tales. At these moments, he slips unconsciously into an alter ego that he refers to—in a playful inversion of Abraham Lincoln's well-known moniker—as "Dishonest Abe" (32). Troublingly, Abe sometimes surfaces in the context of Powell's police work, making the detective appear unstable and impulsive, a shade darker as an antihero. However, Powell also genuinely, often comically, struggles to suppress Abe, and Abe seems as much a release valve developed in response to simmering psychosocial pressures or a quirky side effect of advanced telepathic ability as a sinister aspect of Powell's character. In this respect, Abe's existence actually humanizes Powell, giving him the appearance of an everyman with pardonable flaws rather than an aloof or unassailable superman. Powell is caught up in the throes of change, puzzling out how to navigate an evolving reality just as much as the next person, and the complexities of his society remain complex at the level personal experience—he does not transcend or escape them by virtue of his powers.

Much has been made of the Freudian underpinnings of *The Demolished Man*, largely in terms of the Oedipus complex, but Bester's expansive, sociolinguistic treatment of telepathy actually impels the plot and much of the character development until about two-thirds of the way into the novel, when

Powell's case unexpectedly collapses due to insufficient documentation of Reich's profit motive. In fact, up to this false climax, Bester has mostly borrowed stock incidents from detective fiction—the "good cop, bad cop" routine, the race to locate a key witness, the slick interrogation, and so on. If the language-oriented world-building were to be stripped away, these plot devices would appear formulaic, largely barren of ambiguity and thus of story. However, the same shifting patterns of language and culture that bring the background of the novel to life also serve as an elaborate blind of sorts, allowing Bester to plant clues of Reich's passion motive in plain view and set up the Freudian turn that undergirds the final act of the novel. While repetition of the Man-With-No-Face motif serves as an enigmatic reminder that a repressed trauma lurks in Reich's unconscious mind, these clues crop up visibly in the narrative, as circumstances obliquely suggesting the nature of that trauma. Why has D'Courtney given an estate on Callisto to Reich's mother? Why does Reich hesitate when he has the opportunity to kill Barbara, the sole witness to the murder? Why does Barbara harbor a twisted image of herself and Reich as "Siamese twins" deep in her unconscious? (156) As Powell pieces together his case in fits and starts, he raises these questions, but only in passing, in part because they seem likely to yield circumstantial rather than direct evidence. Through this sort of incluing, Bester gives readers opportunities to make inferences and second-guess Powell's line of reasoning, but he leaves the problem of individual psychology in the far background, only faintly discernible through the looming social concerns introduced via world-building.

Perhaps not surprisingly, Powell's case falls through when he obtains a piece of information that has been accessible to readers from the outset of the novel. His lab finally cracks D'Courtney's coded message to Reich, and much to his consternation, he learns that D'Courtney accepted Reich's offer of a merger. By all appearances, Reich had nothing to gain from D'Courtney's death and much to lose if his battle with the D'Courtney Cartel continued. Because the profit motive for the murder no longer holds, Powell's superiors force him to drop Reich as a suspect. Reich will walk, plain and simple. At this moment, the problem of Reich's unconscious motive moves center stage, and the narrative begins to build toward the real climax. The Man With No Face now haunts Reich more persistently than ever, even crossing over into his conscious perception as a hallucination, and several mysterious attempts on Reich's life occur. Reich blames these incidents on Powell and, in a desperately paranoid state, instigates a violent confrontation with the detective. During this scene, the astonished Powell discovers that Reich truly believes D'Courtney rejected his offer, and he chides himself for missing the evidence of Reich's passion motive, muttering it verbally as he connects the puzzle pieces in his mind. He peeps Reich on the spot in order to confirm his suspicions and discovers the identity of The Man With No Face in the process, but he refuses to divulge it to Reich, saying cryptically: "He's your ancient enemy, Reich . . . A man you'll never escape" (200). By extension, of course, Bester also denies the reader access to Powell's breakthrough. He represents Powell's thought process via dialogue, retracing the trail of breadcrumbs scattered throughout the narrative, but challenges readers to play psychologist and synthesize the clues along with Powell.

Bester also introduces a new complication. As Powell peeps Reich, he recognizes him as one of those "rare Universe-shakers" capable of refashioning reality in his own image (208). Reich stands at a "crucial link" in history, possessed of wealth, social influence, and a compulsive drive that will likely make "his reality become the world's reality" (207). Although Bester imagines him in less fantastic terms than Odysseus Gaul from "Oddy and Id," Reich shares that earlier character's will to power and could achieve a similar sort of dominion, imposing his psychotic mindset on society from the top down by material means. Here, Bester forges a link between the psychosocial landscape built up in previous portions of the novel and Reich's individual psychology, largely through allusion to Freudian contexts, especially the socially oriented theories of *Civilization and Its Discontents* (1930). Freud portrayed the death drive, which he associated with deep-seated human instincts toward aggression and self-destruction, as the "greatest impediment" to society.[22] Reich, with his "killer instinct" (25), not only embodies the death drive, he threatens to enthrone it at the center of the social order. In the face of this terrible possibility, Powell convinces the Guild to allow him to undertake a drastic and dangerous measure, a Mass Cathexis procedure that no telepath has yet survived. He will channel the latent psychic energy of thousands of espers, capitalizing it in order to force Reich into a confrontation with The Man With No Face.

With the Mass Cathexis scene, Bester returns to psychological world-building but purposefully inverts his approach. He brings Reich's fractured psychology into close focus by unbuilding the social world around it. This switchback in the narrative plays out in a series of hairpin turns: an image of a "fearful torrent" of psychic energy descending on Powell is followed by an inscrutable interlude of stream-of-consciousness narration and a quick shift into Reich's viewpoint that proves more complex that it initially seems (214). Reich apparently awakens from a nightmare consisting of jumbled words, equations, and commands, but as the reader later realizes, the stream-of-consciousness segment actually portrays Powell engaging Reich psychically, entering into his mind to attempt to destabilize his delusional reality and lure him into an encounter with The Man With No Face. In a jujitsu-like maneuver, Powell uses Reich's burgeoning god complex against him, drawing him into the "common neurotic" fantasy that "he alone" really exists (242). Basically, Powell recodes Reich's mind, building up an elaborate reality construct within it and then deconstructing it, bit by bit.

Filtered entirely through Reich's perception, this surreal section of the novel shimmers with the paranoia of a waking dream. Reich first notices that the stars have vanished from the night sky, then the planets, but no one else appears to remember that they ever existed. Reich tries to distract himself with work, but when he orders a hostile takeover of the D'Courtney Cartel, his staff gazes at him blankly, fearing for his sanity. It no longer exists, either. He attempts to flee to his home in Paris to regroup, but the ticket agent at the travel office looks up, revealing himself to be The Man With No Face, and says eerily: "There is no Paris" (231). When the external world completely disappears, Reich has nowhere to project his delusions, no society to act out against. He eventually finds himself alone with The Man, forced to look directly at his face, and he sees first himself and then D'Courtney, their faces "blending into one" in an uncanny double image (235). He finally recognizes D'Courtney for what he is: his father.

If this twist sounds like a precursor to the sort of "Luke, I am your father" moment that *Star Wars* (1977) transformed into a cultural archetype, rest assured that Bester pulls it off without excessive melodrama. In the scene, the failure of Reich's identity merely takes the form of an accomplished fact. Powell's disappearing-reality gambit does not cure Reich—it lays bare his megalomania, his propensity to view others as "dolls" and "puppets" in a drama centered on him. Nor is Reich redeemed. No sense of reconciliation with his father or of personal transformation emerges. Though sometimes admirable for his spirit and determination, Reich simply fails the "test" of selfhood. Immersed in his viewpoint, the reader follows him to this dead end. As such, the climax of the novel cuts against the grain of escapist storytelling—power fantasies do not obtain, and the Answer does not come to light. To the contrary, Reich's god complex devolves into neurotic fantasy, and he learns only that he will "never know . . . the solution" to the puzzle-box of his identity (236). In a sharp stab of irony, Powell traps Reich by means of an "escape pattern" (243); yet for Reich, there is no escape, only Demolition.

Meanwhile, Powell's heroic action remains entirely in the background of the scene, a matter of inference rather than a point of identification for the reader. Even the circumstances surrounding the Mass Cathexis Measure deemphasize his individual agency. To be sure, he wields immense power during the procedure, but it is borrowed power, drawn from a social reservoir of psychic energy with the full consent of the Guild. Furthermore, it nearly destroys him. The image of this aftermath, which occurs after a chapter break, likewise works against the valorization of power fantasies and black-and-white thinking, even though it does let in a degree of melodrama. Powell and Reich are found on the ground in a city park, where they have been drawn "together like two magnetized needles." Although near death, Powell clutches Reich, who has "curled into a tight foetal ball," with a tenacity oddly suggestive of a parent protecting a child. Readers are not presented with a good guy and a bad guy—one victorious, the other defeated—but with a complex image of human connection. This image lingers and takes on an air of pathos as officials coldly gather up Reich's "inert body," which they obviously view as a selfless thing, and transport *it* "to Kingston Hospital for Demolition" (238).

This powerful emotional moment segues into a more staid, mystery-style summation justified by Powell's need to *"s-p-e-l-l it out"* for his perplexed superior, Commissioner Crabbe (239). Much of the exposition that follows hinges on a fuzzy-edged but effective Freudian rationalization of Reich's dissociative identity: unable to accept D'Courtney's rejection of him, Reich projected his own hostility on D'Courtney in another context, justifying the murder as a matter of self-preservation in the business world; but Reich's "super-ego" refused to let him "go unpunished for such a horrible crime," manifesting his unconscious guilt by way of The Man With No Face (241). In a plot twist prefiguring more recent handlings of dissociative identity such as Chuck Palahniuk's *Fight Club* (1996), Reich has made unconscious attempts on his own life, booby-trapping his home and office during superego-induced fugue states. His superego also prevented him from killing Barbara D'Courtney, his half-sister. In forcing Reich to confront The Man With No Face, Powell restored Reich's conscience to its rightful place but shattered his id-driven ego in the process.

In detective fiction, a good summation complements rather than completes the plot. It etches the mystery in high relief and deepens its significance rather than retroactively glossing over gaps or fudging points. Bester achieves that effect here, avoiding the sense of letdown often attendant to infodump by focusing the summation less on the facts themselves than on the conceptual framework that makes sense of them—that is, on the theory of the unconscious as an obscure and unpredictable force that influences, even compels, human behavior. Powell does not simply serve up a checklist of resolved clues, he reveals what binds those clues together into a body of evidence and, conversely, what makes them so resistant to interpretation. Although regrettable from the point of view of the contemporary reader because it feels dated, Bester's allusion to Freud holds up technically, as a strategy to add depth and interest to the summation and to showcase the intricacy of the plot.

In a similarly adept show of technical awareness, Bester returns to the immediacy of storytelling mode to conclude the novel, having held in reserve not one but two appreciable plot twists. On the one hand, the romantic subplot involving Powell and Barbara D'Courtney remains unresolved and apparently unresolvable, given that the Guild law barring the marriage of espers and normals stands in the way of their long-term happiness. However, when Powell goes to visit her at Kingston Hospital, it soon becomes clear that clues introduced in the context of the crime also bear on their relationship. Through much of the second half of the novel, Barbara suffers from episodes of traumatic recall. When she hears the word "help," she relives the murder of her father, and the significance of that word, repeated again and again, has finally occurred to Powell. Barbara's father suffered from throat cancer and could barely speak, but asleep in an adjoining room, she heard his cry for help—telepathically. The second and final twist occurs when Powell spots Reich in the distance. Though mentioned frequently and ominously throughout the novel, Demolition never comes under close scrutiny, and Bester lets the most likely assumption about it—that it is a future form of capital punishment—float along the surface of the narrative. However, Demolition refers only to the dismantling of the mind. Though Reich will undergo a procedure that will last a year and destroy all vestiges of his old identity, a new self will eventually emerge from the ashes of his psyche, and Powell welcomes the prospect, thinking that Reich's "talent and guts" will survive the process (249).

When Bester completed the version of *The Demolished Man* published as a serial, he still harbored some doubts about his ability to write SF in the longer form, or at least felt unhappy with the manuscript. Before the first installment of the novel appeared in *Galaxy*, he referred to it indirectly in a December 1951 essay for *The Writer*, calling it "miserable";[23] and later in his career, he confided to William F. Nolan that he felt sure he had "written a dog."[24] However, his lack of confidence in the novel perhaps related in part to another circumstance: his trouble securing a book contract. He began sending the manuscript out during the fall of 1951, but by his account, pretty much "every agent and publisher in New York" eventually turned it down. The novel proved "virtually impossible to sell as a book."[25] Meanwhile, as the rejections piled up, the *Galaxy* serial created all kinds of buzz, most of it quite positive. In an editorial for the magazine's June 1952 issue, Gold claimed that *The Demolished Man* had generated "more comment than any science fiction novel in years." Not only hundreds of *Galaxy* readers but also dozens of "dazzled" SF writers had sent him letters heaping praise on the novel.[26] Surely, Gold engaged in a bit of self-promotion, tooting *Galaxy*'s horn, as it were, but he also noted broader signs of the serial's success. For instance, it had been discussed on mainstream radio, in a segment by none other than Elmer Davis, one of the most widely respected journalists and cultural commentators of the day.

Such acclamation surprised and delighted Bester, who had set out with no "conscious intention of breaking new trails," hoping only "to do a craftsmanlike job."[27] However, it did little in the way of helping him find a major publishing house willing to bring the novel out in hardcover. In the end, against the advice of Boucher but with no other option, he accepted a contract with a small but important SF press in Chicago, Shasta Publishers. Operated by a group of fans turned publishers, most notably Erle Melvin Korshak, T. E. Dikty, and Mark Reinsberg, Shasta had published several important authors, including Heinlein, Campbell, and Murray Leinster, but it generally offered short print runs, and Bester's novel would receive an initial printing of only three thousand copies.[28] Meanwhile, New American Library (NAL) bought the American paperback rights, Sidgwick and Jackson the U.K. hardcover rights.

Bester revised the serial significantly as he shaped it into the book version discussed above, and his choices as he prepared the manuscript for resubmission speak to the circumstances of the novel's republication and its later reception, as well as his ultimate goals. In addition to being pressured to drop the prologue, Bester also experienced other forms of interference from his

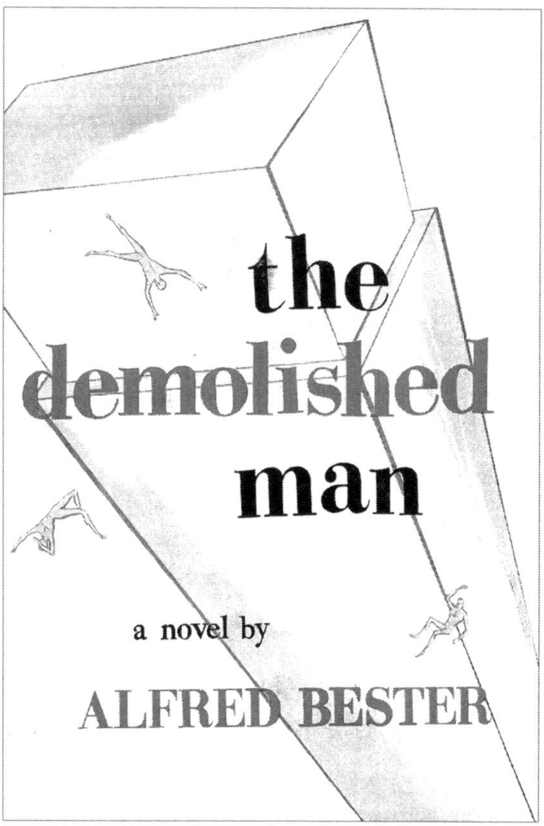

Bester's *The Demolished Man*, first U.S. edition, Shasta, 1953. Jacket design by Martin Herbstman. Reprinted by permission of Erle Melvin Korshak.

Bester's *The Demolished Man*, first U.K. edition, Sidgwick and Jackson, 1953. Courtesy of Pan Macmillan.

publishers, but unfortunately, he did not specify what kinds.[29] This pushback perhaps related to the vein of decadence that ran through the future depicted in the novel, which Bester proceeded to tone down, at least superficially. For instance, he changed the irreverent-sounding name of Reich's corporation, Sacrament, to Monarch Industries, and eliminated all reference to "Pantys," a popular, often racy form of theatrical entertainment common in the twenty-fourth century. However, these changes perhaps stemmed as much from the deletion of the prologue, and the accompanying loss of context for these references, as from blue-nosed editing. Indeed, in some respects, Bester's vision of the future grew even darker as he revised the manuscript. For example, he made the scene in which blind voyeur Keno Quizzard takes advantage of the near catatonic Barbara D'Courtney much more sinister, not only lingering on the description of Quizzard's perverse pleasure in employing his wife as his "eyes" but also underscoring the scene's sexual violence by changing the phrase "kissed her passive mouth" to "fondled her brutally" (124).[30] He likewise made Maria Beaumont more decadent. In the serial version, when she sends Reich an invitation to her birthday party, she does not include a nude portrait of herself with it, nor does her party seethe with orgiastic overtones.

Bester's reasons for undertaking other revisions seem more apparent. He likely changed Powell's name from Preston to Lincoln as part of a larger effort to make the character greyer and rounder, more of an antihero like Reich. If the nickname "Pres" made Powell sound like a natural leader in the *Galaxy* serial, the introduction of Powell's alter ego Dishonest Abe in the book version results in a less stable but more flawed and human Powell, even as it allows Bester to raise ethical questions about the use of telepathy in police work and about the tendency of espers at large to adopt a laissez-faire attitude toward duplicity in their dealings with normals. In addition to creating such interplay of character and context, Powell's name change results in a new nickname, "Linc," that foreshadows his role as the "link" in the Mass Cathexis Measure.

Bester's most striking revisions occurred in respect to his use of nonstandard orthography. Looking back on the *Galaxy* manuscript and perhaps remembering Boucher and McComas's advice concerning his initial overwriting "Of Time and Third Avenue," Bester came to view his heavy use of "symbol-names" in the serial as gimmicky and intrusive, and he decided to scale them back.[31] Most noticeably, he dropped symbols from the names of prominent and frequently referenced characters. $$son, the streetwise Inspector who reports to Powell and who stylizes his last name using a doubled dollar sign that alludes to the slang term for a $20 bill, becomes simply "Jackson."[32] Likewise, Bester spells out T8, the name of the psychologist running interference for Reich, as "Tate." However, Bester also renamed minor characters such as the appraiser ₵try, the forensics expert K½ft, and the doctor ¼maine, who become Graham, DeSantis, and Jordan, respectively.[33]

This concession with respect to orthographical play did not mean that Bester backed away from it in general. To the contrary, he employed it more extensively in instances where it pointed toward telepathy as a language variant and differing mode of communication. For instance, Bester added Powell's jokey reference to Chervil's "(lap)^2" to the esper party. In the serial, Powell simply describes him as "fat."[34] He also sprinkled bits of visual overcoding in contexts outside of the esper party. Much later in the novel, Mary Noyes tells Powell she cannot "thread-needle" through his mind block, and the phrase itself curves below the line and up, imitating the motion of a needle piercing fabric (131). New to the Shasta printing, this textual effect appears in no subsequent edition of the novel, American or British, leaving one to wonder how much of the language play contained in Bester's manuscript disappeared over the years during reprinting.

If Bester played up espers' love of overcoded and compressed language with additions such as these, he also worked out orthographical methods for representing features of telepathic communication such as thought amplification. When Powell tracks Reich in a nature preserve and employs telepathy to start a stampede, he does not simply send *"fear, terror, fear"* as he does in the serial but *"Fear, Fear. Terror. Fear* . . . FEAR - FLIGHT - TERROR - *FEAR - FLIGHT - TERROR -* ***FLIGHT!***" (173).[35] Bester gives Powell's broadcast a dramatic tempo by way of punctuation, and mixes fonts and formatting to simulate its crescendo effect visually. Bester's expanded emphasis on the visual aspects of language also shows in his use of page layout to suggest time distortion. In the book, when Jackson and Powell talk about the case telepathically, their dialogue no longer alternates down the page in a linear sequence. Bester separates it out into columns that force the reader's eyes to jump back-and-forth across the page, evoking the dizzying speed of telepathic conversation. In all likelihood, the two-column layout of *Galaxy* dissuaded Bester from attempting this treatment of telepathic dialogue in the serial, where it might be indistinguishable from regular text or even look like a printer's error rather than an intentional effect. In the end, such attention to the visual dimensions of the printed word not only extended the psychological realism—or perhaps more appropriately, "psychological surrealism"—of the novel, it also foreshadowed Bester's treatment of synesthesia in his later novel, *The Stars My Destination*.[36]

The reception of *The Demolished Man* after it appeared in hardcover in March 1953 proved Gold's earlier assessment of its impact to be no exaggeration. It had become a nodal point for discussion of developments in the field. Groff Conklin presented the novel as a quick and firm answer to "toothless talk" about SF needing to grow up, emphasizing its thematic and technical maturity;[37] and Mark Reinsberg predicted that its psychological themes and literary style would attract new readers to the genre, ones that had "never before taken science fiction seriously."[38] A somewhat crotchety Sam Moskowitz framed his review in terms of a mainstream influence eroding "strong central ideas and plotting" in the field and argued that "gimmicks," particularly Bester's use of "trick typesetting for special effects," carried the novel. He admitted that *The Demolished Man* represented an "important experiment in the evolution of science-fiction writing" but also warned that it signaled a larger, more troubling trend, one that, if it continued, would mean that the clothes would "not only have to make the man, but hold him upright as well."[39] Anthony Boucher gave the novel a glowing review under the pseudonym H. H. Holmes but referred to Bester's use of visual effects as "coy whimsies";[40] and Conklin in turn accused him of ignoring how Bester's style invokes language change: "π on you, Mr. Holmes, for ignoring language development! Many symbols need only formal inclusion to make them part of the alphabet; in actual practice, they are there already."[41]

Neither Bester's outsider status nor the changes to the *Galaxy* serial escaped critical notice. In an otherwise effusive review, Sam Merwin Jr. paused to note that Bester started out writing for the SF pulps but left the field when "Mammon beckoned," and he closed his review by expressing the hope that the book sold well, so that Bester would write more like it. Apparently, the image of Bester as a slick "money writer," as Pohl would later call him, emerged hand in hand with his reputation. Such doubts about Bester's allegiances also surfaced in *The Science Fiction News Letter*. There, Wilson "Bob" Tucker portrayed Bester's revisions as a matter of "dressing up" the novel—of eliminating science-fictional elements and generally toning it down—in an effort to repackage it for mainstream readers.[42]

Despite the ambivalence that sometimes crept into reviews of *The Demolished Man*, few dissented with respect to its quality and importance. "Best of" statements along a spectrum from "best s-f novel of 1953" to one of the "best ever written" cropped up time and again, along with words such as "classic" and "masterpiece."[43] Following a watershed year that also saw the publication of Pohl and Kornbluth's *The Space Merchants*, Theodore Sturgeon's *More than Human*, Ward Moore's *Bring the Jubilee*, and Arthur C. Clarke's *Childhood's End*—all still considered genre masterworks—Bester would go on to win the very first Hugo Award in the novel category.

In October 1951, with *Demolished* in the final stages of production, Bester had submitted a story to Gold under the working title "Time Is the Traitor." This short story occasioned a major disagreement between the two. Part of the trouble stemmed from that fact that Bester also sent it to *Fantasy and Science Fiction* for consideration. After doing so, as he and Gold discussed strategies for submitting his novel to publishing houses, Gold warned him against the dreadful crime of double submission. Within hours of the conversation, Bester had rushed off a letter to Boucher and McComas, professing his ignorance of this aspect of professional etiquette and begging them to forget that he ever sent them the manuscript. Unfortunately, the story had already bowled Boucher over. Days earlier, he had written an enthusiastic editorial note to McComas that read: "Definitely something I want! *You* want it!!! JeSUS!!!"[44] It is no surprise that McComas wanted it, too, and the editors encouraged Bester to withdraw it from consideration at *Galaxy*, in part by upping their usual per-word payment rate. Gold, on the other hand, responded to the story with hesitation, claiming not to understand the ending and offering to accept it on the condition that Bester "fix it" by spelling out the protagonist's fate. Unhappy with Gold's response, Bester explained that the story's point depended on a certain lack of resolution and asked Gold to return the manuscript for submission elsewhere.[45] Gold reluctantly agreed to do so, but not knowing that Bester would sign a contract with *Fantasy and Science Fiction* immediately upon the story's release, he later changed his mind without informing Bester. Bester unexpectedly received a check in the mail, which he returned with regrets. In the end, Bester resented both Gold's indecisiveness and his readerly stance on the story. By Bester's account, Gold harbored resentments as well, proceeding to reject every story that he submitted to *Galaxy* afterward.[46]

Bester developed the story, which eventually became "Hobson's Choice" (1952), from an entry that he made in his gimmick book while writing for *The Paul Winchell Show*. Originally, Bester intended to turn the note into a comedy sketch titled "I Remember Hiroshima" that parodied the 1948 film *I Remember Mama*.[47] Now, however, he turned his intentions in another direction, further exploring a technique that he used to develop Powell's and Reich's characters in *The Demolished Man*: the leitmotif. In Powell's case, other espers constantly bring up a lurid incident in the career of Dishonest Abe by asking the detective, "*Who stole the weather, Powell?*" (140). This question invariably makes Powell blush, but the details of the incident to which the motif refers never come to light: Bester leaves the matter to the reader's imagination and lets comic ambiguity do the work. The repetition of the question in itself reveals Powell's good-natured embarrassment at his own dissembling ways. The darker leitmotif associated with Reich is, of course, The Man With No Face. In "Hobson's Choice," Bester would employ leitmotif with a mixed valence, turning the device to the purposes of dark comedy.

Nothing provides a better entry point into the story and Bester's use of this technique than direct quotation of its opening lines:

> This is a warning to accomplices like you, me, and Addyer.
>
> *Can you spare price of one cup coffee, honorable sir? I am indigent organism which are hungering.*[48]

Bester here layers two forms of direct address, suspending the narrative before it even begins. The narrator offers a terse warning that transitions into a second, more cryptic bit of direct address, presented as the quoted speech of a beggar rather than story proper. Whether the warning of the first line refers to beggar's speech, to the story at large, or to both simultaneously remains unclear, as do the narrator's grounds for implicating the reader as an "accomplice." The conscious displacement of story that occurs in the narrator's warning, which is arguably an instance of metanarration, echoes in a peculiar image of social and cultural displacement. The broken English of the beggar, with its missing articles, odd word choices, and unusual syntax, suggests a nonnative speaker, one forcing newly acquired words into the more familiar grammatical structures of a mother tongue, and the reader is in effect reminded of being accosted on the street, perhaps even passing a beggar by.

In the very next line, the narrative shifts into past tense and takes on a whimsical tone as the reader is introduced to the protagonist Addyer, a Walter-Mittyish statistician who engages in ritualized daydreaming. He constantly imagines going either to the past weighed down with "bestsellers, hit plays and gambling records" that are sure to make him rich and famous, or to a "Golden Age of perfection" in the far future (3). In a way, the reader hardly blames him for wishing himself elsewhere. He lives in a postapocalyptic landscape wracked by war; but Bester handles this common SF premise with jaunty irreverence, undercutting any hint of sympathy for Addyer. As the world lay in ruins, the status quo remains intact, and Addyer serves it naively. The story at first focuses on his comical attempts to suck up to his indifferent boss; on his outbursts of "high statistical passion" as he uncovers a population-growth anomaly that promises to give meaning to his petty existence as a low-ranking bureaucrat; and on his quiet acceptance of the suffering around him as he goes on a quest to discover the source of the anomaly (5). Meanwhile, slight variations of the request for spare change quoted at the head of the story recur periodically, sometimes accompanied by narratorial intrusions. These surreal interruptions not only evolve into a leitmotif, they stand in troubling opposition to Addyer's viewpoint. If the narrative sets Addyer up as a rational, problem-solving hero—albeit an unsympathetic one—it also points toward an excess, an unidentified illogic that simply does not calculate for Addyer.

When Addyer uncovers the reason for the mysterious population spike that has made him so excited—in Finney County, Kansas, an area devastated in the war and still glowing with pockets of radiation—the weird illogic of the leitmotif encroaches on his reality directly. In the small, nearly deserted town of Lyonesse, he witnesses a "horde of happy people" emerge from behind rubble piles and from dark side streets, chatting, laughing, and singing as they board a bus (7). After observing this strange spectacle every day for a week, he comes to a questionable conclusion, one driven by wartime paranoia, namely that the people are "spies" (7). In an attempt to play the hero, he tracks some of them back to a rural farmhouse, and the situation grows even more bizarre. As he crouches near the barn, he watches two naked men trotting back and forth, trying to carry on a conversation. One says "Roo booo foo mooo hwaaa loo fooo," the other "Wd-nk-kd-ik-md-pd-ld-nk," and then both laugh merrily (8). In the meantime, someone sneaks up behind him and knocks him unconscious.

Addyer wakes up to see a man twiddling knobs on a machine resembling a radio as a woman materializes on a copper disc nearby. Despite this fantastic sight, Addyer sticks to his spy theory, in part because the woman appears to speak an unfamiliar language like the men outside; but the man, named Jelling, soon disabuses him of that notion, matter-of-factly explaining that the device is a time machine, the farmhouse a way station, and the woman a traveler experiencing the effects of temporal displacement. Oddly enough, she and the others are also psychotherapy patients. In the future, whenever neurotics who harbor escape fantasies fail to respond to treatment, therapists allow them to emigrate in time. Jelling is essentially an immigration officer who watches the patients come and go on a daily basis, and he does not think much of this form of therapy. In his experience, the patients' idealizations never match the actual conditions of their chosen realities; and rather than facing up to facts, they just continue to run from their problems, becoming little more than "time-bums" drifting from century to century (14).

Rather comically, Addyer accepts this fantastic account of time travel without blinking an eye, but Jelling's outlook riles him. He sees it as an attack on his own escapist fantasies and accuses Jelling of having a "superficial attitude" about the whole matter. The latter responds with weary cynicism, pointing out the many aspects of time travel that the patients—and Addyer—fail to consider: the lack of sanitation, medical care, and other modern conveniences in the past; the often drastic difference between the cultural and political climate of one age and another; and so on. Even with preventative inoculations, patients who return to Elizabethan England or medieval France often die of disease. If Addyer traveled to the future, Jelling tells him, he might never fully understand its advanced technology or master thirtieth-century speech, which conveys meaning through complex strings of rhetorical figures more so than through words themselves. He also dismisses Addyer's idea that in the past, his "superior knowledge" would transform him into a genius ahead of his time. The time machine transports nothing but "flesh" (12). Without a great literary work in hand, could Addyer reproduce it from memory? Could he invent a radio from scratch? Would he not need first to reproduce the "hundred allied technical discoveries that went into it"? (13) Would he not need capital to manufacture it?

This conversation, of course, sets up a plot twist. Jelling suspects that Addyer will "talk and cause trouble" and informs him that he will soon experience the difficulties of time travel firsthand, taking a "one-way" trip to the destination of his choice (14). Despite Jelling's warnings, Addyer receives this news with excitement, convinced he will finally realize his dreams; but as he steps naked into the time machine and makes his choice, he "turns blue and rather unsteady" (15). Then, he disappears. The reader does not find out where he goes.

According to the narrator, who intrudes at this moment, where Addyer went does not matter. We already know: he chose the "land of Our pet fantasy" (15). As the narrator implies, the point of the story is to examine the escapist mindset itself, for readers to reflect on the wish-fulfillment tendency within themselves; or, as Bester put it when he tried to explain this ending to Gold, Addyer "went to the escape-year that the reader favors."[49] If Addyer's name puns on his profession, it at this moment also plays on "add your," as in "add your own fantasy here."

The narrator does reveal one key bit of information: Addyer soon comes to regret his choice, just as Jelling predicted. In a way, Jelling's deconstruction of Addyer's mindset also functions as a preemptive critique of whichever escapist fantasy the reader supplies. Bester generates a writable moment—a place for the reader to co-create meaning—but that moment implicates the reader in Addyer's folly, goads the reader into a pattern of self-recognition much as Powell does Reich in *The Demolished Man*. The narrator's closing words make the reader's entanglement with Addyer's mindset explicit: "We yearn for yesterdays and tomorrows, never realizing that we are faced with Hobson's Choice . . . that today, bitter or sweet, anxious or calm, is the only day for us. The dream of time is the traitor, and we are all accomplices to the betrayal of ourselves" (15). Hobson's Choice, for those who might not be familiar with the phrase, is the illusion of choice when no choice really exists, and escapism is just that sort of illusion. It requires "Our" complicity.

As one might expect, the story ends not on the narrator's words but with a final repetition of the leitmotif, one that reveals the identity of the beggar: a Japanese man who previously stumbled onto the secret of the way station and was transported by Jelling. If Bester leaves Addyer's storyline unresolved in terms of factual details, the leitmotif now offers a haunting approximation of his fate, one charged with both philosophical import and absurdity. This other man is trapped in what he has come to view as a "so-miserable year" in the future—poor, "starveling," and friendless—and his final plea underscores the black irony of being faced with Hobson's Choice, the take-it-or-leave-it conundrum of existence: "I want to go back to year 1945 again. I want to be in Hiroshima again. I want to go home" (15).

In an editorial response, Boucher praised "Hobson's Choice" for its focus on the "linguistics of time travel," portraying it as a slap in the face to "daydreamers & professional authors" who simply ignored this difficulty; and he encouraged Bester to lay further emphasis on this aspect of the story by adding framing statements highlighting what the handling of the Japanese traveler's speech and the episodes of temporal displacement already implied.[50] Bester responded by having Jelling reflect overtly on language change—on the likelihood that no amount of preparation could teach a traveler "how the Romans pronounced Latin" or how to "think" in seventeenth-century Flemish, or what unpredictable twists and turns language might take in the future (13). This emphasis on the social context of language—its close involvement with worldview—underscores the sense of culture shock that lingers in the background of the story and that ultimately becomes a critical lens for the examination of escapism.

Boucher, who fostered a minor obsession with linguistics, loved "Hobson's Choice." In fact, he declared it the "best s-f short of the year" before it even appeared in print—at least according to a young Harlan Ellison, then unknown outside of fan circles, who reported as much in a feature on *Fantasy and Science Fiction* for the fanzine *Pendulum*.[51] Naturally, Boucher and McComas selected the story as the centerpiece for their 1953 installment of *The Best from Fantasy and Science Fiction*, but significantly, despite their exclusive option clause, they had to fend off a host of other anthologists who aggressively sought rights to reprint the story in their own best-of anthologies, including T. E. Dikty and Groff Conklin.[52] No short-story awards specific to the SF field existed at the time, so "Hobson's Choice" had little chance for wider recognition in that respect, but the fact that rising star C. M. Kornbluth titled one of his stories "Time Bum" (1953) shortly after the story's appearance perhaps speaks to its wider impact.

Bester continued to produce variations on the wish-fulfillment theme throughout 1952 and 1953. "Disappearing Act" (1953), perhaps the most political of Bester's short stories, presented escapism in a different light, depicting it not as a foible of human psychology but as a survival strategy for war casualties suffering from severe shock. These patients are lodged in a government hospital, but they slowly begin to disappear from a locked-down ward, only to inexplicably reappear again hours, days, or even weeks later. When a bigwig General learns of the phenomenon, he brings in expert after expert to investigate, hoping to turn teleportation into a weapon in the war. Protecting the "American Dream" is so important to him that he even grants one of these experts a special one-day leave from the "Un-American Ancestors Committee."[53]

Working from bits and snatches of information picked up by disguised observers sent into the ward, these experts infer that the patients travel in time; but readers have reason to question this conclusion. That is to say, Bester involves readers in the mystery through a series of vignettes that allow them, unlike the researchers, to experience the patients' alternate realities directly. One of the patients, Lela Machan, teleports to ancient Rome, where she takes on a Cleopatra-like identity, living a life of luxury and intrigue, but she occasionally whips out a cigarette and smokes it with the flamboyant disinterest of a femme fatale in a mystery novel, and she also conducts an affair with Ben-Hur. Another, Nathan Riley, returns to the Gilded Age, making his living as a gambler and entrepreneur by placing bets on 1950s-era sporting events and elections on the same day that he invests in a young Henry Ford's first automobile prototype. Yet another, George Hanmer, disappears to England, where he delivers a powerful oration to Parliament about the Suez Canal, much to the admiration of William Pitt, Benjamin Disraeli, and Winston Churchill.

Just in case a reader has missed these anachronisms, a historian on the team named Scrim eventually catches on and points them out to the other experts, discrediting the time-travel theory. His name—an allusion to a type of thin screen used for perspective effects in the theater—mirrors his function in the story. When he puts forth his own theory, the perspective of the narrative suddenly flips. The background serves to reinterpret the foreground, to shift the focus from the patients' psychology to the ideology of the government. Scrim suspects that the patients generate their own alternative realities, materially realizing their dreams of escape, anachronisms and all. This creative ability, analogous to that of a "poet" or artist, holds no military value. However, in a turn of events that drips with satire, Scrim convinces the General that such imaginative freedom "is" in fact the "American Dream." In a final effort to discover the mechanism of the patients' gift, the General calls for an expert in creativity, a poet, but he waits in vain. None can be found (20).

Bester here recognizes escape as an active, creative impulse akin to writing—the shock patients keep a horrible reality at bay through their fantasy lives—but he simultaneously reveals the General's version of the American dream as empty rhetoric and his crusade as mindless bureaucracy dressed up in false idealism. This satire of McCarthy-era politics, with its overt reference to the House Committee on Un-American Activities, takes particular aim at the blacklisting of professionals in the entertainment industry and the wider threat to creative freedom that it implied. The disappearance of "beauty and poetry" at the end of the story implies a "fatal" narrowing of the American mind (21).

Bester wrote "Disappearing Act" in response to Frederik Pohl's persistent requests for an original to include in his *Star Science Fiction* anthology series, which printed new works by "star" authors. Although not of the same caliber as "Hobson's Choice," the story definitely lived up to the expectations set by the title, outshining all else in Pohl's collection except perhaps Jerome Bixby's classic "It's a Good Life" (1953), which the Science Fiction Writers of America (SFWA) later selected as one of the twenty best SF short stories published prior to the creation of the Nebula Awards. (Bester's later story "Fondly Fahrenheit" would also be selected.)

Three additional stories engaging in various ways with the idea of wish fulfillment appeared in 1953, all robust but perhaps showing diminishing returns on Bester's investment in the theme. The first, the "The Roller Coaster" (1953), centers on a pair of thrill-seeking time travelers who return to the past in search of a type of rough play and raw emotion that no longer exist in the hypercivilized future. For them, the past is an amusement park, a place to experience primal fear without real consequences—thus the story's title. Boucher and McComas bounced the story, pronouncing its noirish plot "trite" and its content a "little too Mickey Spillane"—that is, too heavy with sexualized violence geared toward shock value.[54] They kindly advised Bester to send it to Howard Browne at *Fantastic*, and in a testament to Bester's growing reputation, the editor not only snapped it up but offered him a whopping five cents per word—well above the most competitive magazine rate in the field. Boucher and McComas accepted the other two stories, one of which had been rejected by Gold with "crushing indignation," but their editorial correspondence shows none of the bubbling enthusiasm with which they greeted "Hobson's Choice."[55] The first of these two stories, "Star Light, Star Bright" (1953), focuses on a child able to make even his most idle wishes come true. In the context of his god-like powers, the notion that "children will be children" takes on frightening connotations. The second, originally submitted under the working title "The Decider," explores wish fulfillment in the context of unconscious compulsion. An important businessman regularly enters into a fugue state at night, conducting a futile search for his dead fiancée, but when his wish to find her does come true, he fails to recognize her. Sadly, the paradox of his compulsion is that it does not drive him to actually find her, only to reenact his loss again and again.

In an interesting side note, the eventual retitling of the last story occasioned a humorous episode between Bester and his editors. Bester, by his own admission, struggled to come up with catchy titles. At this time, no title of his had ever made it into print. In this instance, Boucher and McComas retitled his story using the working title for "Hobson's Choice"—that is, "Time Is the Traitor"—but in an attempt to surprise him, they purposely withheld the fact. Bester found out in a very odd manner. Forrest J. Ackerman, a well-known fan and occasional anthologist, contacted him in an effort to secure rights to "Time Is the Traitor." Thinking Ackerman referred to "Hobson's Choice," Bester informed him that the title had been changed and the story already optioned. At that point, Ackerman wrote him a letter, partly in "Japanese dialect," to demonstrate "that he knew all about" the earlier story and in fact referred to Bester's new story, set to appear in the upcoming issue of *Fantasy and Science Fiction*. Suddenly, the truth of the matter dawned on Bester, and he dashed off an excited letter to Boucher and McComas:

> I am so painfully grateful to you for using one my titles that I'm tempted to refund the fee for the story. All my life editors have been tactfully rejecting my titles and sinking me deeper and deeper into a morass of humiliation. Now, at last, one of my titles is accepted. *Hoch!* For another story, true; but who cares? *Viva!* Boucher and McComas have uncastrated me. . . . My blessings be upon you two dear fillers of scrotums.[56]

Bester would produce one more variation on the wish-fulfillment theme in "5,271,009," a novelette written at the end of 1953 and published in 1954. However, in this instance, he would handle the theme in an original and definitive way that left him ready to turn his attention elsewhere. The story came about under unusual circumstances. Boucher and McComas queried

Bester as to whether he would consider writing a story to match a piece of cover art for the magazine, and he replied that he would but raised concerns about what would happen if the illustration they sent him left him cold. He could not write a story without a "philosophic concept or social criticism" to underpin it, he said, and if he found the cover art "intellectually meaningless," he could not guarantee to write a story in response.[57] Despite his rather equivocal answer and somewhat to his surprise, the editors sent him a reproduction of a cover painting immediately, telling him that he could simply return it at their expense if it sparked no ideas.

Although Boucher and McComas handpicked cover art with a crime-and-punishment theme for Bester, he at first glance thought the illustration "preposterous," a realization of his worst fears about the assignment. It depicted a cosmic convict, whose striped, nineteenth-century-style prison uniform

Cover of *The Magazine of Fantasy and Science Fiction*, March 1954. Art for Bester's "5,271,009" by Fred Kirberger. Reprinted by permission of *The Magazine of Fantasy and Science Fiction*.

doubled as a spacesuit. Rusty chains bound his feet to a tiny, free-floating asteroid, and he leaned back against an oxygen tank with a look of resolve or perhaps embitterment on his face, staring into the distance. Emblazoned across his chest was the number 5,271,009. For Bester, this cover evoked the wild-and-woolly logic of pulp SF, its often anachronistic imagery, shaky science, and sweeping melodrama. Any story written about it would be a "mad camp." Bester determined to "reject the assignment with thanks," but as he went about his daily affairs, the illustration lingered in his mind. He had been satirizing the "clichés and stereotypes of science fiction" since his return to the field. Did the cover not provide a perfect opportunity for "more of the same"? And in the spirit of fairness, should he not also poke some "fun" at himself?[58]

About a week later, Bester accepted the assignment, telling McComas that he planned to combine some "unconventional ideas" with the cover art to "save the story from turning into an AMAZING cliché."[59] Later, in a plot outline he sent to Boucher and McComas for approval, he framed the story as a commentary on the use of wish-fulfillment devices in SF:

> I want to preach a sermon (as usual) in this story, and the theme is an attack on the adolescent wish-fulfillment-type dreaming which blocks us from becoming adults if we indulge it without recognizing it for what it is. It is this same adolescent wish-fulfillment which science fiction so shamelessly exploits; and if SF continues to indulge it, SF will never become an adult form of literature.[60]

In accordance with this premise, the story would center on an artist, Jeffrey Halsyon, who has experienced a psychotic break and is given the choice either to embrace maturity, along with the personal and artistic risks that it entails, or to recede into the "bliss" of insanity.[61]

Though Bester does not say so in the outline, his self-parody would revolve around the mysterious figure who offers this choice, Solon Aquila. A fortune-prone like Oddy Gaul, compulsive liar like Lincoln Powell, and oddball like Boyne, Aquila comes across as a tongue-in-cheek mashup of Bester's earlier characters, a fact that Bester acknowledges with a subtle metafictional reference that identifies him as a composite character. The story begins: "Take two parts of Beelzebub, two of Israfel, one of Monte Cristo, one of Cyrano, mix violently, season with a mystery and you have Mr. Solon Aquila."[62] The highly theatrical Aquila also speaks a comical, disjointed polyglot that caricatures Bester's use of linguistics in previous stories. About three-fourths or more of his speech consists of American English, sometimes used perfectly, even with respect to idiom and slang, and sometimes syntactically mangled or otherwise suggestive of a nonnative speaker, as in the line: "I have in me to buy a picture" (4). The rest is primarily composed of interjections, common sayings, and tag phrases in German, French, and Latin, with small bits of Italian, Spanish, and distinctively British English also cropping up here and there. Aquila switches codes restlessly and sometimes mixes codes, and his speech gives the impression of restless invention even though it is heavy with repetition and purely emotive exclamations that inflect rather than extend meaning. Like the story in general, his dialogue is also larded with allusions to literature, film, art, theater, philosophy, and science that convey meaning indirectly, if at all. Incredibly, Bester manages to encapsulate much of this linguistic oddity in Aquila's very first excited outburst: "HimmelHerrGottSei-Dank! I'm crazy, man, crazy. Eclectic, by God . . . The Weltmann type, nicht wahr? My ideal: Goethe. Tout le monde. God damn" (4). In the span of about twenty-five words, Aquila combines an unusual form of a German idiom, fifties hipster slang, German and French loanwords, a learned reference, and profanity, switching codes ceaselessly along the way. His frequent borrowings from German, especially the repeated tag substitution "nicht wahr," perhaps suggest it as his native tongue, but his cultural origins remain indistinct. From the beginning, Bester ties the mystery of Aquila's identity to language. That is, he continues to employ his preferred strategy for character development even as he satirizes it.

If Aquila's overcoded speech produces an effect not unlike the heavily citational style of "Hell Is Forever," Bester's structuring of "5,271,009" also calls to mind that earlier story. Bester employs a frame narrative that opens out onto five brief episodes perhaps best described as a dream sequence. The frame focuses primarily on establishing Aquila's character and the nature of Halsyon's mental illness, and in developing it, Bester made use of lore about American romanticist painter Ralph Blakelock as source material. He heard the artist's story through Rolly's wealthy uncle Maxim Karolik, a famous opera singer and art collector, who related it to him as follows: Blakelock had suffered a breakdown because of his financial difficulties and, after being institutionalized, spent the rest of his life painting images of money. Somewhere within the frame of each bill, he would insert his usual subject matter, a landscape.[63] Bester rationalized this anecdote through Freud. In contrast to Blakelock, Halsyon uses actual money as his canvass, begging dollar bills from visitors by whining: "Baby wants a dollar!" (8); and he repeatedly sketches portraits of the sinister-looking Aquila over the portrait of George Washington. His desire to deface money, according to his analysts, stems from regression and fear. Unable to handle the pressures of his blossoming career as an artist, he has withdrawn into a state of infantile helplessness (thus, his name, which evokes the phrase "halcyon days of childhood"). He draws on money as a rejection of what it represents: the adult world and the responsibility it entails.

The transition to the episodic middle of the story occurs after Aquila, a collector of Halsyon's work, hears the story of the artist's breakdown from an art dealer and decides to intervene. Having never met Halsyon, he worries about his apparent involvement in the matter, as indicated by Halsyon's grotesque, Bosch-like images of him. From the beginning, Bester surrounds Aquila with an aura of otherness, and now, that otherness takes on hues of otherworldliness. Aquila makes an "appointment" with Halsyon in a most fantastic manner (7). He takes out his lighter and strikes it, and the flame places the art dealer in a trance. He treats a dollar bill with a strange ink, places it in the art dealer's wallet, and instructs him to deliver it to Halsyon, which he does soon after Aquila closes the lighter. When Halsyon touches the bill, he becomes lucid and escapes the asylum, thinking he acts by his own volition, but much to his horror and shock, he arrives on the doorstep of Aquila's "office," right on time for his appointment. A doctor of sorts, Aquila questions him about the drawings, and Halsyon explains that his breakdown occurred after he glimpsed Aquila "wearing no mask." He claims that Aquila, with that one fatal glance, "robbed" him of "everything." Aquila now remembers this "unguarded" moment and acknowledges that his "carelessness" pushed Halsyon over the edge but also insists that Halsyon "fell into a chasm" of his own making (12). Nonetheless, Aquila resolves to help the artist purge his "adolescent" dreams, and the treatment begins with an injection that causes Halsyon to lose consciousness (13–14).

This scene not only contextualizes the episodes to follow, identifying them as the very fantasies that hold Halsyon back, it also sets up Aquila as a symbol of Halsyon's fear without fully resolving the mystery of his identity. As further context for this dream sequence, it is worthwhile to quote Bester's plot outline for the story:

> Below are listed the childhood fantasies which SF exploits and which I'd like to cover:
>
> 1. The sexual urge . . . The Freudian yearning to fuck the world.
> 2. Injustice collecting . . . The schizoid desire to feel sorry for one's self because of unjust treatment by others. This is the misunderstood hero of classic pulp fiction. Also high-type fiction . . . witness Monte Cristo.
> 3. The desire to escape reality through discovery that reality is a hoax, a put-up job. In this episode I had intended my protagonist to discover that he and everybody he knew were characters in a book.
> 4. The revenge complex . . . That is, the desire of children to go back in time with their present knowledge for a reencounter with old situations in which they fancied themselves humiliated. In this episode the protagonist would find himself a boy of ten once again, living the life he lived then, but with the advantage of possessing his present knowledge.
> 5. The escape from the obligations and discipline of a society through the Adam & Eve dream.[64]

If Bester's outline seems somber and severe, he developed these plot notes tactfully in the writing of the story, invoking obviously dated pulp SF devices and deconstructing them with irony and a sense of humor. For instance, he developed the second note into a parody not only of the one-man-to-save-the-world trope but also of the pulpy cover for the story. The episode based on it opens with Halsyon in the same circumstances as the prisoner in the illustration—floating in space "chained to what had once been the wall of Cell 5, Block 27, Tier 100, Wing 9 of the Callisto Penitentiary"—but it also discloses the reason for his embittered expression: his false conviction. Readers soon learn another astonishing fact: he is "the one man with the one secret" capable of saving the galaxy from a menacing alien race, which Bester comically names the "Grrsh" in analogy to "Grr" (18–19). However, after his unlikely rescue and unexpected exoneration, both of which mock the quick reversals of fortune so common to pulp SF, he refuses to reveal the secret, pouting and brooding instead over the injustice done him. To assuage his persecution complex, his girlfriend apologizes for abandoning him during the trial. The judge (coincidentally her father) apologizes. Even the United Nations General Assembly, despite its lack of direct involvement in the affair, apologizes. Halsyon finally relents; but as he builds up to his revelation in a windy manner characteristic of pulp exposition, terse communiques disclosing the secret pour in from all quarters of the globe. Even a bottle tossed into the midst of the Assembly from the street contains an illiterate note revealing it. This massive, absurd infodump steals Halsyon's thunder. As he mutters about this new injustice, his girlfriend ignores him, and the judge exclaims: "HimmelHerrGott! . . . You are all alike. You dream you are the one men" (22). Within seconds, a growling Grrsh appears and devours Halsyon—and the next fantasy begins.

As the judge's dialogue in this scene suggests, the frame narrative continually bleeds through into the individual episodes, primarily through surreal intrusions of Aquila's voice, which remind the reader of his presence in the background, busily recoding Halsyon's fantasies and bringing them to naught. The metafictional impulse apparent in this slippage between the narrative levels comes into full view in the most interesting of the episodes, which Bester bases on Ophelia's burial scene in Shakespeare's *Hamlet*. Halsyon appears as the second clown digging the grave, and he soon begins to suspect that no matter what he does, he invariably ends up back before the grave, with shovel in hand, answering the question: "Is she to be buried in Christian burial that willfully seeks her own salvation?" As a result, he refuses to answer and explains his feelings of déjà vu to the first clown, who grows agitated and snaps back in Aquila's manner of speech: "Old ham & eggs . . . you have answered it 5,271,009 times. God damn. Answer again." When Halsyon still refuses, the first clown chastises him for his ignorance, unveiling the puzzle-box of their reality: "God damn. Don't you realize? We are . . . We are all characters in a book. As the book is read, we dance our dances; when the book is read again, we dance again. E pluribus unum" (27). Now, Halsyon asks how they could possibly hold a conversation of this sort in such a deterministic reality, and the other clown attributes it to the reader's imagination going off script, supplementing the text. Halsyon (at the behest of the reader?) decides to stage a revolt, to find the reality beyond the text at whatever cost. He shouts, "Stop reading the book . . . Let me out of the pages. I'd rather be in a world of my own making. Let me go!" No other characters follow him, but in contrast to the resolution of every other fantasy in the dream sequence, he now succeeds. After the reader slams the book shut, he is cast briefly into the seventh circle of Dante's Inferno as punishment, but he is thereafter allowed to "devise a text of his own" (28).

In this episode, Bester employs metafiction to make a comment about readerly and writerly imagination. He acknowledges reading as an act that recodes the text—even the reader's inattention or intrusive fantasies alter it. The first clown wants to stay in the book, dully scripted by the text itself. He dismisses his writable nature, but Halsyon embraces it, and he transcends the text by way of the reader's imagination.

Accordingly, in the next and final fantasy, Halsyon takes control of the narrative's development. He finds himself the last man on Earth, with "5,271,009 houses" to shelter him, but howls with loneliness—or so the reader is likely to presume. (He actually howls in pain.) When Halsyon discovers the only other survivor, he immediately asks her, "Are you a dentist?" "No," she says, "I'm a beautiful woman with an I.Q. of 141, which is more important for the propagation of a brave new beautiful race of men to inherit the good green earth." "Not with my teeth," Halsyon answers, as he raises a gun to his head and squeezes the trigger (29). In a move that resonates strongly with the previous episode, which invokes Ophelia's suicide as a heroic act, Halsyon saves himself through a kind of self-demolition, the rejection of his wish-fulfillment desires. From the outset of the dream, he recognizes one of the many mundane but often ignored complications attendant to the Adam-and-Eve trope—dental hygiene—and recodes the fantasy to fail. When he awakes, Aquila stands above him and congratulates him: "Bravo, my liver & onions . . . The last one you did by yourself, eh? No assistance from yours truly required. Meglio tarde che mai" (29–30).

With this return to the larger narrative frame, the emphasis shifts from an examination of Halsyon's psychology as an individual to his mindset as an artist. Halsyon contends that his fantasy life feeds his creativity—that his art is made up of dreams. Without them, he fears, nothing remains. Aquila acknowledges this point but portrays wish-fulfillment dreams as common to "all" and thus "empty" of art in the first place. By reiterating them, the artist offers nothing. The responsibility of the artist lies in the direction of uncommon imagination; or, as he tells Halsyon, "It is you, the artists, who must lead [others] out as I have led you. I purge you; now you purge them" (30). Ultimately, however, he leaves Halsyon to decide his future, and Halsyon's choice is made real by the consequences of the treatment, which Aquila reveals by handing him a mirror. Gazing into it, the thirty-three-year-old Halsyon sees a "fifty-year-old face" staring back at him (31). Aquila gives him a choice not unlike Neo's in *The Matrix*. He may either regain his youth and the illusions that go with it, forgetting that he ever met Aquila, or wake up to the risks of a new reality and walk the "hard road to maturity" (31).

Here, the mystery of Aquila's identity reemerges with force. Prompted by disbelief, Halsyon asks him how he could possibly possess such powers, and Aquila both scoffs at his naïveté and makes a painful confession. He is no more than a "remittance man," an exile paid to stay away from his home, and it was his indulgence of his own fantasies that ruined his life. He combs the "beaches of this planet for a little amusement, a little hope, a little joy to while away the weary desolate years" (31). Bester's characterization of Aquila could not differ more from the sort of alien he parodies in the Grrsh. Aquila's unplaceable linguistic difference and Halsyon's terrifying glimpse of his true form culminate in an understated narrative tell embedded in two words: "this planet." Aquila's name perhaps takes on added significance now—hinting that his home lies somewhere in the far reaches of the northern sky, near the constellation of the same name—but he is hardly unveiled. Though fully realized as a character, Aquila remains a countenance, front-lit against a dark and vast background; and it is this background of inscrutable otherness that frames Halsyon's decision. When he makes his choice, he accepts the existential risk it entails, saying simply: "I'll take it the hard way" (32).

The ending leaves little doubt that Halsyon has made the right decision, and this firm resolution of meaning, so uncharacteristic of Bester's fiction of this period, underscores that the story is a parable about the imagination. However, it is not a heavy-handed one. The story works as a story because Bester realizes his imminent critique of wish-fulfillment fantasy through self-conscious play with reading protocols rather than overt moralizing. Aquila's excited harangues fit with his comic affect and penchant for overstatement, forming a part of his character rather than turning him into a mouthpiece for the author, and the real destabilization of stereotypes and clichés occurs at the level of narrative—through the ironic citation, disruption, and even recoding of genre machinery itself.

Bester had attempted to carry out a similar critique in "The Trematode: A Critique of Modern Science-Fiction" (1953), an essay written just before this story, but when "Trematode" appeared, both Boucher and McComas thought that it fell flat in comparison. Partly in order to warn Bester that he had written a negative notice of the essay, Boucher brought the matter up in a letter concerning "5,271,009": "It seems to me that BEACHCOMBER [Bester's working title] establishes fictionally, with subtlety & validity, exactly the same points which your non-fiction piece failed to make convincing."[65] McComas would later agree, suggesting that whereas the story succeeded in showing, the essay managed only to tell.[66] Neither Boucher nor McComas took umbrage at Bester's impulse to critique SF—both viewed "5,271,009" as "completely wondrous, Bester in Excelsis"—but Boucher did express distaste at Bester's tone in "The Trematode," making it the subject of an unflattering comparison.[67] A couple of months earlier, in a short but controversial article for *Harper's Bazaar*, Arthur Koestler had dismissed the idea that science fiction would ever "grow up," portraying it as "good entertainment" that would never become "good art." He had also, without a trace of irony, referred to *Tom Corbett, Space Cadet* as though it represented the genre at large.[68] Boucher told Bester that "The Trematode" made him "sound like Koestler & the other outsiders who know all about SF from a few samples." While this comment did not necessarily place Bester atop Koestler's literary high horse, it did imply that he had engaged in a similar type of posturing, adopting a condescending attitude toward SF.[69] If Bester did climb on a high horse of his own, it was psychology. At moments in "The Trematode," he discusses SF almost as though he were its psychiatrist and it his analysand, and it is not hard to imagine why this clinical posture did not sit well with Boucher.

Interestingly, a noticeable shift in Bester's outlook occurred in the wake of "5,271,009" and "The Trematode." Perhaps the story made a definitive statement that brought about this change in approach. In much the same manner that it purged Halsyon of his wish-fulfillment fantasies, it appeared to put an end to Bester's preoccupation with wish fulfillment as a theme. Perhaps Boucher and McComas's side-by-side comparison of the story and essay inflected Bester's point of view, encouraging him to focus on transforming the genre from the inside rather than critiquing it like an outsider. Or perhaps both story and essay simply led to a catharsis, allowing Bester to get his gripes—some of which dated back to his conflict with Campbell—out of his system and move on. Whatever the case, this moment marked the beginning of a distinctive stage in Bester's career, one characterized by changing priorities and a softer touch.

CHAPTER 5

TIGER, TIGER, BURNING BRIGHT

The change of outlook that characterized the next period of Bester's career was not a sea change. Bester continued to show an interest in the workings of the mind and employ language play in his fiction, and he did not leave satire behind. However, he seemed less intent on dismissing pulp clichés through parody than on transforming aspects of pulp aesthetics in earnest. His next story, "Fondly Fahrenheit" (1954), would not poke fun at but revamp the mad-robot story, working around the rational view of technology encompassed in Asimov's Three Laws of Robotics to do so. *The Stars My Destination* (1956), the novel to follow, would see Bester embrace space opera but handle the form with baroque flourishes of artistry and psychological depth that made it sleeker and headier than ever before. Despite their satirical elements, both works convey a feeling of ironized attachment to older forms more so than of ironic detachment from them. They show Bester in rapport with the SF of his youth but transforming it with the wit and wisdom of a seasoned writer.

It is little wonder that these two works have proved his most popular and enduring, attaining a cult status in the field that continues to this day.

As ever, Bester picked and pulled at an existing thread in his work as he moved forward. Both the dream sequence of "5,271,009" and, to a lesser extent, the Mass Cathexis scene of *The Demolished Man* depicted one character's viewpoint encroaching on another's perceived reality, pointing toward Bester's developing interest in mixed-viewpoint narration. In "Fondly Fahrenheit," Bester brought this technique front and center. A good portion of the story is told from third-person omniscient point of view, but the viewpoint of one of the characters repeatedly intrudes on and eventually displaces this objective viewpoint entirely. The character creating this interference pattern refers to himself sometimes in first, sometimes in third person; and in consequence, questions about his identity, reliability, and state of mind emerge from the outset. Bester encapsulates these ambiguities in a brief moment of direct address that reads almost like an epigram to the story: "He doesn't know which of us I am these days, but they know one truth. You must own nothing but yourself. You must make your own life, live your own life and die your own death . . . or else you will die another's."[1] Four shifts in narrative point of view occur within the first sentence alone, which ranges from third-person objective to first-person plural to first-person singular to third-person subjective. These lines not only establish this character's uncertainty about his own identity, they show him oscillating between discrete viewpoints. The shift into the second-person hypothetical "you" in the next statement underscores this feature of the narration, revealing a truth that the narrator understands not as "I" or "he" individually, but only as "they." This slippage of point of view, derived mostly from pronoun confusion, recurs to varying degrees throughout the story but with particular intensity from middle to end, where it parallels the character's rapidly deteriorating state of mind.

The two characters possibly responsible for the mixed viewpoint do not appear until several pages into the story, introduced in the wake of a lyrical third-person omniscient account of a search party looking for a missing girl and finding her dead, by all appearances murdered by an android. One of these characters is the homicidal android, the other its owner, James Vandaleur. The android, despite its serve-and-protect conditioning and apparently docile manner, has a sordid history of vandalism, arson, and assault, and has now graduated to murder. Vandaleur, because of the android's crimes, teeters on the brink of financial ruin. As Vandaleur "savagely" beats the android and it sits obediently, the narrative noticeably wavers between points of view, and illogical dialogue attributions crop up here and there, as in the following exchange:

> "Why did you do it? Why did you kill her?" I asked.
> "I don't know," I answered. (6)

Although the reader now knows the "I" and "he" composing the "they," the mystery revolves around whether Vandaleur or his android narrates in these instances, and Bester does not fail to cultivate ambiguity around this issue through overdetermination. Some first-person statements clearly identify one or the other as the speaker, but these instances obviously contradict one another. Sometimes, a sentence even slips from third-person subjective to first-person singular midway through, or vice versa. At the start of the sentence "Its owner watched me miserably," neither Vandaleur nor the android narrates, but the "me" indicates that the sentence ends in the latter's voice (7). Elsewhere, the point of view shifts to the inclusive "we" but depicts the two engaged in distinct activities. When the first-person narrator says, "There we were weeping and counting and calmly watching," context dictates that Vandaleur weeps and counts while the android looks on indifferently—that "we" is not really applicable to the situation—and the character behind the "we" remains unidentifiable as a result (6). Surprisingly, these curves and switchbacks do not interrupt the flow of the narrative much at all. The overall effect is similar to that of a conceptual painting such as Marcel Duchamp's *Nude Descending a Staircase, No. 2*, in which the proliferation of viewpoints distorts the viewer's sense of time, space, and form, but not of motion.

After forging new papers and establishing residence on another planet, Vandaleur and the android settle down to business as usual, the android appearing incapable of autonomous action, much less murder. Vandaleur's backstory surfaces when a client who rents the android from him guesses his real identity, and he tries to gain her pity to prevent her from turning him in. His father, he tells her, was wealthy but lost his fortune and died, leaving him with no means of support except the android. Vandaleur lives his life on the run because the android's seizure would force him to work for a living, and he refuses to sell it because its rare multiple-aptitudes fetch the highest rates on the labor market. As Bester once noted, he based this aspect of Vandaleur's character on a Mark Twain anecdote about a slave owner motivated by greed to conceal a slave's criminal history, and he intended to depict Vandaleur as a "master" in an "android-slave society."[2]

The android's calm soon ends under telling circumstances. As it works near a smelting furnace on an especially hot summer day, its fingers writhe, a mad gleam appears in it eyes, and it begins to sing: "Oh, it's no feat to beat the heat. / All reet! All reet! / So jeet your seat / Be fleet be fleet / Cool and discreet / Honey" (9). Then, it pours a crucible of molten gold over Vandaleur's client's head and repeats the process several times, its song growing more frenzied all the while. Vandaleur and the android predictably flee the locale of the crime, yet such scenes of violence recur, growing more bizarre along the way. Bester punctuates each with some variant of "And the thermometer that day registered 92.9° gloriously Fahrenheit" (6), a tag line that becomes a leitmotif and underscores the source of the android's malady: heat. In general, Bester develops the android's character through a schizophrenic, up-and-down tempo that manifests at the level of language and style. In its calm phases, the android sits motionless and repeats the same bland statements about its status as "valuable property," largely to dissuade Vandaleur from beating it, but during its lunatic phases, it enters into an agitated state reflected at the level of narrative in the frantic tempo of the mad song it chants and in animated images of it "capering" and "dancing a lunatic rumba" as it kills (12). The mixed viewpoint irrupts with force during these scenes, adding to the disturbing sense of alterity and grotesque motion that defines them.

Vandaleur, who at one point admits he is "not very smart," fails to grasp the correlation between the temperature and the android's deranged fits (8); but once he learns the truth, he poses as a researcher and visits a psychometric consultant in hopes of learning how to manage the android's condition. She explains that the android suffers from synesthesia. When the temperature rises, it experiences sensory confusion that produces a violent emotional response. Further, it poses a threat to its owner. Through projection, the android could draw its owner into its own "psychotic pattern" (18). The concept of projection originated with Freud, and Bester encountered it in the work of Karen Horney. It refers to a process of psychological displacement that occurs to some degree in all people. Individuals externalize what they dislike or reject about themselves, attributing it to others; and sometimes, especially in traumatic relationships, such projection elicits counterprojection or other forms of acting out.[3] Bester puts a science-fictional spin on this concept, imagining the possibility of android-human projection, but more important, he offers up a hazy rationale for the mixed-viewpoint narration, which appears to represent this process of identity confusion in some way.

The psychometrician's explanation clearly implicates the android, and Vandaleur readily accepts her account, more than willing to accept the status of victim. However, in a manner characteristic of Bester, this all-too-easy answer foreshadows a writable twist. The build toward the climax consists of pure pulp action sprinkled with bits of mixed-viewpoint narration. The psychometrician recognizes Vandaleur, and he guns her down, apparently channeling the android as he does so. The authorities spot Vandaleur and the android as they flee from her office, and a chase ensues that ends in a spectacular crash. They flee on foot into a marsh and hide, but the burning car sets fire to the reeds. As the flames creep near their hiding place, the android, not without a degree of dark comedy, begins to exclaim "All reet! All reet!" It jumps up and dances a "horrid dance," unfazed by gunfire and bullet wounds, until the flames consume it; but Vandaleur escapes in the confusion, apparently still "crazy" after the android's death (21).

Had the story ended here, it could easily be read as a slightly nostalgic mad-robot story, updated with a humanlike android and an interesting psychological twist, but Bester adds a paragraph, narrated entirely by Vandaleur, that draws out another possibility subtly raised by the story as a whole: that the android's behavior mirrors Vandaleur's brutal and selfish master mentality. After he escapes, Vandaleur buys a "cheap labor robot" to support him, and it too has started "twitching and singing" even though Vandaleur has taken the precaution of living on a frozen planet. In a subtle bit of narrative irony, the "they" at the beginning of the story actually refers to Vandaleur and this robot. Here identified as "we," they "know one truth": that the psychometrician was "wrong." Bester initially wanted to include a second paragraph to drive this point home, but Boucher and McComas wisely advised him to cut it and retain only the final repetition of the leitmotif.[4] As it stands, the ending confirms the suspicions of readers who have taken pause at Vandaleur's violent, imperious treatment of the android, and it switches the newly purchased robot's trigger from heat to cold, leaving Vandaleur's mindset the only real constant in the equation. As the robot wanders off with a child "for a solitary walk," the narrative closes: "Cool and discreet, honey, in the dancing frost while the thermometer registers 10° fondly Fahrenheit" (21). In terms of what will happen, the final repetition of the leitmotif says it all.

Clifford D. Simak's story "Time Quarry" (1950; later incorporated into *Time and Again*, 1951) played a key role in introducing the android into the 1950s SF idiom and also depicted a slave society;[5] but it focused on the android slave within a wider context and achieved very little psychological depth. Bester, by contrast, handles this trope specifically in terms of the psychodynamics of the master-slave relationship; and in the end, he presents the android's insanity as the true counterprojection, a mirroring back of Vandaleur's cruelty and egotism. Bester puts the trope in the service of a subtle satire of technological dependence, perhaps even of the technophilic mindset. His handling of it shifts the focus from the technological object to the technological subject, laying bare some of the more sinister psychological implications of cognitive entanglement with technology; but he places responsibility for the resulting impoverishment of self squarely on human shoulders. Vandaleur's laziness, complacency, and general sense of entitlement cause all the trouble. It is human nature that corrupts technology in the story, not the other way around.

When Bester submitted "Fondly Fahrenheit," Boucher noted that it contained "a lot of repetition" and jokingly described it as "not . . . the bester of Bester" but added "who cares?" in a tone indicating that he actually liked it very much.[6] Later, in his introduction to the story in *Fantasy and Science Fiction*, Boucher naturally emphasized its merits, indicating that it carried out a "literary experiment" not only as riveting as any in *The Demolished Man* but also "more psychologically significant" (3). Whether Boucher came to appreciate the story more over time or simply felt obliged to write a good plug for the pages of the magazine, his comment speaks to the story's uncommon integration of meaning and form.[7] Bester's psychological theme plays out in the structure, language, and rhythms of the story itself more so than in conventional exposition. Even the psychometrician's clunky lecture reads like an embedded footnote intended mostly to put a name to the story's mixed point of view. The magic of the story resides in the alchemy by which Bester transmutes a psychological principle into a narrative technique without strained intellectualism and invokes the pulp SF and mystery formats without slipping into nostalgia. The story itself is a composite of forms perhaps best described as "Pulp Modernism."[8]

After Boucher accepted "Fondly Fahrenheit," Bester revealed his particular investment in the story, saying: "My heart really was in that experiment";[9] and later in his career, he selected it for Harry Harrison's *Author's Choice* anthology series, including an unusually detailed account of his writing process. The story originated when he recorded the Twain anecdote in his commonplace book alongside a note to extrapolate the situation into an android-slave society. Though he thought about this entry occasionally, it remained there for "years" before he once again gave it "serious attention," outlining several scenes unsuccessfully and then leaving the matter to stew in his "unconscious." Several months later he looked back over his notes and realized that the android was the equivalent of a murderous robot. He had not considered what would cause it to circumvent its conditioning, and he pulled a note from elsewhere in his commonplace book concerning spikes in the crime rate during heat waves. He went back and changed the settings to match the "temperature gimmick" but felt that the story still lacked suspense and put it aside again until "much later."[10] Though Bester does not mention as much in his account, he probably started thinking about the story idea again in September 1953. A lighthearted note preceding his outline of "5,271,009" reads:

> Since I suffer from synesthesia . . . and am deluded into believing that I am a jellied eel whenever the temperature rises above 78°, I have not been able to think until our heat spell broke. Now the temperature is 73°, and in that range I suffer from the delusion that I am a writer.[11]

When he later came across a quote about projection transcribed from one of Horney's books, the pieces finally clicked together: the climax would reveal the master as the criminal. He dropped his other projects and sat down at the typewriter, realizing in the process that this framework would allow him to attempt "multiple point of view," a technique he had "been toying with for years." By his account, the story was already written. After years of synthesizing ideas and sporadic bouts of outlining, he "typed it" in two days.[12]

Bester rarely remembered the specifics of his writing process in such detail, especially with regard to short stories, and that fact makes his account of "Fondly Fahrenheit" all the more valuable. It deepens the picture of him as a bricoleur who gathered together "odds and ends" and crafted them into unlikely and, for that very reason, unique creations.[13] His practice of keeping a commonplace book factored into his artistic process, perhaps even more heavily than self-pastiche. From 1941 on, as he moved through and straddled mediums, he recorded any oddment of knowledge that he thought might "produce or contribute to a story," always with the goal of allowing ideas to mix and marry in his mind over time.[14] The short sections of his commonplace book edited and published by Eric Solstein demonstrate both Bester's wide-ranging interests and the persistent influence of the Renaissance ideal on his outlook. The various entries span criminology, psychology, parapsychology, chemistry, film, medicine, literature, the history of coinage, popular lore, and much, much more. Bester's self-concept as a writer centered on the impulse to collect and merge ideas. At various points in his career, he described himself as a "professional magpie," a "packrat," and even a "cesspool" in which nothing went "to waste."[15]

Bester started gearing up to write his second SF novel, *The Stars My Destination*, in November 1953, but due to two circumstances, he would end up writing it abroad in England and Italy.[16] First, *Who He?* sold to paperback at a substantial sum, and actor Jackie Gleason optioned the film rights on top of that. Second, the Besters sold their home on East Sixty-Eighth Street to a land developer, who would soon knock down houses on their block to make way for an apartment complex.[17] Finding themselves at once flush and soon to be homeless, the Besters decided to put all of their belongings into storage and live abroad in Europe for a year or two. When they set sail for the United Kingdom on May 22, 1954, Bester took with him only a portable typewriter, his commonplace book, a thesaurus, and a vague notion for the novel—namely, that it would center on teleportation and employ a revenge plot resembling the one in Alexandre Dumas's *The Count of Monte Cristo*.[18]

If Bester at first thought the notion of writing a novel abroad romantic, he soon encountered a host of practical difficulties that led him to believe otherwise. Once settled in a cottage in the English countryside, he found that he could not write on a portable, but when he tried to rent a standard type-

Bester circa 1954. First published in *Science Fiction News* (UK) 11, no. 1, November/December 1954.

writer, he could not locate one with an American keyboard. He also struggled with his research, even asking Boucher and British editor John Carnell to send him recent issues of SF magazines so that he would be able to read in the genre as he wrote.[19] He made some headway by using British maps and phonebooks to cultivate a sense of place for scenes and come up with a list of character names, but afterward, his work progressed slowly and eventually stalled. After relocating to London failed to help him gain momentum, he and Rolly packed their car and left for Rome in November 1954. Although he still struggled with his research, finding the collections of the American and British libraries there woefully dated, he finally hit an ignition point with the manuscript and completed it during spring of the next year.[20]

Following the pattern established in "Fondly Fahrenheit," Bester had again undertaken his work with an eye toward the past even as he experimented with new techniques. Although he embraced the space opera idiom, he steeped it in modernism and postwar skepticism about science. The novel's protagonist, Gully Foyle, superficially resembles a pulp-style superman, but as a "stereotype Common Man" awakened by traumatic experience and a burning desire for revenge, he possesses darker qualities more in line with Olaf Stapledon's John Wainwright, the angst-ridden and amoral superhuman protagonist of *Odd John*.[21] Foyle's interplanetary quest for vengeance, which occurs amid social upheaval brought on by the advent of teleportation and a war between the inner and outer planets of the solar system, refashions the adventure plot and associated tropes such as the hero's indomitable will into a vehicle for a philosophical meditation on the unpredictable logic of evolution and transcendence.

Bester's research troubles perhaps made it necessary for him to look backward and forward all at once. He noted that as he worked at the English-language libraries in Rome, he generally found himself constrained to using texts published "before 1930";[22] and he also acknowledged that he at moments simply relied on earlier research, some that dated all the way back to his days as a pulp writer. For instance, in preparing to write his *South Sea* stories some fifteen or so years before, he had encountered an anecdote about an English remittance man who underwent a facial-tattooing ritual in order to marry a native woman but later inherited his family's fortune. Unwilling to return to England with either tattoo or spouse, the man somehow had the tattoo removed and abandoned the woman, but as he sailed away, he saw her lovingly embracing another man. As his face flushed with rage, the scars from the tattoo stood out against his red face, effectively making him "the Englishman who could never lose his temper."[23] This anecdote not only fed into the creation both of the antihero Foyle and the tribe of Scientific People, Bester also derived a meaningful plot device from it. After Foyle's own unwanted facial tattoo returns in ghostly form, the plot hinges on whether or not he will learn to control his rage.

If "Fondly Fahrenheit" had minimized the importance of psychology as context, realizing its psychological theme primarily at the level of technique, *Stars* would go even further in this direction, more or less dismissing psychology as an overt rationalization for characterization or story elements. Jane Hipolito and Willis E. McNelly recognized this shift in Bester's handling of psychology when they described the thematic connections between *Stars* and *The Demolished Man* as "quite invisible,"[24] and the long-term reception of the two novels also bears witness to it. *Stars* remained fresh and relevant long after its initial publication, while *Demolished*'s Freudian references made it date more quickly. By the early 1970s, the former would be praised as the "best science fiction of its kind ever written," the latter viewed as a "tour de force" marred by its "formal approach" to psychology.[25]

Bester does not simply drop formal psychology in *Stars*—he brackets it off in a way that shows him in dialogue with the earlier novel. In *The Demolished Man*, even though a troubling ambivalence surrounds the Guild, Bester in the end aligns it hesitantly with social progress. In *Stars*, on the other hand, institutional psychology smacks of monstrosity. When Charles Fort Jaunte accidentally catches himself on fire and spontaneously teleports across a lab to gain access to a fire extinguisher and save his life, he gives rise to the first documented instance of teleportation, and his "fellow researchers," all of them from various branches of applied psychology, study him "savagely" (7). After he fails to manifest the power again, they reproduce the original life-or-death situation by placing him in an escape-proof tank and irreversibly flooding it with water—with his consent, of course. After he succeeds under these circumstances, they send out a "call for suicide volunteers" and then proceed for years to drown, hang, and burn them, inventing "new forms of slow and controlled death" in an effort to identify and refine the trait in others. These experiments produce results but at an immense cost, and though the story of them "would make a fascinating and horrible study," the narrator informs readers to turn their attention elsewhere, in effect away from formal psychology as an explicit narrative concern (8).

This moment of metanarration occurs early in the novel's prologue and offers up a reading cue, one realized through a scene that in all likelihood resonated strongly with readers of the day. The account of the gruesome clinical study reads like an exaggerated parody of popular rumors about behaviorism, the dominant psychological framework of the 1950s. It takes aim in particular at Julian Huxley's notion of "evolutionary humanism."[26] Not without controversy, Huxley proposed that humans should attempt to "exert an operative effect" on human evolution and strongly advocated eugenics as a principle means of doing so.[27] The prologue to *Stars* depicts scientific intervention in this vein as gruesome and misguided, and instead lays emphasis on evolution as a mysterious process, one indifferent to human concerns and driven by an unpredictable clash of extremes, an unlikely "marriage of pinnacle freaks" (13). Jaunting, as teleportation quickly becomes known, likewise remains shrouded in ambiguity. Jaunte's very name contains a reference to Charles Fort, who gained celebrity and notoriety for his writings on phenomena that science could not explain; and the explanations of jaunting that do appear in the prologue by way of the narrator's sometimes-comic secondhand reportage really only represent rationalizations of it. The Jaunte Schools that gradually emerge make a motto of "*Cogito ergo jaunteo*," borrowing the unassailable logic of René Descartes's famous argument about consciousness without illuminating the mechanism of jaunting at all; and Royal Society scientists connect "Nissl bodies . . . in the nerve cells" to jaunting ability but make no headway in revealing how they function (10). Far from positioning psychology or any other specialized register of knowledge to rationalize the plot, theme, or even specific literary techniques, the prologue opens the door to mysticism and visionary experience, promising an unmediated glimpse of impersonal forces that lie beyond scientific understanding. It is little wonder that Bester employs a stanza from William Blake's "The Tyger" as an epigraph for the novel. The poem poses a series of questions that, even though they go unanswered, gesture ambivalently toward the mysterious creative power behind nature—toward the "immortal hand or eye" that could "frame" the "fearful symmetry" of the tiger and place it alongside the lamb.[28]

Even so, a quasi-psychological framework does implicitly shape the plot of the novel and relate to Foyle's character—but not necessarily on even terms with the focus of Bester's earlier work. (Unlike Reich, Foyle will not, in the end, be a case study.) Bester once acknowledged his youthful fascination with P. D. Ouspensky's *Tertium Organum* (1912), a key text within an early twentieth-century spiritual psychology movement that borrowed ideas from various sources ranging from Buddhism to theoretical physics but invariably centered on "cosmic consciousness."[29] This concept differed from thinker to thinker after Richard M. Bucke introduced it in 1901; but it generally referred to transcendent awareness involving both the elimination of egotism and a sublime consciousness of the cosmos as an All in an absolute and unknowable sense. In the minds of its proponents, cosmic consciousness represented the next step in the evolution of humankind, and Bester takes it up accordingly in the novel, connecting it in particular to Foyle's character.

In *Tertium Organum,* Ouspensky presents cosmic consciousness in terms of a developmental narrative, dividing the stages of consciousness into four "forms": potential consciousness based in unconscious "animal" awareness; simple consciousness based in active perception, basic learning, and emotion-driven decision making; self-consciousness based on reflection, a sense of good and evil, and "three-dimensional" perception; and cosmic consciousness based on intuition and a growing awareness of the complex "metageometry" of the universe. In this latter stage, individuals begin to experience time spatially—as the existence of the "past and future together with the present" rather than just as time's arrow.[30]

Ouspensky's four forms parallel the development of Foyle's character in the novel closely. Early on, his Merchant Marine record acknowledges his "intellectual potential" but places him at a developmental "dead end," and the narrator likens him to a "heavily armored creature, sluggish and indifferent," who has drifted mindlessly "from moment to moment of existence" for its entire life (15). The reader first sees him engaged in a bitter struggle for survival amid the wreckage of the spaceship *Nomad*, having spent one hundred and seventy days alone in space, but even this harrowing experience has left him unchanged.[31] Then, when the *Vorga*, a sister vessel to the *Nomad*, spots him and passes him by, his fury unlocks his mind, and he pursues revenge with blind impulsiveness, at one point even attacking the empty, docked ship "like a wild beast trying to punish the trap that injured it" (58). He emerges into a state of self-consciousness much later, only after the ghostly image of his tattoo appears, and he realizes he must control his emotions to exact his revenge. Late in the novel, in the course of a stream-of-consciousness scene involving synesthesia, Foyle develops "fourth dimensional awareness" of the cosmos that allows him to jaunte not only through three-dimensional space but "space-time" itself (178). In the end, Bester not only places Foyle at the forefront of a major evolutionary leap in consciousness, he also leaves him among the Scientific People, who practice a strange mysticism all their own.

Ali Nomad, another thinker associated with this form of spiritual psychology, went further in the direction of religious mysticism than Ouspensky. He invoked a similar revelatory framework, describing cosmic consciousness as a breaking free from sensory limitations and monadic self-awareness to attain "cosmic *perception*," but in the end, he presented the concept in less rational terms.[32] If the brutish and vengeful Foyle seems an unlikely candidate to climb upward through Ouspensky's forms, Nomad contended that in matters of mental evolution, "stupidity is closer to deliverance than intellect."[33] His account of cosmic consciousness also relies heavily on fire and light imagery of the sort employed throughout *Stars*. He not only cites instances of divine revelation from the Bible but quotes passages from Bucke's *Cosmic Consciousness: A Study in the Evolution of the Human Mind* (1901) that describe the onset of higher awareness as a "sense of being emerged in a flame or brilliant light" and "wrapped in a flame-colored cloud."[34] Arguably, Bester weaves direct allusions to Nomad's work into the novel. For instance, the final scene almost seems an illustration of the subtitle of Nomad's *Cosmic Consciousness: The Man-God Whom We Await* (1913). After Foyle's enigmatic return to the wreck of the *Nomad* and the Scientific People, J♂seph and M♀ira somberly "await the awakening" of the "god-man" from his trancelike state (197). More conspicuously, the tattoo emblazoned across Foyle's forehead for a good portion of the novel reads "N♂mad" and perhaps represents one of the most clever and humorous vehicles for an obscure allusion in the history of SF.

The point here is not to suggest that Bester had any real investment in cosmic consciousness but rather that he adapted elements of the intellectual framework associated with it to narrative ends. The developmental, visionary, and evolutionary emphases of spiritual psychology allowed him to integrate the novel in terms of form and content, to experiment with technique on science-fictional terms, but also to foster a philosophical tone and epic sense of time reminiscent of Olaf Stapledon's *Star Maker* (1937). Take, for instance, Bester's established interest in extrapolating psychological change through stylistic devices. Approaching Foyle's character in developmental terms allowed him to retain this focus but to turn his attention from language change at the social level to language development in the individual. At the start of the novel, Foyle speaks "nothing but the gutter tongue," a social-class dialect invented by Bester (14); but as the narrative progresses, his desire for revenge drives him to reinvent himself linguistically and socially, largely with an eye toward passing as nouveau riche among elites with access to the information he needs. Along the way, he learns to control his passions and put his own ego aside. Foyle transforms steadily throughout the narrative, and the visionary synesthesia episode near the end of the novel represents a culmination of this process. The evolutionary imperatives already at work in his mind and evidenced in his inexplicably advanced jaunting ability combine with this ongoing purging of ego and the near-death situation in which he finds himself to catapult him into a new state of awareness. Unlike so many scenes of transcendence that derive from some quick contrivance and thus feel forced and artificial, this one emerges organically from a series of smaller, carefully framed language- and perception-based transformations earlier in the narrative.

Bester similarly builds Ouspensky's notion of four-dimensional consciousness into the novel at the level of technique, revisiting a type of narrative metageometry he first introduced into his fiction in "The Probable Man" (1941). Though it does not appear to have been noted previously, *Stars* contains a time paradox that takes shape through the literary device of parallax, or the re-representation of the same narrative event through another point of view. This time paradox revolves around the Burning Man, a figure who looks like a hellish version of Foyle and appears alongside him in the narrative on several of occasions, four of them involving the interrogation and torture of *Vorga* crew members possessing knowledge of who gave the order to pass him by. The nature of these visitations becomes apparent during the synesthesia scene, as Foyle himself—shrouded in flames and jaunting frantically through space-time in an attempt to escape a raging, PyrE-induced inferno—re-experiences them from an alternate point of view. The paradox consists in Foyle's influence on his own timeline. His appearances in the Gouffre Martel and on the Spanish Stairs create distractions that help him escape, and he dissuades himself from killing the captain of the *Vorga* by transferring information about who actually gave the order across points on his own timeline. He also jauntes into the future, and as he floats in what he perceives as a vast, empty "Nowhere," Robin Wednesbury makes telepathic contact with him, telling him how to make his escape. She has been taught how to do so by an "expert," possibly Foyle himself (186–87). Foyle's leap into the fourth dimension not only disrupts the narrative's linearity, it retroactively reconstructs the sense of time in the narrative as a whole. More than a series of flashbacks, Foyle's point of view creates loops or folds in narrative time that reshape the reader's sense of earlier events.

Bester foreshadows this complexity of point of view from the very beginning of the novel, disrupting the chronological sense of time through bricolage, or the cobbling together of narrative modes. In the prologue and first chapter alone, the narrative offers up a quote from Blake as intertext; a pastiche of Dickens's "best of times, worst of times" opening to *A Tale of Two Cities* (1859); a script of a press conference, in which a PR person mostly evades questions; a bit from a scientific report to the Royal Society on jaunting; a blank employment application that demonstrates how "jaunte class" figures into hiring decisions; and Gully Foyle's merchant marine record. Perhaps most significant, borrowing from Joyce's *A Portrait of the Artist as a Young Man* (1916), Bester introduces a leitmotif that in its form resembles a book rhyme.[35] As Foyle struggles to survive on the wreck of the *Nomad*, his mind occasionally jumps "backward thirty years" to a "nursery jingle" from his childhood:

> Gully Foyle is my name
> And Terra is my nation.
> Deep space is my dwelling place
> And death's my destination. (14)

Variations of this rhyme recur periodically throughout the first chapter, interrupting the narrative's linear motion, and if Bester previously employed relatively static leitmotifs, this one conveys a sense of changing point of view, transitioning from a statement to a series of questions that recall the interrogative tone of Blake's "The Tyger" and point toward Foyle's new sense of purpose. The repetition that ends the chapter reads:

> "Who are you?"
> "Where are you from?"
> "Where are you now?"
> "Where are you bound?" (22)

Arguably, the leitmotif also shifts the point of view and time in a way that only becomes apparent much later. Just before the synesthesia scene near the end of the novel, Regis Sheffield reveals that the Outer Satellites (OS) ship responsible for destroying the *Nomad* actually picked up Foyle, patched him up, and attempted to use him as a decoy to lure in Inner Planets (IP) ships and destroy them—but Foyle jaunted back through space to the *Nomad*, then some six hundred thousand miles away. This new context, established long after the fact, introduces a writable moment, suggesting that at least one of the repetitions of the leitmotif, probably the one that follows, depicts Foyle's interrogation on the OS ship:

> "Who are you?"
> "Gully Foyle."

"Where are you from?"
"Terra."
"Where are you now?"
"Space."
"Where are you bound?" (17)

This detail is not just an Easter egg for the clever reader. Sheffield's disclosure points toward the ambiguous time of the leitmotif and the mixed modality of the early chapters, looping back to an earlier point in the narrative and structurally foreshadowing the synesthesia episode. It is a formal clue to the shift in reading protocols about to occur.

The synesthesia scene itself results in an outgrowth of Bester's use of typography as a stylistic device. Bester still employs nonstandard orthography in *Stars*—the gender symbols in the names of the Scientific People being the most obvious example—but his handling of synesthesia uses typographical faces and patterns to suggest altered states of perception, Foyle's near-hallucinatory stream of consciousness. Words become images in a manner resembling concrete poetry, or simulate sensory experience, or do both at once (181).

```
T
 H      E
  E    M   A
   R  A    S
    EC     H
           O
           U
           T LIKE A
                  Z
                 I
                G
                 Z
                  A
                   G OF L
                         I
                        G
                       H
                      T
                     N
                    I
                   N
                  G
```

Illustrations act as text or even intertwine with text (186).

> He was in a scintillating mist a snowflake cluster of stars
>
> 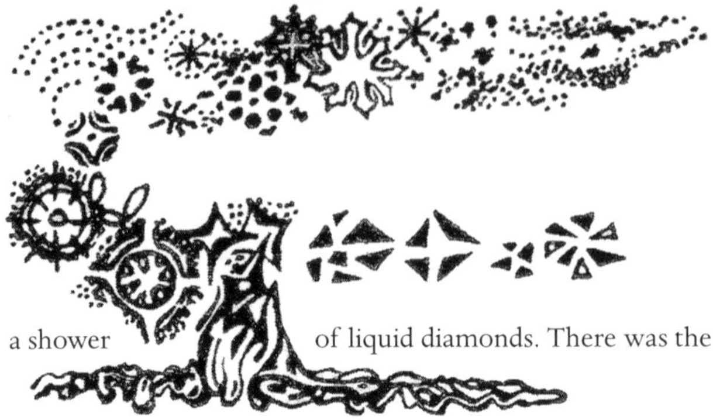
>
> a shower of liquid diamonds. There was the
>
> touch of butterfly wings on his skin. There was the
>
> 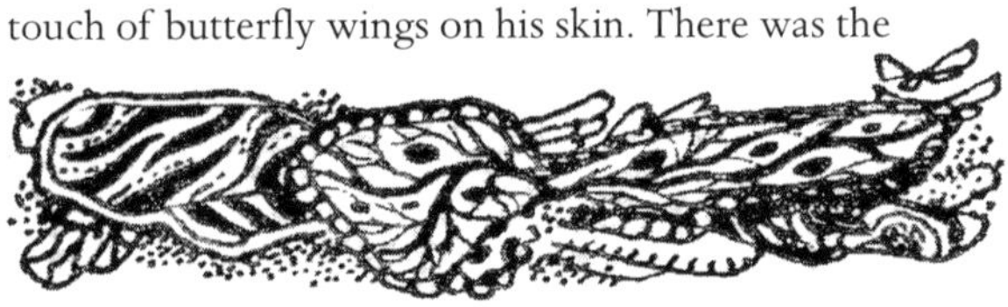

Rhythmic, Dadaesque nonsense language crosses over into the more straightforwardly narrative portions of the scene. Bester also skews the logic of dialogue attributions, assigning dialogue not only to people but to phenomena, as in the following example:

> "BURUU GYARR?" the steam asked.
>
> "Asha. Asha, rit-kit-dit-zit m'gid," the quick shadows answered. (176)

Mostly, such dialogue reads like onomatopoeia meant to represent the sound or motion of the phenomenon, but sometimes Bester makes use of a blend of German and English words to produce a vague sense of meaning. For instance, the flames on Foyle's clothes roar "MANTERGEISTMANN," loosely suggesting "man to spirit man" and perhaps even alluding to Friedrich Hegel's use of "Geist" to designate Absolute Spirit in *The Phenomenology of Spirit* (177). More constructions of this sort occur in the British version of the novel, *Tiger! Tiger!* (1956), including "GANZELSSFURSTINLASTENBRUGG," which contains the German words "Ganz" (whole or undivided) and "Brugg" (a variant of "Brücke," or bridge), and the English words "first" (phonetically) and "last";[36] but Bester cut this instance and others in the American version, possibly to avoid such linguistic decipherability and emphasize rhythm and sound. In any case, this section of the novel gives the impression of language emanating from the object world, of a noumenon operating beyond the threshold of ordinary human perception. This warping of narrative space and time represents yet another instance of mixed-viewpoint or composite narration, but here the cosmos itself bleeds through into Foyle's consciousness through his crossed senses. Bester decenters the human point of view, gesturing toward a gap between the cosmos in itself and the human experience of it, but that decentering signals Foyle's budding awareness of a larger reality.

If the synesthesia scene offers a glimpse of this reality through modernist technique, Bester also adapts pulp machinery to similar ends. In the wake of Foyle's jaunte through space-time, as others question him about whether or not he will give up the PyrE in his possession to the war effort and teach others how to jaunte through space, he finds himself the One Man poised to influence the course of humanity's future. He knows he must settle on some course of action, but as the others try to influence him with promises of profit and heroism or appeals to his conscience, the doubtful Foyle turns their self-interested and idealistic arguments back on them. In the midst of this heated debate, a low-grade robot bartender with a ridiculous "Irish grin" carved into its metal face hurls a drink across the room in response to one of Foyle's questions and interrupts the meeting (188).

Earlier in the scene, the robot has shown evidence of very basic programming, responding to any statement with the word "day" in it with the stock response "Always a lovely day somewhere, sir," and Foyle has even used it as a point of reference in characterizing the human predicament: "That's all of us. We prattle about free will, but we're nothing but response . . . mechanical reaction in prescribed grooves" (188); but now, apparently affected by Saul Dagenham's radiation-poisoned body, the robot starts to sound like a sage philosopher or even a mystic. All of the other characters discredit it, and Dagenham calls for someone to switch it off, but the captivated Foyle tells them to wait and carries on a dialogue with the "mad" robot, one that ends with it telling him: "You're all freaks, sir. But you always have been freaks. Life is a freak. That's its hope and glory" (191–92). While the other characters frame Foyle's decision in terms of human ends—wealth, honor, fame, good conscience, and redemption—the robot switches the register to the evolutionary framework invoked in the prologue, offering a cosmic rather than social perspective on human potential. To borrow the language of a well-known evolutionary psychologist, it points out that "in the larger, unfolding scheme of things, we are all extraordinary, all strange—freaks every last one of us."[37] The robot functions in the narrative as another instance of the object world surreally speaking to Foyle, and for a moment, it even resembles Foyle, itself catching a glimpse of a larger truth. Then, after its strangely oracular tirade, it bleeps and whirrs, sparks and sizzles, and collapses in a heap, just like a haywire robot straight out of the pulps.

In narrative terms, the conversation between Foyle and the robot reshapes the One Man trope in a very distinctive way. Foyle rejects the conventional heroic rationales offered by the other characters, turning to them and saying simply, "You're wrong. Who are we, any of us, to make a decision for the world?" (192). He decides to lead without becoming a leader, to hand "life and death back to the people who do the living and dying" (193). He quickly jauntes to the hidden PyrE with the other characters following close behind, and after he extracts it, he shouts a destination and leads them on a chase around the globe, throwing slugs of PyrE into crowds of people gathered near major jaunte stages all along the way. Although Foyle opens the door to anarchy, perhaps even holocaust, he explains this action as an attempt to shock the populace "awake" and to give them a chance to take control of their own destiny rather than live their lives "whipped and led . . . by driven men" (193–94). As one commentator has cleverly noted, this moment in the novel teems with ambiguity, representing either the "greatest empowerment dream ever" or a "horrific prelude to a tale that can consist only of the words 'Everything blew up.'"[38] However, in terms of Bester's narrative craft, it matters most as a gesture. Unlike the One Man, Foyle rejects his own uniqueness. When Dagenham accuses him of handing a "loaded gun to children," he says, "No, I believe in them. I was one of them" (194–95); and then, he jauntes to the top of Eros in Piccadilly Circus and rants in the gutter tongue like a mad street prophet, ultimately telling the jeering crowd: "Blow yourselves to Christ gone or come and find me, Gully Foyle, and . . . I give you the stars" (195).

As the phrase "come and find me" implies, Foyle plans to withdraw from human society. Now however, he abruptly disappears, hurling himself through space-time, determined to reach the stars himself and make good his promise;

and after several feverish and suspenseful attempts, he does, hanging in open space before Rigel, Vega, Aldebaran, and Antares like the "first gilled creature to come out of the sea and hang gulping on a primeval beach in the dawn-history of life on earth" (196). This narrative jump cut—from a claustrophobic close up of the human affairs hemming Foyle in to a series of stunning, wide-angle vistas of the cosmos—produces a sense not only of wonder but also of scale and contrast. The human sphere of activity and consciousness appears small and narcissistic against the unfathomable depths of the universe. Bester again decenters the human point of view, now through a swift and final thrust of perspectivism. The fire and light imagery of the novel, at first associated with Foyle's passions and hatred, culminates in a crisp vision of evolutionary transcendence.

This decentering also plays out in Foyle's return to the "womb" of the *Nomad*, where he will once again gestate and awaken (196). The wreck of the *Nomad* rests on the asteroid of the Scientific People, a tribe of space-dwellers handled comically early in the novel because of the pseudoscientific basis of their culture (22). The descendants of a scientific expedition lost in the asteroid belt some two hundred years earlier, they fetishize scientific instruments and texts left behind by their ancestors, treating them as sacred objects within a mystical religion, but they really only understand science intuitively, as it pertains to their survival in space. After their rediscovery by human civilization, they choose to continue living in isolation, according to their own customs, and the world at large "promptly" forgets them (23). Like primitive bricoleurs, they build their habitat from flotsam and jetsam, and they enrich their genetic pool by taking in the rare survivors among the debris, a practice they refer to as "arrival of the fittest" (24). By returning to the wreck of the *Nomad*, Foyle does not necessarily choose the way of the Scientific People; but in narrative terms, Bester does align him with the savage creativity of their harsh, uncodified, and piecemeal existence, as a higher expression of the same sort of excess.

Hipolito and McNelly have read Foyle's "evolving consciousness" in terms of the "four Jungian psychological categories"—sensation, intuition, thinking, and feeling—and portrayed him as striving toward an "individuated selfhood" that poises him to become a "new Christ, the Saviour-Lamb."[39] Another critic has presented Foyle as a "hero" who "grows up to civilized, moral adulthood."[40] J♂seph and M♀ira's reception of him as a "god-man" supports the one reading, and the willingness of the future Robin Wednesbury to save Foyle the other, but Bester has refused such top-heavy allegory throughout the novel, and the ending positions Foyle ambivalently with respect to conventional morality. Though not necessarily untenable, moralistic readings of Foyle seem beside the point. In narrative terms, Bester leaves Foyle's character unresolved, awakening but not awakened. The ending of *Stars* resembles that of "The Probable Man" in the sense that it offers the reader an imaginative vista, an ambiguous new beginning, rather than a straightforward resolution. In this respect, it also resembles Blake's "The Tyger," raising moral questions but leaving them up in the air for the reader to contemplate. The moral content of Foyle's transcendence and its implications for his world remain uncertain, writable by the reader. One need only consider Bester's handling of epochal change in the novel to take in this point. In Foyle's age, jaunting has resulted in wide-ranging "knock-on consequences" for human society, producing economic disorder, crime waves and jack-jaunting, a new purdah for women, land riots, plagues and pandemics, and the rewriting of laws and customs in general.[41] What will space-jaunting bring? No reading of the novel's ending that ignores Bester's savage and undomesticated sense of wonder really does justice to it, or to Foyle.

An odd string of announcements concerning the publication of *Stars* made it an object of wider interest before it even appeared in print. In the March 1956 issue of *Fantasy and Science Fiction*, a flash news item in an advertising space across from Ray Bradbury's "The Dragon" indicated that Bester's new novel "The Burning Spear" would appear serially in the magazine, starting in June; and the next month, a correction citing "editorial considerations" retracted the announcement and postponed the appearance of Bester's novel.[42] Then, in August, *Galaxy* announced the serialization of *Stars* by way of a lengthy subscription advertisement and followed up with a three-quarter-page repeat of the advertisement in September, along with a gushing coming-next-month section that mentioned none of the contents of the October issue except *Stars*. According to one observer of the period, readers suspected an editorial wrangle over rights to the novel and had watched both magazines' coming-soon announcements with "more than the usual interest" throughout the summer and fall.[43]

Such suspicions had a basis in reality. Between the two announcements, an ugly dispute over serialization rights raged behind the scenes. Bester originally submitted the manuscript to Boucher under the title "Tyger! Tyger!" The editor enthusiastically accepted it in December 1955, telling Bester: "Jesus boy, you've gone & done it again!" Boucher clearly planned to publish the novel as soon as possible. He requested only minor revisions and suggested several new titles in the acceptance letter, including "Wide World's End" (taken from "Tom-a-Bedlam," which Bester quoted as an epigraph to the second part of the novel), "The Burning Man," and "The Burning Spear."[44] Bester responded in kind, agreeing to all the revisions and addressing the suggested titles in his return letter. He identified Boucher's first title as his abandoned working title, rejected the second as derivative of *The Demolished Man*, expressed a preference for the third, and threw into the mix a fourth, "Forest of the Night."[45] The novel's publication was essentially a done deal before the end of the year. By early January, Boucher had already slated "The Burning Spear" as a four-part serial to run from June to September of 1956 and just managed to insert the announcement in the March issue before it went to press.

However, when Gold learned of the sale, he responded with outrage, alleging that Bester had committed the novel to *Galaxy* in the course of their correspondence. He also threatened legal action. Though Bester vehemently denied promising the novel to Gold, he possessed no carbons of the letters in question, and his legal counsel informed him that without them, there was no way of knowing whether or not Gold had a case based on an offhand comment he might have made. In a letter to Boucher, Bester described Gold as entirely "off-balance and unpredictable" and a lawsuit as "inevitable" unless he withdrew the novel from *Fantasy and Science Fiction* and transferred the rights to *Galaxy*. By Bester's account, Gold later even claimed credit for the novel's "story and treatment," an assertion of "squatter's rights" that made Bester so livid that he lost his temper and told Gold that he would "tear him apart" if he ever breathed a hint of it again, either in "public or private."[46]

In the end, of course, Boucher lost the rights to the serial; but he behaved with the highest professional dignity, promising not to sue or start a public feud with Gold, and he encouraged Bester to take advantage of his editorial comments on the manuscript despite the circumstances. Bester in fact did so, and by his account, his contract with Galaxy Publishing forbad Gold from requesting revisions or changing "one word" of the manuscript he submitted.[47] As such, all the changes to the manuscript after it left Boucher's hands would have resulted from a combination of Boucher's advice and Bester's interactions with Truman "Mac" Talley, the editor overseeing the paperback publication at NAL. The new title very likely originated with Talley. Although NAL originally announced the book as "And Hell's My Destination" in a winter 1956 catalog, Bester had given Talley carte blanche with respect to the retitling in March 1956.[48] Incidentally, no publishing house accepted *Stars* for hardcover publication. Though Boucher included the novel in the second volume of his anthology *A Treasury of Great Science Fiction* in 1959, the first stand-alone hardcover of *Stars* in the United States did not appear until 1975, with the Gregg Press edition.

Because of delays associated with this dispute, which pushed back both the serial and paperback publication dates about six months, the Sidgwick and Jackson hardcover edition in the United Kingdom came out first, under the title *Tiger! Tiger!* in the summer of 1956. It met with overwhelmingly positive reviews. In *New Worlds*, for instance, Leslie Flood said the novel read as if "Olaf Stapledon had finished a manuscript by Heinlein and Kornbluth and Spillane," and ranked it "among the top ten science-fiction novels of all time."[49] The U.K. Science Fiction Book Club quickly picked it up for hardcover reprinting, and a review in the club's official news outlet, *Science Fiction News*, heralded it as an "inferno of a novel." It also placed its originality beyond even the highest of superlatives, saying: "The fertility of Alfred Bester's imagination cannot be adequately described. He has created an entire new mythology of the future."[50]

The novel's reception in the United States proved lukewarm by comparison. Hans Stefan Santesson, the editor of *Fantastic Universe*, gave the novel a negative review, boiling it down to "violence (or rather blind, dogged hate), plus basic English, plus Sex and deliberately exaggerated characterizations." In his view, the novel courted shock value and "commercial possibilities" but lacked plotting in the "classic sense."[51] At the opposite end of the spectrum lay P. Schuyler Miller, who thought *Stars* among the "top rank" of books released that year but found it not quite up to the standard of *The Demolished Man*.[52] In the middle were James Blish and Damon Knight, both of whom gave the novel sharply mixed reviews. Blish disliked the serial in *Galaxy* but

Bester's *Tiger! Tiger!*, first U.K. edition, Sidgwick and Jackson, 1956. Courtesy of Pan Macmillan.

later chalked up his negative response to reading the novel in chunks. After sitting down with the paperback and reading it straight through, he revised his position, describing *Stars* as better than *The Demolished Man* but marred by its "typographical tricks," especially those of the synesthesia scene. From his perspective, Bester included them only because readers expected "such tricks of the author of *The Demolished Man*."[53] Knight took Bester to task for scientific inaccuracies and "bad taste," calling him a "literate maso-Spillane," but he also acknowledged Bester's bricolage technique as a source of strange and unexpected beauty. At the end of his lengthy and largely negative review, he likened Bester to a "California hobbyist who builds graceful towers out of old bottles and rusting iron" and admitted that *Stars* was undeniably a "work of art" even though made "out of junk."[54] *Stars* appeared after the 1956 Hugo

Awards, and the 1957 Hugo ballot included no awards for fiction, but a 1957 *Fantasy Times* reader poll did hint at the novel's wider reception in the United States. The newszine's readers selected the *Galaxy* serial as the best novel of 1956 in a landslide vote.[55]

After the dustup surrounding *Stars*, Bester started the brainstorming process for a new novel almost immediately. In return for *Fantasy and Science Fiction*'s release of his manuscript, he had promised Boucher a replacement under the title "The Burning Spear," and by late March 1956, he was "work-

Bester's *The Stars My Destination*, first U.S. edition, Signet, 1957. Courtesy of Penguin Random House.

ing intensively" on the plot, piecing it together by the "mosaic method" he generally used. Though he assured Boucher that he would send a "long, long summary" of his ideas within a week or so, he also complained that his plotting method, despite its ability to "enrich" a novel, took "forever."[56] By all appearances, he abandoned the project not long after, for reasons unknown. His correspondence with Boucher simply ends at this point, and he published no further stories in *Fantasy and Science Fiction* until Robert P. Mills, his literary agent at the time, took over as the magazine's editor.

Commentators have cited a variety of circumstances that led to Bester's departure from SF at the end of the fifties, ranging from his "fulltime" focus on journalism to his "disgust" with the field,[57] but the conflict over the serial rights to *Stars* surely played a key role in his change of focus. Bester—understandably it seems on the basis of his account—severed his ties with Gold,[58] and the lingering awkwardness of the situation strained his working relationship with Boucher until it reached a breaking point. Though Bester had not necessarily set the fire, he found the bridges to his two main SF markets effectively burned.

Before the end of the decade, Bester produced two more superior SF stories, both published in *Fantasy and Science Fiction* by Mills, but his slowing output clearly showed that he once again considered SF a sideline activity. Nonetheless, both stories evinced the glitzy pulp modernism of "Fondly Fahrenheit" and *Stars*. "The Men Who Murdered Mohammed" (1958) features a mad professor who flies into a rage after he finds his wife in the arms of another man. Named Henry Hassel, probably in lighthearted allusion to pulp writer Henry Hasse, he builds a time machine in a matter of minutes, goes back in time, and murders his wife's grandfather. When that fails to erase her from existence, he kills her grandmother. When that also fails, he aims higher, killing George Washington, Christopher Columbus, Napoleon, Mohammed, and a host of other major historical figures in an attempt to change the course of history. He even teaches Madame Curie how to build an atomic bomb, after which she accidentally wipes nineteenth-century Paris from the face of the earth—but nothing works. Meanwhile, subtle hints indicate that Hassel himself is slowly fading out of existence. Bester here revisits the same mad-science trope he employed in his very first story. In "The Broken Axiom" (1939), a matter-transmission experiment that goes wrong causes a professor to become semi-invisible and slip into a liminal space between dimensions. However, Bester now handles the vanishing-man trope with calculated insincerity, representing science indirectly, through a pastiche of encyclopedia entries about Ludwig Boltzmann, Jacques Charles, and André-Marie Ampère, and littering the text with equations and scientific laws of little importance to the plot. He also undercuts the power fantasy that Hassel entertains, reinventing the shopworn grandfather paradox in a surprisingly novel fashion. In the end, Hassel manages only to erase his own timeline from existence. Bester imagines time as entirely subjective—a time traveler travels only along his or her time-strand within a larger continuum—and when Hassel wrecks his personal timeline, he becomes like the sauce in a pot of spaghetti. He is able to visit any strand in the pot but not to exist inside it. He has unwittingly committed existential suicide, or "chronocide," as Bester terms it.[59]

In "The Pi Man" (1959), which appeared in *Fantasy and Science Fiction*'s special tenth anniversary issue, Bester reimagines the clairvoyant mutant of tales such as Muriel Jaeger's *The Man with Six Senses* (1927) through the lens of pattern compulsion. Bester's protagonist, Abraham Storm, shows an extreme sensitivity to patterns of any sort—whether natural or social, terrestrial or cosmic—and he experiences them through intuition more so than perception. They influence him across vast distances and sometimes control him. That is, he finds himself compelled to "compensate," or counterbalance evolving patterns through his thoughts and actions, and frequently, he behaves in eccentric or violent ways that do not reflect his individual will.[60] His language comes and goes, but he speaks mostly broken English interspersed with bits of French, German, Italian, and Latin, and his obsession with numbers also means that equations, mathematical notation, and numbers feature prominently in his discourse. As a character, he very much resembles Aquila from "5,271,009." However, he narrates the story in first person, and word flows and concrete poetry-style word pictures give readers direct access to his patterned perception. The story hinges on Storm's developing relationship with Lizzie Chalmers, whom he tries to drive away for fear he will harm her, but she argues that their love will shield them from the unpredictable patterns that possess him. Here, unlike the mystical ending of *Stars*, Bester does not quietly pass over the moral implications of a character bound up in impersonal, cosmic forces indifferent to human hopes and desires. Storm replies:

"We're part of a universe that's big beyond knowledge. What if it turns out to be too gigantic for love?" (94).

"The Men Who Murdered Mohammed" and "The Pi Man" garnered Hugo Award nominations in 1959 and 1960, respectively; and Bester's "Murder and the Android" (1959), an adaptation of "Fondly Fahrenheit" that aired as an episode of NBC's *Sunday Showcase* and starred a young Rip Torn as the android, also received a nomination in the "Best Dramatic Presentation" category in 1960; but despite his high visibility, Bester had already left the field. In his absence, his reputation would grow steadily—not necessarily among general readers but among up-and-coming writers and aficionados, who would come to regard him as an enfant terrible of the Golden Age whose verve and originality had opened new avenues for the development of the genre. Broader changes in the marketplace, including new venues such as *Galaxy* and *Fantasy and Science Fiction* and the increasing demand for hardcovers and paperbacks, had contributed to a sense of postwar transformation in the field, as had other writers such as C. M. Kornbluth, Theodore Sturgeon, and Robert Sheckley; but Bester, whose idiosyncratic fiction perhaps pushed the envelope further than the rest, would receive particular attention. Though now an outsider in earnest, he would become the insider's outsider, a figure on the margins that movers and shakers would point to as an exemplar of meaningful difference.

CHAPTER 6

HIATUS AND SEARCH FOR A NEW STYLE

The period that followed "The Pi Man" and extended until Bester's full-fledged return to SF in 1971 saw his fiction output dwindle and then come to a halt entirely. Although commentators often present Bester as simply shifting his attention to journalistic endeavors after he became a regular columnist for *Holiday* in 1956, he in fact wrote another contemporary novel around 1959 and every major publisher rejected it. Charles Platt, who some thirty-odd years later shepherded the novel to publication under the title *Tender Loving Rage* (1991), sensed that it represented Bester's "bid for serious acceptance as a novelist" and that its failure to sell turned Bester's "dream" to "ashes."[1] If so, disappointment perhaps factored into Bester's decision to put fiction aside almost completely after 1963. His nonfiction from this period suggests as much. Although he distinguished himself at *Holiday*, expertly interviewing celebrities such as Sir Laurence Olivier, Sophia Loren, and John Huston, and contributing arts and travel features of uncommon depth and interest, he appeared disappointed in his career. He wrote a satirical piece about his own lack of productivity in 1961, flippantly labeling himself a sellout, a "parasite attached to the underbelly of the arts." Though full of bravado, this essay's humor takes on troubling undertones considered in the context of his unsold novel. Bester describes himself as a failed writer who has "produced no worthwhile fiction in the last five years" and "lost the habit of creative thought, and the discipline of creative work."[2] In another equally strained self-sketch from 1962, he gibes about the discontents of the writer, referring to Trigorin's monologue on the same topic in Anton Chekhov's *The Seagull*, and sardonically asks for a special holiday gift: a piece of writing that will not "disappoint" him in the end.[3]

Bester did produce several new SF stories early in this period. The strongest, "They Don't Make Life Like They Used To," appeared in *Fantasy and Science Fiction* in 1963 and represented yet another of Bester's clever recomplications of the Adam-and-Eve motif. After the last man and woman cross paths in postapocalyptic New York City, they prove not only highly incompatible but also of questionable sanity. Not unlike "Adam and No Eve," the story's plot hinges on psychological horror, but here that horror derives at first from black comedy related to the protagonists' weird quirks and budding but dysfunctional romance. It takes on broader dimensions only at the climax. Throughout the story, the source of the disaster remains unclear, even to the protagonists, but disquieting signs of a possible menace accumulate, creating an atmosphere of paranoia and impending doom that relates either to the main characters' ambivalent desire for each other, a real threat, or both. Bester's mosaic approach persisted in this story but largely played out in the story's setting, which he identified as a montage of some of his "favorite places" in the city.[4]

By all appearances, Bester wrote two other stories for a very practical purpose: to fill out his forthcoming story collection *The Dark Side of the Earth* (1964). The short "Out of this World" (1964) has the feel of quick filler or bottom-of-the-drawer material, but Bester showed a greater sense of investment in "The Flowered Thundermug" (1964), which he took the time to submit for consideration to Pohl at *Galaxy*. Though Pohl rejected the story almost immediately, finding it too "slow," and Bester wondered if writing it specifically for book publication resulted in the relaxed pace, it ranks among the better stories of Bester's later career, cleverly riffing on the moronic-future theme of C. M. Kornbluth's "The Marching Morons" (1951).[5] Nonetheless, it does show the first signs of a tendency toward overwriting and empty parody that undermined much of Bester's later work.[6]

The story drops the reader into a bizarre reality, one that creates a sense of both familiarity and dislocation through heavy allusion to Hollywood films and the "L.A. Way of Life." Most of the characters speak in clichéd film dialogue spanning the crime, mystery, and adventure genres, and bear the names of famous actors, actresses, and characters. In "Great L.A.," as the United States is now called in 2464, Muzak rings from every tree, vending machines dispense autographs, and Klieg lights beam atop every structure.[7] In general, the setting conveys a sense that some perverse interpretation of Hollywood values organizes life at large. The plot hinges on two unwilling and homesick time travelers trapped in this "Hollywood nightmare" (99). They discover each other as they attempt to steal a flowered thundermug, a piece of twentieth-century Americana that they both covet out of nostalgia. The intelligence quotient of the future becomes apparent when they encounter a "burglar-proof" safe with twenty-seven possible combinations (91); and their discussions reveal that during the war only Hollywood survived the massive bombings that nearly wiped out human civilization. The punchline, of course, is that it then became the cultural hub of the United States and produced the strangely anachronistic and dumbed-down society that the two are now forced to inhabit.

Bester approaches cultural change at the level of language, overcoding the future through a veritable inundation of film and lifestyle references, but the narrative conveys no sense of process or historicity. In the future, the glossy surface of culture and the psychology of society coincide, and that flatness is part of the joke. However, this approach to extra-coding differs substantially from Bester's earlier uses of the technique. It borders on an empty mode of pastiche that "cannibalizes" styles and combines them into "overstimulating ensembles" without meaningfully transforming them.[8] Bester also arguably passes over an opportunity to create a writable dynamic in the story. The protagonists' nostalgia leads them to reconstruct safe havens out of remnants of their own culture, and though they do so in a more active and discriminating manner than their future counterparts, they engage in a similar type of cultural montage. Nevertheless, no narrative tensions take shape around this issue. The story does not slip into nostalgia itself, but neither does it, in

Bester's usual fashion, necessarily involve the reader in a layered cross-play of meanings.

If "The Flowered Thundermug" hints that Bester grew somewhat less concerned with the reader's agency at this stage in his career, his essay "My Private World of Science Fiction" (1963) confirms as much. When Robert Mills asked him to contribute his favorite story to *The Worlds of Science Fiction* (1963), Bester refused on the grounds that he disliked *all* of his own work. He contended that the "joy" a writer derived from "creating a piece" bore no relationship to the finished work itself. All of his "best works" were "still notes" in his commonplace book, and as soon as he wrote stories based on them, they would "become disappointments, too."[9] This author-centered concept of story shifts noticeably from Bester's a decade earlier, when he explained story as a dialogue between the writer and reader, one in which the reader co-produces meaning and resembles a theatergoer who "shares a play in its making."[10] It likewise shows him in a very discouraged state of mind with respect to his own fiction, perhaps further confirming that his dashed hopes for his novel strongly affected the direction of his career.

Even Bester's disastrous but hilarious stint as *Fantasy and Science Fiction*'s book reviewer (October 1960–July 1962) demonstrates this shift in his outlook. In his reviews, he employed the royal "we," a point of view that gave his voice a comic, high-hat tone, and he at first selected a strange mélange of popular science, borderline novels, and genre offerings for review. Then, five months into his tenure, he sloughed all but one of the books he received, declaring all the others too "bad" for serious consideration, and wrote a polemic more or less summarized by the following line: "It is the authors who are killing science fiction."[11] Predictably, a major backlash followed, and Bester in his next column attempted to form an all-star composite SF author from a number of authors he admired, probably in an attempt to smooth the controversy over, but he later continued in much the same vein. On various occasions, in lieu of actually reviewing books, he deferred to guest reviewers by way of tetchy introductions, wrote a profile of an SF fan, and wrote a haughty but damning self-profile. Although Bester often proved insightful and entertaining while on these tangents, his tendency to turn the books column into a personal soapbox showed more than a trace of self-indulgence and not a little disregard for the magazine's readers.

Up until 1966, Bester perhaps remained somewhat connected to the SF world through his work as an arts correspondent for *Rogue*, a *Playboy*-style magazine whose regular contributors included Harlan Ellison and Robert Bloch, among others. However, after the publication of *The Dark Side of the Earth* in 1964, he produced virtually no SF for the rest of the decade. He wrote an SF short, "Ms. Found in a Champagne Bottle" (1968), for the short-lived lifestyle magazine *Status* but with the express purpose of taking an unusual news item and playing with it in the "science-fiction manner" for the magazine's "elite" readers.[12] Within the field proper, he remained visible primarily by way of new reprints and reviews of his novels, but his reputation nonetheless grew exponentially due to the rising influence of the New Wave. When Michael Moorcock took the helm of *New Worlds* in 1964 and determined to set the magazine—and SF in general—on a bold new course, he championed Bester's work, representing it as one of the few bridges between the Golden Age and the new future he and other New Wave writers imagined for SF. From 1963 forward, Moorcock would cite *The Stars My Destination* in particular as an example of "grown up" science fiction that could be held to the highest literary standard and withstand all but the "most rigorous criticism."[13] Other writers associated with the New Wave on both sides of the Atlantic, including Charles Platt, Ellison, Norman Spinrad, and Samuel R. Delany, followed suit, with Delany even representing *Stars* as the "single greatest SF novel" ever written.[14] When Bester returned to SF in the early 1970s, he found himself the "granddaddy of the New Wave," as one critic put it.[15] However, when asked in 1971 what he thought of the New Wave, he replied: "I know almost nothing about New Wave science fiction. . . . All I can say is that I welcome anything new, am always most sympathetic to the breaking away from old traditions which have a tendency to fossilize."[16]

Bester reentered the field for a very different reason than he had in the 1950s. Then, he sought a venue for experimentation and creative release. Now, mere circumstance led him back. After a change in ownership in 1970, *Holiday* magazine relocated to Indianapolis, and Bester declined to move with it. Instead of seeking another editorial position, he drifted back into SF. He also returned in poor health. In 1971, he underwent a major cataract surgery on his failing eyes, and in his commonplace book, he described the previous year as the "worst" of his life, noting that he still struggled to read or to use a typewriter.[17] He brought little current knowledge of the field with him, as evidenced by his comment about the New Wave, and it showed in his first story, "The Animal Fair" (1972), a quaintly moralistic talking-animal satire in the vein of Orwell's *Animal Farm* (1945). The story dabbles in local color—the first line sets the story in Bucks County, Pennsylvania, where Bester owned a home—and explores questions about both euthanasia and the relative merits of militant action versus education in redressing social ills, but it ultimately suffers from thematic incoherence. Even so, the SF community welcomed Bester back with open arms. In 1973 the story garnered one of the most puzzling Nebula nominations in the history of the award and went on to appear in the annual *Best from Fantasy and Science Fiction* before falling out of print entirely.

Editors quickly began to solicit work from Bester. When his friend Harry Harrison asked him to contribute to *Astounding: John W. Campbell Memorial Anthology* (1973), he reacted with surprise, having never considered himself one of Campbell's authors, but he eventually accepted the assignment, even agreeing to write a story with an emphasis on hard science.[18] In 1966 he had written a popular science book titled *The Life and Death of a Satellite*, and he parlayed his research for that project into "Something Up There Likes Me" (1973), a story about a sentient satellite that takes up an antagonistic stance toward humanity but spares its creators, whom it considers its parents. This story represented Bester's first genuine attempt at hard SF in his career, but he would not continue in this direction. When Harlan Ellison requested a story for the *Last Dangerous Visions*, Bester returned to the pastiche style of "The Flowered Thundermug" in a story with the working title "Santayana Said It." Ellison found it "unsatisfactory" and returned it with extensive comments, but Bester did not abandon the story. He went on to develop it into his madcap novel *The Computer Connection* (1975).[19]

Though even Bester himself considered *The Computer Connection* a "disaster," it warrants brief discussion because of the way it illustrates how his changing concept of story affected his return to SF.[20] The novel's plot centers on several immortals, led by first-person narrator Edward Curzon, who want to end political oppression on earth and "just have a good time for themselves" along the way;[21] but a supercomputer with telepathic powers turns the tables by possessing one of them, a Cherokee physicist named Sequoya Guess. As a result, the immortals must figure out how to kill Guess. The novel brims with neologisms, blend words, puns, and invented dialects. Outrageous characters, ranging from a recurring BEM with no apparent relevance to any part of the novel to Jesus Christ, are introduced almost by the page. The background, foreground, and all the nooks and crannies are filled with anachronisms related to the immortals' origins in various eras reaching back to the Stone Age. Tropes and genre devices related to immortality, time travel, transcendence, hyperintelligence, supercomputing, and much, much more are sprinkled liberally and mixed up at will. To call the novel extra-coded hardly captures its three-ring-circus atmosphere, and Bester perhaps offered a better term when he described his later work as "extravaganza."[22]

Though some reviewers kindly emphasized the novel's restless invention and stylistic flourishes, most classed it no better than readable. Doubtless, Bester faced impossibly high expectations, his comeback having been, as one reviewer put it, "more heralded than Gloria Swanson's in *Sunset Boulevard*,"[23] but his approach clearly leaned in a strongly author-centered direction. The novel reads as though Bester understood it as a personal playground for his pet ideas rather than a place for readers to share in the story. One reviewer, George Warren, flatly declared that Bester had "lost his voice" or at least his "faith in it,"[24] but Gerald Jonas very likely came closer to the truth when he winnowed the problem down to self-indulgence, saying: "The trouble with books like *The Computer Connection* is that they cannot be as much fun to read as they are to write."[25] By all appearances, Bester had receded into his private world of science fiction completely.

Bester did regain a sense of creative discipline and reader awareness in "The Four Hour Fugue" (1974), the strongest story of his late career. "Fugue" cross-pollinates SF, mystery, and horror, and shows Bester turning to a mode somewhat akin to the weird tale. If *The Computer Connection* feels dated, like a cold stew of SF clichés warmed over in Bester's imagination, "The Four Hour Fugue" opens with an arresting image of urban sprawl more in line with the cyberpunk sensibility to emerge ten years later than the SF of the day:

> By now, of course, the Northeast Corridor was the Northeast slum, stretching from Canada to the Carolinas and as far west as Pittsburgh. It was a fantastic jungle of rancid violence, inhabited by a steaming, restless population with no visible means of support and no fixed residence, so vast that census-takers, birth-

> control supervisors, and the social services had given up all hope. It was a gigantic raree-show that everyone denounced and enjoyed. Even the privileged . . . never thought of leaving. The jungle grabbed you.[26]

This image forms the first part of a miniature prologue that demonstrates Bester's continuing flair for edgy world-building and introduces the story's central extrapolative conceit. Because of pollution, overcrowding, and sheer, unmanageable sprawl, the supply of water to the Corridor inevitably falls well short of demand, making it a carefully regulated and expensive commodity, one sometimes available only through black markets. As a result, the general populace of the Corridor not only stinks to high heaven but also buys perfume in volume, making the scent industry one of the most lucrative in the world.

At once off-beat and cleverly rationalized, this premise opens the door to comedy and horror, and Bester seizes on both possibilities in the course of the story. Early on, Bester engages in a jaunty satire of corporate culture, portraying the scent industry as over-reliant on experts, in love with gimmicky advertising, and top-heavy with semi-competent executives prone to throw money at problems. This sendup of the corporate world emerges by way of introducing a mystery. Dr. Blaise Skiaki, the premier scent expert in the industry, is in a slump and executives want to know why. Eventually, they call in Gretchen Nunn, a revered fixer and investigator who is also the protagonist, and when she arrives on the scene, the tone of the story grows much darker. In the course of her investigation, she and Skiaki fall for each other, but she also learns that he slips into fugue states on a regular basis, leaving his home in the middle of the night, apparently to commit murder. When she follows him on one of these fugues, he speaks to her in an eerie trance, identifying himself as "Mr. Wish," and she suspects that he follows human pheromone trails of a particular sort: those produced by an individual's unconscious "death-wish" (97–98). Bester returns to psychology with force here but in the service of context-driven psychological horror. Though the source of Skiaki's fugues remains undetermined, the story vaguely suggests that the Corridor itself in some way possesses him—that the "jungle" has "grabbed" him quite literally, reawakening some violent, primal urge deep in his unconscious.

"Fugue" includes a rather forced twist related to Nunn's character that almost causes it to veer out of control; but it ends with a well-executed surprise that partly redeems Skiaki—or at least clears him of the murders. Brutal killers able to sense his pheromone trail use him as a "bird dog" to locate victims before they send him away and commit the murders themselves (101). On the whole, the story represented a return to form, and it clearly reconnected Bester with his audience. The SF community at large selected "Fugue" as one of five finalists for the Hugo Award in the short story category, and *Locus* readers voted it the sixth best story of the year in the magazine's 1975 poll. In June of the same year, Bester's reputation also benefited from the appearance of the first hardcover of *Stars* in the United States. This Gregg Press edition included a well-researched introduction by Paul Williams that positioned the novel as the forbear of Kurt Vonnegut's *The Sirens of Titan* (1959) and Philip K. Dick's *The Three Stigmata of Palmer Eldritch* (1965), and Bester as the seminal influence on writers who came of age during the sixties.

Bester at this moment put aside new projects and turned his attention to revising his stories for hardcover republication in *The Light Fantastic* (1976) and *Star Light, Star Bright* (1976). Though he mostly added stylistic touches and updated cultural references, he also made extensive changes to two stories, "Hell Is Forever" and "The Pi Man." In revising the latter, one of his personal favorites, he renamed the main characters, developed minor scenes,

Bester circa 1976. Publicity photo by Roger Field. First published in *The Light Fantastic*, 1976. Courtesy of Penguin Random House.

removed most of the in-text typographical effects, and expanded typographical effects occurring in white space, largely in the direction of word pictures. For example, in the original, the first typographical effect involves a simple trail of words that cuts back across the page and brilliantly complicates the standard two-column magazine layout, letting readers directly experience a switchback in the Pi Man's perception. In the later version, the same effect represents the Pi Man symbolically, as such:

Sometimes

I I I
am am am
3.14159 +
from from from
this other that
space space space

Othertimes not.[27]

Neither version of the story proves clearly superior at the technical level: the original emphasizes the external pressures that shape the Pi Man's existence, the latter version his compulsion to balance patterns; but the revised story doubtless profited from Bester's removal of numerous stale references to beatnik culture, which clearly dated it, and from a more mature, contemplative tone.

Arguably, Bester made a very market-savvy move when he scrubbed his stories of dusty historical markers and highlighted his technical achievements. These two volumes, especially after collected in the more affordable SFBC omnibus edition *Starlight* (1976), boosted Bester's reputation even higher, in part because reviewers found the stories as fresh and relevant as ever. Harlan Ellison placed Bester among the big names of the field—the "Asimovs, Heinleins, Bradburys"—but depicted his work as ageless in comparison.[28] Challenging the representation of Bester as a precursor to the New Wave, Richard E. Geis described him as a "post–New Wave writer all the way back in the 1950s," by which he meant a writer "vastly sophisticated in content and technique" but still interested in "character and dramatic values." He also added: "I'm not sure the rest of the field has caught up with him yet."[29] Though John Clute found Bester's decision to dedicate *The Light Fantastic* to

Bester's *The Light Fantastic*, Berkley, 1976. Courtesy of Penguin Random House.

the "wonderful demented fans" ingratiating and self-indulgent, he perhaps put the matter most succinctly when he said of the stories in the two collections: "They define the genre they inhabit."[30]

With his reputation at a career high, Bester started a new project, perhaps inevitably returning to the well-received "Fugue" with plans to expand it into an SF horror novel titled *Golem*[100] (1980). In an interview conducted in 1976 at MidAmeriCon, Bester spoke excitedly of the project, suggesting that it tackled the question of perception from an original and ambitious angle, but he also worried that he was "not good enough of a writer to handle it."[31] Closer to the release date, he spoke with greater confidence, describing his "new style" as one that would involve readers more than ever before. By his account, it combined "*all the art forms*," moving beyond even synesthesia to offer readers a "total" sensory experience, and portions of the novel even took place inside the characters' minds, below the threshold of conscious perception.[32]

Though difficult to describe, the novel follows "The Four-Hour Fugue" in associating the urban landscape with the release of primal psychic energy. Here, Bester introduces the "Guff," an area of the Northeast Corridor once known as New York City, as a "poisonous" region riddled with "psychopathic and psychedelic crime."[33] The storyline centers on a wave of murders that are grisly even by the Guff's standards, and though the killer remains a mystery for much of the novel, the Guff itself is in a sense the culprit. Early in the novel, a group of bored, decadent women dabbling in witchcraft for a thrill try to summon Satan into their midst, apparently without success, but it is later revealed that they have provided a focal point for the roiling collective unconscious of the Guff's inhabitants and unwittingly conjured up a malevolent Golem instead. Bester had just revised "Hell Is Forever" extensively for *The Light Fantastic*, and as this aspect of the plot suggests, that earlier story still lingered in his mind, but his psychological rationalization of the Golem also resonates strongly with another possible source, Gustav Meyrink's *The Golem* (1915). In that novel, the Golem is an urban elemental of sorts, born of the pent-up subconscious energy and misery of Prague's sprawling Ghetto:

> Just as, in thundery weather, the electric tension in the atmosphere will increase to a point past endurance, and eventually give birth to the lightning, may it not be that the whole mass of stagnant thought infecting the air of the Ghetto needs clearing from time to time by some kind of mysterious explosion, something potent in its workings—something that forces the dreams of the subconscious up into the light of day.[34]

Though more in the vein of a horror-film creature than Meyrink's, Bester's Golem takes form in much the same manner. The exponent included in the novel's title in fact underscores that the Golem derives from the oversaturated collective psyche of the Guff. Bester takes the premise of the id-induced phantasm in films such as *Forbidden Planet* (1956) and imbues it with a gritty, urban realism.

Bester's "new style" would hinge on extensive sections of graphic sequential narrative, in which images rather than words advanced the story. Most of these episodes, originally drawn by Bester and reinterpreted by Jack Gaughan, represent the subconscious "Phasmaworld" from which the Golem originates (154). For instance, chapter 13 depicts Blaise Shima's and Gretchen Nunn's distorted perceptions within this other reality. It contains some dialogue but consists primarily of images that stylistically reference comics, film, and a range of modernist and abstract art forms. Chapter 17 consists mainly of twenty-six Rorschach blots, purportedly drawn and captioned by Gretchen Nunn in an attempt to recount her journey to the sub-world. However, Bester also expanded his citational style to include computer binary code, musical notation, barcodes, religious iconography, chemistry notation, and other nonverbal narrative elements.

The novel's murder-mystery plot at first resembles that of "Fugue," centering on suspicions of Blaise that are dispelled when the protagonists figure out that the Golem merely uses him to sniff out victims, but here, this twist transitions into a hunt for the Golem that traverses both the Guff and the sub-world and continues until about two-thirds of the way into the book. Then, depending on how generously one looks at it, the plot either fragments into a postmodern house of mirrors or simply implodes. Even if Bester intended for the plot to break down, one aspect of the novel's development remains beyond debate. It ends with a flourish of blank parody and shock tactics not far distant from those of *The Computer Connection* and even more problematic with the element of slash-and-gore horror thrown into the mix.

Golem¹⁰⁰ found a defender in Norman Spinrad, who argued that come what may, Bester had intended to transgress readers' dearest "conceptions about novelistic reality," and it won a rave from *Analog*'s Spider Robinson for its use of images as narrative, which Robinson portrayed as a truly new development in the field.[35] (Years later, China Miéville would similarly praise the novel's "disrespect for text" and call it "surpassingly strange and rather underrated," a fact that could place it tentatively in the lineage of the New Weird.[36]) However, it largely met with negative reviews. More than one reviewer portrayed its combination of "cuteness" and horror as a toxic brew, one likely to permanently damage Bester's reputation.[37] Others reflected that Bester slipped into a mode of self-caricature that cheapened and diminished the heady style of his classic novels.[38] Algis Budrys compared the novel to Heinlein's by-then-notorious *The Number of the Beast* (1979), accusing both of meaningless "reader-cheating," of using idiot plotting, smoke-screen pyrotechnics, and funny-hat characterization to finish a manuscript that promised a quick payday.[39] In one of the harshest reviews, Damien Broderick made perhaps the most interesting observation about why *Golem*[100] put readers off. He noted that Bester's work of the fifties conveyed a sense of Nature in the background "shaking the bottle of *elan vital*," maybe even rooting for the underdog to move up the evolutionary ladder first. In his view, regardless of Bester's subject matter, evolution at some level lingered in the background as a thematic principle, offering structure and coherence to Bester's experiments in characterization and style. In contrast, *Golem*[100] left cosmic and even social realities behind, causing the story to collapse into a "potpourri of gaudy images with no underlying texture."[40]

Bester responded to the negative reception of *Golem*[100] publically, in a letter addressed to Budrys. He acknowledged that the novel made "tremendous demands on the reader" but also expressed resentment that another "professional" such as Budrys would not sympathize with his attempt to break new ground. He portrayed himself as a "courageous, creative" artist and said of the novel: "If it was a failure I bitterly regret it, but I'm not sorry I tried." Throughout his later career, Bester repeated an anecdote about Pablo Picasso several times, one related to him by producer Jerry Wald. When Wald met the seventy-seven-year-old artist, he asked: "What are you doing now?" Picasso replied without hesitation: "I'm looking for a new style." Bester came to understand his return to SF in precisely the same terms, but arguably, when he returned to the field, he internalized the widespread view of him as a trailblazer. He seemed to want to one-up his earlier stylistic experiments but lost sight of the reader—and writable storytelling—in the pursuit of novelty. If his work had once balanced style and content with inimitable results, *Golem*[100] subordinated content to style altogether. It closed the reader out; even Spinrad and Robinson admitted as much, though they applauded him for his effort to enlarge the possibilities of the field.

Bester completed one more novel, *The Deceivers* (1981), but even though the cover of the TOR edition touted it as the "true successor to *The Stars My Destination*," it read more like a busy, overwritten pastiche of *Stars* than an original novel. One reviewer called it "mildly good fun" but also outlined its borrowings from the plot of Bester's classic and placed some passages on par with "Heinlein's recent excesses," pointing out that a reviewer could strike "no lower blow" than a such a comparison.[41] Bester started another novel, *Psychoshop* (1998), but he later abandoned it and left the SF field.[42] He left New York also, retiring to his farmhouse in Ottsville, Pennsylvania. Charles Platt visited him there in 1984, the same year Rolly died of cancer, and he found Bester leading a "reclusive" life, drinking heavily, and tinkering with a play based on "Fondly Fahrenheit." According to Platt, Bester had been working on the play for six months, and when asked about it, he acknowledged that it "was virtually impossible to produce" but said "he'd felt like writing it anyway." Bester also seemed embittered about *Golem*^{100}. In Platt's words:

> He said he knew, beyond any doubt, that *Golem*^{100} was his best book, but readers were too short-sighted to grasp this. He felt rejected, and unwilling to write anything more for them. It was the first time I had ever heard him complain about the reception of his work, and I felt embarrassed.[43]

If Bester lost heart after his failed attempt to return to SF, his reputation nonetheless blossomed once again in his absence. In the mid-eighties, writers associated with cyberpunk widely cited him as an inspiration. Bruce Sterling, for instance, placed him on a shortlist of SF's "native visionaries" alongside Philip José Farmer, John Varley, Philip K. Dick, and Thomas Pynchon, while William Gibson noted *The Stars My Destination* as a primary influence on *Neuromancer* (1984), *the* touchstone novel of the eighties.[44] If New Wave writers had invoked Bester mostly in defense of "literary" experimentation, this loosely defined group of writers embraced his fictional sensibility, mixing and marrying the gaudy, pop-culture feel of pulp fiction with high style. They produced a glossy pulp postmodernism, one rooted in a sense of future shock and posthumanism on which *Stars* only verged. Bester apparently knew little about these developments at the time. He spent his final years in deteriorating health, cared for primarily by his friend and bartender, Joe Suder, to whom he left his literary estate. However, he did become aware of renewed interest in his work just before the end of his life. He accepted an invitation to serve as Guest of Honor at the 1987 WorldCon in Brighton, England, though a serious fall and its lingering consequences prevented him from attending; and later in the same year, the Science Fiction Writers of America named him the 1988 Nebula Grand Master, an honor that Bester is said to have learned of before his death in September 1987.

CONCLUSION

In the mid-sixties, a young Alexei Panshin offered up a dissenting view of Bester's fiction. He dismissed it as a superficial mixture of thirties pulp SF and slick "Manhattan" style, and he criticized Bester for knowing too little about the development of "modern SF." According to Panshin, when Bester returned to SF in the fifties, he "had been away a long time, and he didn't know how the pros were working out their problems . . . so he made up his own solutions."[1] Although Panshin perhaps underestimated Bester's awareness of trends in the field and certainly offered this comment by way of critique, he inadvertently hit on part of what made Bester unique: his outsider perspective. Though Bester's desire for creative freedom led him to experiment on his own terms, he did ignore the science-centered, answer-driven paradigm dominant in the field upon his return—a part of his approach that he summarized late in his career by saying, "To hell with the science if it can't produce fiction."[2] He did draw on the pulp SF of an earlier era, retaining its bustling energy and alluring weirdness, but he also transformed it by crossbreeding it with other forms of genre writing, recoding its machinery, and employing modernist style in the service of science-fictional extrapolation. In fact, his early stories, especially those published in *Astounding* and *Unknown*, show him developing a pulp-modernist aesthetic before he even left the field for the first time. In the fifties, he largely picked up where he left off, and his conflict with Campbell, as well as the emergence of new markets such as *Galaxy* and *Fantasy and Science Fiction*, helped him unlock his approach's full potential.

To discuss Bester as an outsider is not to romanticize him or label him, but to emphasize the outsider effect that defined his impact on the field. He approached SF from an oblique angle—with gaps in his knowledge of its development, a background in other mediums, a distinctive artistic process, a relative disregard for markets and trends, a love of the decadents and modernists, a postwar urban sensibility, and a whole lot of attitude. He brought a fresh set of eyes and a unique toolbox to the field, and he produced a wider sense of its merits and possibilities for that very reason. Georges Bataille once observed: "Knowledge implies chronically going astray."[3] Bester led the field astray again and again during the fifties but produced new knowledge all along the way. Although some accounts of his career portray him as almost singlehandedly giving rise to a competing vision of SF that culminated in the "new thing" of the sixties, he was not the only wanderer. A host of writers ranging from veterans like Sturgeon and Pangborn to relative newcomers like Dick and Sheckley were also busily recomplicating the genre and, arguably, producing a revolutionary paradigm shift; but Bester perhaps went further afield than most—and definitely in more idiosyncratic directions. There are grounds for giving credence to Barry N. Malzberg's portrayal of him as a figure on par with Campbell in terms of lasting influence on the genre.

The phrase "writer's writer" often comes up with respect to Bester,[4] and doubtless he contributed much to the field in terms of technique and style, but he is perhaps better understood as an uncommon variety of reader's writer. His writable approach to fiction, which took shape in his early career and peaked in the late fifties, resulted in open texts with layered, incongruous meanings that invited the reader to coproduce, even finish, his stories through active imagination. This sort of narrative metageometry made Bester's stories like proofs solvable by more than one set of steps, or games of chance in which probability weighs against odds and patterns of play. His fiction of the fifties is rereadable not merely because of its inventiveness but also because of this complex patterning, which overdetermines the reader's experience, even the second or third time around. Bester produced this sense of excess through bricolage and pastiche that mixed up and hybridized reading protocols, and through various types of extra-coding—allusion, nonstandard orthography, language confusion, synesthesia, and mixed-viewpoint narration, to name just a few of his narrative strategies—but the reader-centered, writable patterns he created mattered more than any of these "pyrotechnics" alone, as his later career demonstrates. His inventiveness lasted to the end, but when the structural compulsion that defined his work up to the late fifties fell away, so did much of his fiction's magic.

Bester was fond of quoting Hungarian biologist Albert Szent-Györgyi's comment, "Discovery consists of seeing what everybody has seen, and thinking what nobody has thought," and he did precisely that in his SF.[5] He did not press the genre forward as much as he engaged in a self-conscious transvaluation of its codes and reading protocols that expanded it sidewise and put it in a highly productive dialogue with itself. His fiction is a compendium of comments on the field that un-wrote the limits, and Bester is rightly remembered as a lodestar for SF's venturers and nomads.

AN ALFRED BESTER BIBLIOGRAPHY

NOVELS (IN CHRONOLOGICAL ORDER)

The Demolished Man. Chicago: Shasta, 1953 [serialized in *Galaxy*, January–March 1952].

Who He? New York: Dial, 1953 [variant title *The Rat Race*, New York: Berkley, 1956].

Tiger! Tiger! London: Sidgwick and Jackson, 1956 [variant title *The Stars My Destination*].

The Stars My Destination. New York: Signet, 1957 [serialized in *Galaxy*, October 1956–January 1957; variant title *Tiger! Tiger!*].

The Computer Connection. New York: Berkley/Putnam, 1975 [serialized as *The Indian Giver* in *Analog*, November 1974–January 1975; variant title *Extro*, London: Eyre Methuen, 1975].

Golem^{100}. Illustrated by Jack Gaughan. New York: Simon and Schuster, 1980.

The Deceivers. New York: Wallaby/Simon and Schuster, 1981.

Tender Loving Rage. Houston: Tafford, 1991.

Psychoshop. Completed by Roger Zelazny. New York: Vintage, 1998.

STORY COLLECTIONS AND OMNIBUS EDITIONS (IN CHRONOLOGICAL ORDER)

Starburst. New York: Signet, 1958.

The Dark Side of the Earth. New York: Signet, 1964.

An Alfred Bester Omnibus. London: Sidgwick and Jackson, 1967 [collects *The Demolished Man, Tiger! Tiger!* and *The Dark Side of the Earth*].

The Light Fantastic: The Great Short Fiction of Alfred Bester, Volume I. New York: Berkley, 1976.

Star Light, Star Bright: The Great Short Fiction of Alfred Bester, Volume II. New York: Berkley, 1976.

Starlight: The Great Short Fiction of Alfred Bester. Garden City, N.Y.: Nelson Doubleday, 1976 [collects *The Light Fantastic* and *Star Light, Star Bright*].

Virtual Unrealities: The Short Fiction of Alfred Bester. New York: Vintage, 1997.

Redemolished. New York: ibooks/Simon and Schuster, 2000.

SHORT FICTION

"5,271,009." *Magazine of Fantasy and Science Fiction* 6, no. 3 (March 1954): 3–32 [variant title "The Starcomber," *Starburst*, 1958].

"Adam and No Eve." *Astounding* 28, no. 1 (September 1941): 35–45.

"And 3½ to Go." In *Virtual Unrealities: The Short Fiction of Alfred Bester*, 287–91. New York: Vintage, 1997.
"The Animal Fair." *Magazine of Fantasy and Science Fiction* 43, no. 4 (October 1972): 5–37.
"The Biped, Reegan." *Super Science Stories* 3, no. 2 (November 1941): 66–75.
"The Black Nebulea" [*sic*] [as Sonny Powell]. *Magazine of Fantasy and Science Fiction* 17, no. 3 (September 1959): 50.
"The Broken Axiom." *Thrilling Wonder Stories* 13, no. 2 (April 1939): 64–73.
"Death of a Bandit." *Rogue* 7, no. 6 (June 1962): 37–38, 79–80.
"The Devil's Invention." *Astounding* 45, no. 6 (August 1950): 133–45 [variant title "Oddy and Id"].
"The Devil without Glasses." In *Virtual Unrealities: The Short Fiction of Alfred Bester*, 334–66. New York: Vintage, 1997.
"The Die-Hard." In *Starburst*, 148–52. New York: Signet, 1958.
"Disappearing Act." In *Star Science Fiction Stories No. 2*, edited by Frederik Pohl, 1–21. New York: Ballantine, 1953.
"Emerging Nation." Unpublished. [For *The Last Dangerous Visions*, edited by Harlan Ellison.]
"The Flowered Thundermug." In *The Dark Side of the Earth*, 74–116. New York: Signet, 1964.
"Fondly Fahrenheit." *Magazine of Fantasy and Science Fiction* 7, no. 2 (August 1954): 3–21.
"The Four Hour Fugue." *Analog* 93, no. 4 (June 1974): 88–102.
"Galatea Galante, The Perfect Popsy." *Omni* 1, no. 7 (April 1979): 42–46, 124–32.
"Guinea Pig, Ph.D." *Startling Stories* 3, no. 2 (March 1940): 116–19, 124+.
"Hell Is Forever." *Unknown Worlds* 6, no. 2 (August 1942): 8–45.
"The 'HEs,' the 'SHEs,' and the 'ITs.'" In *Frontier Crossings*, 23–26. London: Robert Jackson for Science Fiction Conventions, 1987.
"Hobson's Choice." *Magazine of Fantasy and Science Fiction* 3, no. 4 (August 1952): 3–15.
"I Will Never Celebrate New Year's Again." *Rogue* 8, no. 2 (February 1963): 10, 87.
"The Julias." *Escapade* 13, no. 5 (June 1968): 11.
"Life for Sale." *Amazing Stories* 16, no. 1 (January 1942): 166–89.
"The Lost Child." *Rogue* 9, no. 2 (March 1964): 8, 80.
"The Mad Molecule." *Thrilling Wonder Stories* 19, no. 1 (January 1941): 29–35.
"The McGrabb Bag." *Detective Fiction* 148, no. 2 (October 1, 1941): 16–21.
"The Men Who Murdered Mohammed." *Magazine of Fantasy and Science Fiction* 15, no. 4 (October 1958): 118–29.
"Ms. Found in a Champagne Bottle." In *Status*, 1968. Reprinted in *The Light Fantastic*, 54–57.
"MS Found in a Coconut." *Analog* 99, no. 6 (June 1979): 104–10.
"Never Love a Hellhag." In *The Seventh Omni Book of Science Fiction*, edited by Ellen Datlow, 359–408. New York: Zebra, 1989.
"No Help Wanted." *Thrilling Wonder Stories* 14, no. 3 (December 1939): 89.
"Oddy and Id." In *The Best Science Fiction Stories: 1951*, edited by Everett F. Bleiler and T. E. Dikty, 208–23. New York: Frederick Fell, 1951 [variant title "The Devil's Invention"].
"Of Time and Third Avenue." *The Magazine of Fantasy and Science Fiction* 2, no. 5 (October 1951): 3–9.
"Out of This World." In *The Dark Side of the Earth*, 45–55. New York: Signet, 1964.
"The Pet Nebula." *Astonishing Stories* 2, no. 3 (February 1941): 33–39.
"The Pi Man." *Magazine of Fantasy and Science Fiction* 17, no. 4 (October 1959): 80–94.

"The Probable Man." *Astounding* 27, no. 5 (July 1941): 75–104.
"The Push of a Finger." *Astounding* 29, no. 3 (May 1942): 108–29.
"The Roller Coaster." *Fantastic* 2, no. 3 (May–June 1953): 80–88.
"Slaves of the Life-Ray." *Thrilling Wonder Stories* 19, no. 2 (February 1941): 62–77.
"Something Up There Likes Me." In *Astounding: John W. Campbell Memorial Anthology*, edited by Harry Harrison, 49–72. New York: Random House, 1973.
"Star Light, Star Bright." *Magazine of Fantasy and Science Fiction* 5, no. 1 (July 1953): 113–27.
"They Don't Make Life Like They Used To." *Magazine of Fantasy and Science Fiction* 25, no. 4 (October 1963): 100–127.
"Time Is the Traitor." *Magazine of Fantasy and Science Fiction* 5, no. 3 (September 1953): 103–22.
"Travel Diary." In *Starburst*, 110–13. New York: Signet, 1958.
"Treachery on Camoia." *South Sea Stories* 1, no. 5 (October 1940): 40–62.
"The Unseen Blushers." *Astonishing Stories* 3, no. 4 (June 1942): 84–89.
"Voyage to Nowhere." *Thrilling Wonder Stories* 17, no. 1 (July 1940): 12–30.
"The White Man Who Was Tabu" [as Alexander Blade]. *South Sea Stories* 1, no. 5 (October 1940): 118–27, 142.
"Will You Wait?" *Magazine of Fantasy and Science Fiction* 16, no. 3 (March 1959): 125–29.

INTERVIEWS

"Alfred Bester and Frederik Pohl—The Conversation." Recorded June 26, 1978, at the Tyneside Cinema, Newcastle upon Tyne, U.K., by Kevin Williams. In *Inca* 5 (December 2009): 4–19.
Interview by Charles Platt, conducted in London, September 1979. In *Dream Makers: The Uncommon People Who Write Science Fiction*, 93–102. New York: Berkley, 1980.
Interview by Darrell Schweitzer, conducted at Philcon, December 1974. In *SF Voices*, 6–16. Baltimore: T-K Graphics, 1976 [abridged versions appeared in *Amazing*, June 1976, and *Science Fiction Voices #1*, 1979].
Interview by David Truesdale. In *Tangent* 6 (Winter 1977): 25–33.
Interview by Guy Lillian III. In *Challenger* 25 (Winter 2007). Available at www.challzine.net/25/25alfie.html (accessed February 12, 2012).
Interview by James Phillips, conducted in 1984. In *Starlog* 128 (March 1988): 34–36, 72.
Interview by Jim Steranko. In *Mediascene* 36 (March/April 1979): 12–13.
Interview by Lou Mougin. In *Comics Interview* 32 (1986): 6–19.
Interview by Paul Walker, conducted by mail, November–December 1971. In *Luna Monthly* 35/36 (April/May 1972): 15–20.

SELECTED NONFICTION

"Books" [Decline of SF]. *Magazine of Fantasy and Science Fiction* 20, no. 2 (February 1961): 105–8.
"Books" [All-Star SF Author]. *Magazine of Fantasy and Science Fiction* 20, no. 3 (March 1961): 77–81.
"Books" [Fans, or the Fen]. *Magazine of Fantasy and Science Fiction* 22, no. 3 (March 1962): 90–93.

"The Compleat Hobbyist." *Holiday* 38, no. 6 (December 1965): 140+.
"The Demolished Man." *Magazine of Fantasy and Science Fiction* 21, no. 3 (September 1961): 93–95.
"Here Come the Clones: A Short History of SF Writing with Fifty All-Purpose Footnotes." *Algol* 28 (Spring 1977): 35–37.
"Horace, Galaxyca." In *Galaxy: Thirty Years of Innovative Science Fiction*, edited by Frederik Pohl, Martin H. Greenberg, and Joseph D. Olander, 410–12. New York: Playboy, 1980.
"How a Science Fiction Author Works." In *SF Symposium/FC Simpósio*, edited by José Sanz, 117–24. Rio de Janeiro: Artes Gráficas Gomes De Souza / Instituto Nacional Do Cinema, 1969.
Introduction to *Odd John: A Story Between Jest and Earnest*, by Olaf Stapledon. Norwalk, Conn.: Easton, 1987.
"Journey to Limbo." *Thrilling Wonder* 17, no. 1 (July 1940): 122–23.
The Life and Death of a Satellite. Boston: Little, Brown, 1966.
"My Affair with Science Fiction." In *Hell's Cartographers*, edited by Brian W. Aldiss and Harry Harrison, 46–75. New York: Harper and Row, 1975.
"My Private World of Science Fiction." In *The Worlds of Science Fiction*, edited by Robert P. Mills, 340–49. New York: Dial, 1963.
"My World with Harry Harrison." In *Novacon 12 Program*, 13–17. Birmingham: Birmingham Science Fiction Group, 1982.
"Science Fiction and the Renaissance Man." Speech delivered February 22, 1957, University of Chicago. In *The Science Fiction Novel: Imagination and Social Criticism*, edited by Basil Davenport, 102–25. Chicago: Advent, 1959.
"Selections from the Gimmick Books." Edited by Eric Solstein. *New York Review of Science Fiction* 14, no. 1 (September 2001): 11–14.
"The Shame of Skiffy." *Patchin Review* 2 (September 1981): 30–32.
"The Trematode: A Critique of Modern Science-Fiction." In *The Best Science-Fiction Stories: 1953*, edited by Everett F. Bleiler and T. E. Dikty, 11–22. New York: Frederick Fell, 1953.
"What's the Difference?" *Science Fantasy* 12 (February 1955): 2–5.
"Writing and *The Demolished Man*." *Algol* 18 (May 1972): 4–8.
"Writing the Radio Mystery." *The Writer* 64, no. 12 (December 1951): 391–95.
"Yes, Santa, There Is an Alfie." *Rogue* 7, no. 12 (December 1962): 6, 80.

SELECTED MEDIA

"The Lost Child." WPIX, New York. August, 15, 1949.
"The Man with No Face." *The Shadow*. November 27, 1949.
"Murder and the Android." *NBC Sunday Showcase*. October 18, 1959. Repeat September 5, 1960 [adaptation of "Fondly Fahrenheit"].
"The Walking Dead." *CBS Radio Mystery Theater*. May 20, 1976 [adaptation of "Fondly Fahrenheit"].

NOTES

INTRODUCTION

1. Delany, introduction to *The Cosmic Rape*, vii. See also Hartwell and Cramer, *Ascent of Wonder*, 790.

2. Knight, review of *Stars*, 107; Moskowitz, *Seekers of Tomorrow*, 422.

3. Aldiss, introduction to *Galactic Empires, Volume II*, viii.

4. Bishop, introduction to "In Memoriam," 24; Jeter, interview, 30.

5. Malzberg and Resnick, "Resnick/Malzberg Dialogues X," 43.

6. Bester, "My Affair," 57, 69.

7. Bester, *Star Light, Star Bright*, 48–49. See also Bester, interview by Truesdale, 29–31, and "My Affair," 57–60.

8. Warner, letter in *Tangent*, 126.

9. Bester, *Star Light, Star Bright*, 49.

10. Phillips, "Club House," 145.

11. Campbell, "Third Eastern Science Fiction Convention Speech," 8.

12. Asimov, "Introduction: The Father of Science Fiction," xii.

13. Wollheim, introduction to *Novels of Science*, x–xii.

14. Campbell, "Science of Science Fiction Writing," 85.

15. Boggs, "Hat Trick," 1, 6.

16. Hines, "Belles-Lettres," 9.

17. Phillips, "Club House," 145–46.

18. Bester, "Trematode," 12. Hereafter cited parenthetically in the text.

19. Campbell, "Science of Science Fiction Writing," 84. Bester, *Star Light, Star Bright*, 167.

20. Knight, review of *Stars*, 106.

21. Boucher, letter to Bester, October 20, 1953. Mercury Press Records, Special Collections Research Center, Syracuse University Libraries.

22. Bester, letter to Boucher, Thursday [October 30 or November 5, 1953]. Mercury Press Records, Special Collections Research Center, Syracuse University Libraries.

23. Bester, "What's the Difference?" 3. Hereafter cited parenthetically in the text.

24. Pohl, introduction to *Galaxy*, x.

25. Nicholls, "Alfred Bester," 9.

26. Bester, "Science Fiction and the Renaissance Man," 124.

27. Bester, *Light Fantastic*, 151.

28. Bester, "Science Fiction and the Renaissance Man," 113, 117, 123–24.

29. Barthes, *S/Z*, 4. Barthes's term "*scriptible*" has been translated into English by some as "writerly," by others as "writable." Throughout this study, I employ "writable" when discussing texts, "writerly" when discussing readers.

30. Bester, interview by Paul Walker, 19.

31. Ashley, *Transformations*, 160.

32. Eco, *Theory of Semiotics*, 136.

CHAPTER 1. BEGINNINGS

1. Bester, "My Affair," 47.

2. Bester, "Journey to Limbo," 123.

3. Pohl, *Way the Future Was*, 1–2, 6; Knight, "Beauty," 68; Bester, "Journey to Limbo," 123. See also Westfahl, *Mechanics of Wonder*, 260.

4. Bester, "Compleat Hobbyist," 141–42.

5. Bester, "My Affair," 46.

6. Bester, "Science Fiction and the Renaissance Man," 103. Bester identified himself as a pre-med student in "Writing the Radio Mystery," 391.

7. Alfred M. Bester Student Information Card and Alumni Information Sheet. Alumni Records Collection, folder title: Bester, Alfred M. Courtesy of the University of Pennsylvania Archives, Philadelphia, Pennsylvania. See also Philomathean Society of the University of Pennsylvania, "Roll of Moderators."

8. Bester, introduction to *Odd John*, n.p.

9. "Recorder's Diary," 385. See also Bester, "Science Fiction and the Renaissance Man," 103.

10. Bester, "My Affair," 49.

11. Bester, "Science Fiction and the Renaissance Man," 104.

12. Bester, "My Affair," 48.

13. Bester, "Science Fiction and the Renaissance Man," 104.

14. Bester, "My Affair," 49.

15. Schwartz, *Man of Two Worlds*, 46.

16. Bester, "My Affair," 49.

17. "Meet the Author," 64.

18. Bester quoted in Heinlein, interview by Alfred Bester, 44.

19. Schwartz, *Man of Two Worlds*, 46.

20. Bester, "No Help Wanted," 89.

21. Bester, "My Affair," 49–50.

22. Schwartz, "Bester Years of My Life," 56.

23. Ibid.

24. Bester, "How a Science Fiction Author Works," 122.

25. Bester, "White Man Who Was Tabu," 116, 123. Hereafter cited parenthetically in the text.

26. Bester, interview by James Phillips, 35.

27. Bester, "Science Fiction and the Renaissance Man," 104.

CHAPTER 2. OF THINGS TO COME

1. Bester, "McGrabb Bag," 20–21.

2. Bester, *Light Fantastic*, 157.

3. Bester, "Probable Man," 75. Hereafter cited parenthetically in the text.

4. Edwards and Stableford, "Time Paradoxes."

5. *Friedrich Schiller: The Triumph of a Genius* was released in 1940 and drew parallels between the eighteenth-century poet and Hitler. The anthem of the Nazi Party, "The Flag on High," was popularly known as "The Horst Wessel Song."

6. See Deutsch, "Quantum Mechanics," 3211.

7. Wendell, *Alfred Bester*, 42.

8. See Langford, "Shaggy God Story."

9. Bester, "Biped, Reegan," 75.

10. Bester changed the spelling of the protagonist's name to "Steven Krane" when the story appeared in *Starburst* (1958), possibly to make the allusion more subtle.

11. Bester, *Star Light, Star Bright*, 2.

12. Baudelaire, "Carcass," 201.

13. Bester, "Adam and No Eve," 45.

14. Bester, *Star Light, Star Bright*, 1.

15. Bester, "Push of a Finger," 108. Hereafter cited parenthetically in the text.

16. Campbell, "Elimination," 124.

17. Harrison and Aldiss, *Astounding-Analog Reader*, 1:202.

18. Schwartz, "Bester Years of My Life," 57.

19. Hamilton, "Edmond Hamilton," 40.

20. Bester, "My Affair," 50–51.

21. Joyce, *Finnegans Wake*, 194.

22. Bester, "Unseen Blushers," 84. Hereafter cited parenthetically in the text.

23. Drake, "Manly Wade Wellman," 9.

24. Bester, *Star Light, Star Bright*, 168.

25. Bester, *Light Fantastic*, 155.

26. Schwartz, *Man of Two Worlds*, 47.

27. Bester, *Light Fantastic*, 155–56.

28. Ibid., 154.

29. Bester, "Hell Is Forever," 9. Hereafter cited parenthetically in the text.

30. Beardsley, interview with Lawrence, 198.

31. Both names are anagrams of "Sardi," an allusion to one of Bester's favorite restaurants in New York City: Sardi's.

32. Bester, "Hell Is Forever" (revised), in *Light Fantastic*, 210.

33. Bester, letter to Boucher, May 4, 1943. Courtesy, Lilly Library, Indiana University, Bloomington, Indiana.

34. See Wendell, *Alfred Bester*, 45.

35. Schweitzer, *Windows of the Imagination*, 66.

36. Bester, interview by Darrell Schweitzer, 14.

CHAPTER 3. COMICS, RADIO, AND THE RETURN TO SF

1. Pohl, "Alfie, Part 2." See also Pohl, "Alfred Bester: 1913–1987," 311.

2. Bester, interview by Paul Walker, 17.

3. Bester, "Science Fiction and the Renaissance Man," 104.

4. Bester, interview by Lou Mougin, 10.

5. 1940 U.S. Federal Population Census for Manhattan Assembly District 11, Block K, New York. Enumeration District 31-984B, Sheet 4, April 18, 1940.

6. Bester, letter, *New York Times*, May 30, 1971.

7. Bester, interview by Guy Lillian.

8. Bester, "Science Fiction and the Renaissance Man," 79.

9. See, for instance, interviews by Guy Lillian, n.p., and Lou Mougin, 7–8.

10. Bester, "My Affair," 54–55. See also Schwartz, "Bester Years of My Life," 57.

11. "Who and Where," 33.

12. Schwartz, "Bester Years of My Life," 57–58.

13. Bester, "My Affair," 55.

14. Bester, interview by Lou Mougin, 17.

15. Rose, review of "Lost Child," 32.

16. Bester, "My Affair," 56; interview by David Truesdale, 33.

17. Bester, "Alfred Bester and Frederik Pohl," 18.

18. Ibid., 9.

19. Bester, "Writing the Radio Mystery," 395.

20. Bester, "Alfred Bester and Frederik Pohl," 8.

21. Bester, "My Affair," 57.

22. Pohl, "Alfred Bester, 1913–1987," 312.

23. Bester, *Star Light, Star Bright*, 49–50.

24. Bester, "Devil's Invention," 133. Hereafter cited parenthetically in the text.

25. Bester, interview by James Phillips, 34.

26. Bester, "Oddy and Id," 223.

27. See, for instance, Bester, *Star Light, Star Bright*, 48–49; Bester, interview by Truesdale, 30–31; Bester, "My Affair," 57–60.

28. Boucher and McComas, introduction to "Not with a Bang," 123.

29. Bester, letter to Boucher, March 22 [1950]. Mercury Press Records, Special Collections Research Center, Syracuse University Libraries.

30. Bester, *Star Light, Star Bright*, 151.

31. Stockwell, *Poetics of Science Fiction*, 82–83.

32. Bester, "Of Time and Third Avenue," 3. Hereafter cited parenthetically in the text.

33. Bester, letter to Boucher and McComas, April 19 [1950]. Mercury Press Records, Special Collections Research Center, Syracuse University Libraries.

34. Boucher, letter to Bester, April 27, 1950. Mercury Press Records, Special Collections Research Center, Syracuse University Libraries.

35. Bester, letter to McComas, April 18 [1950]. Mercury Press Records, Special Collections Research Center, Syracuse University Libraries.

36. Boucher, letter to Bester, April 27, 1950. Mercury Press Records, Special Collections Research Center, Syracuse University Libraries.

37. Bester, letter to Boucher, May 8 [1950]. Mercury Press Records, Special Collections Research Center, Syracuse University Libraries.

38. Malzberg, *Engines of the Night*, 161.

CHAPTER 4. THE EUREKA YEARS

1. Gold, "Gold on Galaxy," 7.

2. Bester, "Horace, Galaxyca," 410.

3. Gold, "Gold on Galaxy," 8.

4. Bester, "My Affair," 63.

5. Ibid., 61.

6. Bester, "Writing and *The Demolished Man*," 6.

7. Ibid.

8. Ibid.

9. Asimov, introduction, *Asimov's Mysteries*, x. See also Carter, "Science Fiction Mystery Novels," 109.

10. Bester, "Writing and *The Demolished Man*," 7.

11. Ibid.

12. Bester, *Demolished Man* (Shasta), 20. Hereafter cited parenthetically in the text.

13. Bester, interview by David Truesdale, 26–27.

14. Bester, "My Affair," 63.

15. Bester, "Demolished Man" (part 1), *Galaxy* 3, no. 4 (January 1952): 6–7.

16. Bester, letter to Boucher, Friday [1953]. Mercury Press Records, Special Collections Research Center, Syracuse University Libraries.

17. See, for instance, Williams, introduction, xi; Langford et al., "Telepathy"; Wendell, *Alfred Bester*, 15; Walton, "Telepaths"; Hlavaty, review of *American*, 6; Moskowitz, "Perpetual Cadenza," 27.

18. Langford et al., "Telepathy."

19. Bester, interview by Guy Lillian.

20. Turner, "Double Standard," 19.

21. Bester, interview by Darrell Schweitzer, 12.

22. Freud, *Civilization and Its Discontents*, 81.

23. Bester, "Writing the Radio Mystery," 391.

24. Nolan, *Human Equation*, 5.

25. Bester, "Horace, Galaxyca," 412.

26. Gold, "Random Notes," 2–3.

27. Bester, "My Affair," 63.

28. Eshbach, *Over My Shoulder*, 387.

29. Bester, letter to Boucher, Friday [1953]. Mercury Press Records, Special Collections Research Center, Syracuse University Libraries.

30. Bester, "Demolished Man" (part 2), *Galaxy* 3, no. 5 (February 1952): 137.

31. Bester, letter to Boucher, Friday [1953]. Mercury Press Records, Special Collections Research Center, Syracuse University Libraries.

32. Bester, "Demolished Man" (part 2), *Galaxy* 3, no. 5 (February 1952): 103.

33. Bester recycled ¼maine for Reich's less-frequently referenced attorney.

34. Bester, "Demolished Man" (part 1), *Galaxy* 3, no. 4 (January 1952): 37.

35. Bester, "Demolished Man" (part 3), *Galaxy* 3, no. 6 (March 1952): 113.

36. Conklin, "Galaxy's 5 Star Shelf," 122.

37. Ibid., 121.

38. Reinsberg, "Future of Breath Catching Pace," 13.

39. Moskowitz, "Perpetual Cadenza," 27.

40. Boucher quoted in Conklin, "Galaxy's 5 Star Shelf," 122.

41. Conklin, "Galaxy's 5 Star Shelf," 122.

42. Merwin, "Universe in Books," 191; Pohl, "Alfie, Part 2"; Tucker, review of *Demolished*, 10.

43. For instance, see Miller, review of *Demolished*, 150; Reinsberg, "Future of Breath Catching Pace," 13.

44. Boucher, editorial note to McComas, October 15, 1951. See also Bester, letter to Boucher, Tuesday [October 16, 1951]. Mercury Press Records, Special Collections Research Center, Syracuse University Libraries.

45. Bester, letter to Boucher and McComas, Tuesday [October 30, 1951]. Mercury Press Records, Special Collections Research Center, Syracuse University Libraries.

46. Bester, letter to Boucher and McComas, Wednesday [1953]. Mercury Press Records, Special Collections Research Center, Syracuse University Libraries.

47. Bester, "My Private World," 348.

48. Bester, "Hobson's Choice," 3. Hereafter cited parenthetically in the text.

49. Bester, letter to Boucher and McComas, Tuesday [October 30, 1951]. Mercury Press Records, Special Collections Research Center, Syracuse University Libraries.

50. Boucher, editorial response to Bester, November 2, 1951. Mercury Press Records, Special Collections Research Center, Syracuse University Libraries.

51. Ellison, "In the Limelight," 20.

52. Boucher, editorial note to McComas, July 31, 1952. Mercury Press Records, Special Collections Research Center, Syracuse University Libraries.

53. Bester, "Disappearing Act," 15. Hereafter cited parenthetically in the text.

54. McComas, letter to Bester, September 26, 1952. Mercury Press Records, Special Collections Research Center, Syracuse University Libraries.

55. Bester, letter to Boucher and McComas, Wednesday [1953]. Mercury Press Records, Special Collections Research Center, Syracuse University Libraries. The rejected story was very likely "Star Light, Star Bright."

56. Bester, letter to Boucher and McComas, Wednesday [July 29, 1953]. Mercury Press Records, Special Collections Research Center, Syracuse University Libraries.

57. Bester, letter to Boucher and McComas, Monday [June 15, 1953?]. Mercury Press Records, Special Collections Research Center, Syracuse University Libraries.

58. Bester, *Light Fantastic*, 10–11.

59. Bester, letter to McComas, Wednesday [June 24, 1953?]. Mercury Press Records, Special Collections Research Center, Syracuse University Libraries.

60. Bester, Outline of "5,271,009," 1, circa June 24, 1953. Mercury Press Records, Special Collections Research Center, Syracuse University Libraries.

61. Ibid.

62. Bester, "5,271,009," 3. Hereafter cited parenthetically in the text.

63. Bester, letter to Boucher and McComas, September 16 [1953]. Mercury Press Records, Special Collections Research Center, Syracuse University Libraries.

64. Bester, Outline of "5,271,009," 4, circa June 24, 1953. Mercury Press Records, Special Collections Research Center, Syracuse University Libraries. Bester also included a lust for unlimited power on this list but ultimately excluded it, fearing a sixth episode would belabor the point and make the story too long.

65. Boucher, letter to Bester, October 28, 1953. Mercury Press Records, Special Collections Research Center, Syracuse University Libraries.

66. McComas, letter to Bester, November 22, 1953. Mercury Press Records, Special Collections Research Center, Syracuse University Libraries.

67. Boucher, letter to Bester, October 20, 1953. Mercury Press Records, Special Collections Research Center, Syracuse University Libraries.

68. Koestler, "Boredom of Fantasy," 309.

69. Boucher, letter to Bester, October 20, 1953. Mercury Press Records, Special Collections Research Center, Syracuse University Libraries.

CHAPTER 5. TIGER, TIGER, BURNING BRIGHT

1. Bester, "Fondly Fahrenheit," 3. Hereafter cited parenthetically in the text.

2. Bester, *Light Fantastic*, 86. Bester guessed that he encountered the anecdote about Glasscock's Ben in *Life on the Mississippi*, but it actually appeared in *Mark Twain's Notebooks* (1935).

3. Bester, *Light Fantastic*, 87.

4. Boucher, letter to Bester, February 17, 1954. Mercury Press Records, Special Collections Research Center, Syracuse University Libraries.

5. Stableford, "Androids."

6. Boucher, editorial note to Bester, January 23 [1954]. Mercury Press Records, Special Collections Research Center, Syracuse University Libraries.

7. Though McComas's departure as editor had not yet been announced, Boucher doubtless wrote this introduction solo. In a letter to Bester dated August 11, 1954, he indicated that he had taken over all editorial duties near the beginning of the year. Mercury Press Records, Special Collections Research Center, Syracuse University Libraries.

8. See Earle, *Re-Covering Modernism*, 3.

9. Bester, letter to Boucher, Monday [February 1, 1954]. Mercury Press Records, Special Collections Research Center, Syracuse University Libraries.

10. Bester, *Light Fantastic*, 86–87.

11. Bester, outline of "5,271,009," 1, circa June 24, 1953. Mercury Press Records, Special Collections Research Center, Syracuse University Libraries.

12. Bester, *Light Fantastic*, 87.

13. Bester, "Selections from the Gimmick Books," 11. See also Levi-Strauss, *Savage Mind*, 17–18.

14. Ibid., Bester, "Selections from the Gimmick Books."

15. Bester, "My Affair," 46; Bester, interview by Darrell Schweitzer, 14.

16. Bester, letter to Boucher and McComas, November 14 [1953]. Mercury Press Records, Special Collections Research Center, Syracuse University Libraries.

17. Weiler, "Noted on the Local Screen Scene," X9; Bester, letter to Boucher, Monday [February 1, 1954]. Mercury Press Records, Special Collections Research Center, Syracuse University Libraries.

18. Bester, letter to Boucher, May 12 [1954]. Mercury Press Records, Special Collections Research Center, Syracuse University Libraries.

19. Bester, letter to Boucher, July 7 [1954]. Mercury Press Records, Special Collections Research Center, Syracuse University Libraries.

20. Bester, letter to Boucher, March 16 [1955]. Courtesy Lilly Library, Indiana University, Bloomington, Indiana.

21. Bester, *Stars My Destination*, 15. Hereafter cited parenthetically in the text.

22. Bester, "My Affair," 67.

23. Bester, interview by James Phillips, 35.

24. Hipolito and McNelly, "Statement Is the Self," 79.

25. Platt, "Attack-Escape," 211, 215.

26. "Humanism Hailed as New Religion," 4.

27. Huxley, "Evolution and Genetics," 289.

28. Blake, quoted in Bester, *Stars*, n.p.

29. Bester, "Journey to Limbo," 123.

30. Ouspensky, "Table of the Four Forms of the Manifestation of Consciousness," *Tertium Organum*, n.p.

31. The story of Poon Lim, a merchant marine who survived alone on the open sea for 133 days after the torpedoing of the *S. S. Benlomond*, partly inspired this opening. See Bester, "My Affair," 65, and Samuel F. Harby's "They Survived at Sea" in the May 1945 issue of *National Geographic*, particularly 637–40.

32. Nomad, *Cosmic Consciousness*, 47.

33. Ibid., 23.

34. Ibid., 108, 110.

35. For the connection to Joyce, see McCarthy, "Science Fiction as Creative Revisionism," 60.

36. Bester, *Tiger! Tiger!* 213.

37. Blumberg, *Freaks of Nature*, 7.

38. Hlavaty, review of *American*, 6.

39. Hipolito and McNelly, "Statement Is the Self," 80–81, 84;

40. Wendell, *Alfred Bester*, 28.

41. McHale, "Popular Genres," 190.

42. "Flash!" 124; "Correction," 123.

43. Dikty, introduction, 11.

44. Boucher, letter to Bester, December 16, 1955. Mercury Press Records, Special Collections Research Center, Syracuse University Libraries.

45. Bester, letter to Boucher, Monday [December 19, 1955]. Mercury Press Records, Special Collections Research Center, Syracuse University Libraries.

46. Bester, letter to Boucher, [February 1956]. Mercury Press Records, Special Collections Research Center, Syracuse University Libraries.

47. Ibid.

48. Bester, letter to Boucher, Monday [March 12, 1956]. Mercury Press Records, Special Collections Research Center, Syracuse University Libraries.

49. Flood, review of *Tiger! Tiger!* 128.

50. "Tiger! Tiger!" *Science Fiction News*, 30, no. 3 (January/February 1958): n.p. The SFBC inserted a copy of this newszine in each book released in the series. This issue mailed to subscribers with James Blish's *Earthman, Come Home*.

51. Santesson, review of *Stars*, 113.

52. Miller, review of *Stars*, 148.

53. Blish, review of *Stars*, 6.

54. Knight, review of *Stars*, 107.

55. "Alfred Bester and Eric Frank Russell Best Authors of 1956," 1–2.

56. Bester, letter to Boucher, Monday [March 12, 1956]. Mercury Press Records, Special Collections Research Center, Syracuse University Libraries.

57. Wendell, *Alfred Bester*, 11; Spinrad, *Modern Science Fiction*, 267.

58. Bester, letter to Boucher, [February 1956]. Mercury Press Records, Special Collections Research Center, Syracuse University Libraries.

59. Bester, "Men Who Murdered Mohammed," 129.

60. Bester, "Pi Man," 80. Hereafter cited parenthetically in the text.

CHAPTER 6. HIATUS AND SEARCH FOR A NEW STYLE

1. Platt, *Loose Canon*, 88, 89–90.

2. Bester, "Demolished Man" [see nonfiction], 93, 95.

3. Bester, "Yes, Santa, There Is an Alfie," 6, 80. See also Bester, "My Private World," 341–42.

4. Bester, *Star Light, Star Bright*, 109.

5. Bester, letter to Pohl, Tuesday [October 1963]. Frederik Pohl Papers, Special Collections Research Center, Syracuse University Libraries.

6. Wolfe, review of *Virtual Unrealities*, 60.

7. Bester, "Flowered Thundermug," 80, 97.

8. Jameson, *Postmodernism*, 19.

9. Bester, "My Private World," 341–42.

10. Bester, "Science Fiction and the Renaissance Man," 123.

11. Bester, "Books" [Decline of SF], 107.

12. Bester, *Light Fantastic*, 54–5.

13. Moorcock, "Play with Feeling," 125. See also Gillespie, "J. G. Ballard and the New Wave."

14. Delany, introduction to *Cosmic Rape*, vii.

15. Paul Walker, *Speaking of Science Fiction*, 303.

16. Bester, interview by Paul Walker, 20.

17. Bester, "Selections from the Gimmick Books," 13.

18. Bester, *Star Light, Star Bright*, 191.

19. Bester, *Light Fantastic*, 89–90.

20. Bester, interview by Charles Platt, 95.

21. Back flap of dust wrapper, *Computer Connection*, n.p.

22. Bester, interview by Jim Steranko, 13.

23. Searles, review of *Computer Connection*, n.p.

24. Warren, "Plugged In," 29.

25. Jonas, "Of Things to Come," BR3.

26. Bester, "Four-Hour Fugue," 88. Hereafter cited parenthetically in the text.

27. Bester, "Pi Man" (revised), *Star Light, Star Bright*, 170.

28. Ellison, "Best of Bester," 17.

29. Geis, review of *Light Fantastic* and *Star Light, Star Bright*, 75.

30. Clute, review of *Light Fantastic* and *Star Light, Star Bright*, 48.

31. Bester, interview by David Truesdale, 33.

32. Bester quoted in Henderson, "Book Views," 15; Bester, interview by Jim Steranko, 13.

33. Bester, *Golem^{100}*, 25.

34. Meyrink, *Golem*, 45.

35. Spinrad, review of *Golem^{100}*, 255; Robinson, review of *Golem^{100}*, 173.

36. Miéville, "Forward Thinking," 81; and "China Miéville in Da Lair," interview by Angela Slatter.

37. Searles, review of *Golem*^{100}, 20; Hall, review of *Golem*^{100}, 11.

38. Sturgeon, review of *Golem*^{100}, 8; Stableford, review of *Golem*^{100}, 98.

39. Budrys, "Obstacles and Ironies," 5.

40. Broderick, "Lately Great Alfred Bester," 12.

41. Langford, "Zapping Uri Geller," 25.

42. In an odd turn of events following Bester's death, Roger Zelazny was asked to finish the manuscript.

43. Platt, *Loose Canon*, 93–4.

44. Sterling, preface to *Mirrorshades*, x; Gibson, "Alfred Bester, SF, and Me," 29.

CONCLUSION

1. Panshin, "Alfred Bester," 18–19.

2. Bester, *Star Light, Star Bright*, 168.

3. Bataille, *Guilty*, 68.

4. Nicholls, "Alfred Bester," 9.

5. Bester, interview by Phillips, 72.

Bibliography of Secondary Sources

Aldiss, Brian W. Introduction to *Galactic Empires, Volume II*. Edited by Brian W. Aldiss. New York: St. Martin's, 1977. vi–viii.

"Alfred Bester and Eric Frank Russell Best Authors of 1956." *Fantasy-Times* 12, no. 269 (second issue, April 1957): 1–2.

"Analytical Laboratory." *Astounding* 28, no. 1 (September 1941): 45.

Ashley, Mike. *Transformations: The Story of the Science-Fiction Magazines from 1950 to 1970*. Liverpool: Liverpool University Press, 2005.

Asimov, Isaac. Introduction to *Asimov's Mysteries*. Garden City, N.Y.: Doubleday, 1968. ix–xi.

———. "Introduction: The Father of Science Fiction." In *Astounding: John W. Campbell Memorial Anthology*, edited by Harry Harrison, ix–xiv. Book club edition. New York: Random House, 1974.

Barthes, Roland. *S/Z*. Translated by Richard Miller. New York: Hill and Wang, 1974.

Bataille, Georges. *Guilty*. Translated by Bruce Boone. San Francisco: Lapis, 1988.

Baudelaire, Charles. "A Carcass." In *Baudelaire: His Prose and Poetry*, edited by T. R. Smith, translated by Richard Herne Shepherd, 201. New York: Boni and Liveright, 1919.

Beardsley, Aubrey. Interview by Arthur H. Lawrence. *Idler* 11 (March 1897): 188–202.

Bishop, Michael. Introduction to "In Memoriam: Alfred Bester, 1913–1987," by Isaac Asimov. In *Nebula Awards 23*, 22–24. New York: Harcourt Brace Jovanovich, 1989.

Blish, James. Review of *The Stars My Destination*, by Alfred Bester. *Science Fiction Times* 12, no. 275 (second issue, July 1957): 6.

Blumberg, Mark S. *Freaks of Nature: What Anomalies Tell Us about Development and Evolution*. Oxford: Oxford University Press, 2009.

Boggs, Redd. "The Hat Trick . . . The Tides of TIME. . . ." *Bloomington News Letter* 11 (August 1949): 1, 6.

Boucher, Anthony, and J. Francis McComas. Introduction to "Not with a Bang," by Damon Knight. *Magazine of Fantasy and Science Fiction* 1, no. 2 (Winter–Spring 1950): 123.

Broderick, Damien. "The Lately Great Alfred Bester." *SF Commentary* 62–66 (June 1981): 11–14.

Brooks, Ned. *Fanzine Index*. April 2012. Available at www.fanac.org/Fannish_Reference_Works/NedBrooks/z102.html.

Budrys, Algis. "Obstacles and Ironies in Science-Fiction Criticism." *Patchin Review* 2 (September 1981): 5–15.

Campbell, John W., Jr. "Elimination." In *The Best of John W. Campbell*, edited by Lester del Rey, 122–38. Garden City, New York: Nelson Doubleday/SFBC, 1976.

———. "The Science of Science Fiction Writing." In *Of Worlds Beyond*, edited by Lloyd Arthur Eshbach, 84–94. Reading, Pa.: Fantasy Press, 1947.

———. Third Eastern Science Fiction Convention Speech. Delivered by R. V. Happel. October 31, 1937. Printed in *Skyhook* 14 (Summer 1952): 8–9.

Carter, Steven R. "Science Fiction Mystery Novels." *Clues: A Journal of Detection* 1, no. 1 (Spring 1980): 109–15.

Clute, John. Review of *The Light Fantastic* and *Star Light, Star Bright*, by Alfred Bester. *Magazine of Fantasy and Science Fiction* 52, no. 2 (February 1977): 45–48.

Conklin, Groff. "Galaxy's 5 Star Shelf." *Galaxy* 6, no. 6 (September 1953): 120–24.

"Correction." *Magazine of Fantasy and Science Fiction* 10, no. 4 (April 1956): 123.

Delany, Samuel R. Introduction to *The Cosmic Rape*, by Theodore Sturgeon, v–xxxiv. Boston: Gregg, 1977.

Deutsch, David. "Quantum Mechanics near Closed Timelike Lines." *Physical Review D* 44, no. 10 (November 15, 1991): 3197–217.

Dikty, T. E. Introduction to *The Best Science-Fiction Stories and Novels: 1956*, edited by T. E. Dikty, 9–17. New York: Frederick Fell, 1956.

Drake, David. "Manly Wade Wellman and Alfred Bester." *New York Review of Science Fiction* 97 (September 1996): 9.

Earle, David M. *Re-Covering Modernism: Pulps, Paperbacks, and the Prejudice of Form*. Burlington, Vt.: Ashgate, 2009.

Eco, Umberto. *A Theory of Semiotics*. Bloomington: Indiana University Press, 1976.

Edwards, Malcolm, and Brian M. Stableford. "Time Paradoxes." In *SFE: The Encyclopedia of Science Fiction*, edited by John Clute and Peter Nicholls. 2011. Available at http://www.sf-encyclopedia.com/entry/time_paradoxes (accessed September 24, 2014).

Ellison, Harlan. "Best of Bester." *Los Angeles Times*, July 11, 1976.

———. "In the Limelight." *Pendulum* 1, no. 3 (September 1952): 17–20.

Eshbach, Lloyd Arthur. *Over My Shoulder: Reflections on a Science Fiction Era*. Philadelphia: Oswald Train, 1983.

"Flash!" *Magazine of Fantasy and Science Fiction* 10, no. 3 (March 1956): 124.

Flood, Leslie. Review of *Tiger! Tiger!* by Alfred Bester. *New Worlds* 50 (August 1956): 126–28.

Freud, Sigmund. *Civilization and Its Discontents*. 1930. Edited and translated by James Strachey. New York: Norton, 1989.

Geis, Richard E. Review of *The Light Fantastic* and *Star Light, Star Bright*. *Science Fiction Review* 22 (August 1977): 75.

Gibson, William. "Alfred Bester, SF, and Me." In *Frontier Crossings*, 28–30. London: Robert Jackson for Science Fiction Conventions, 1987.

Gillespie, Bruce. "J. G. Ballard and the New Wave." *e.I* 13 (April 2004): n.p.

Gold, Horace. "Gold on *Galaxy*." In *Galaxy: Thirty Years of Innovative Science Fiction*, edited by Frederik Pohl, Martin H. Greenberg, and Joseph D. Olander, 4–9. New York: Playboy, 1980.

———. "Random Notes." *Galaxy* 4, no. 3 (June 1952): 2–3.

Hall, Melissa Mia. Review of *Golem*^{100}, by Alfred Bester. *Fantasy Newsletter* 27 (August 1980): 11, 30.

Hamilton, Edmond. "Edmond Hamilton." In *The Legion Companion*, edited by Glen Cadigan, 38–42. Raleigh, N.C.: TwoMorrows, 2003.

Harrison, Harry, and Brian W. Aldiss, eds. *The Astounding-Analog Reader, Volume One.* Garden City, N.Y.: Doubleday, 1972.

Hartwell, David G., and Kathryn Cramer, eds. *The Ascent of Wonder: The Evolution of Hard SF.* New York: TOR, 1994.

Heinlein, Robert A. Interview by Alfred Bester. *Publisher's Weekly* 204, no. 1 (July 2, 1973): 44–45.

Henderson, C. J. "Book Views." *Questar* 2, no. 3 (June 1980): 14–15.

Hines, William. "Belles-Lettres Go Out of This World as Science Fiction Grows Up." *SF* 1 (September 1952): 5–12.

Hipolito, Jane, and Willis E. McNelly. "The Statement Is the Self: Alfred Bester's Science Fiction." In *The Stellar Gauge: Essays on Science Fiction Writers*, edited by Michael J. Tolley and Kirpal Singh, 63–90. Carlton, Australia: Norstrilia, 1980.

Hlavaty, Arthur D. Review of *American Science Fiction: Nine Classic Novels of the 1950s*, edited by Gary K. Wolfe. *New York Review of Science Fiction* 293 (January 2013): 1, 4–7.

"Humanism Hailed as New Religion." *New York Times* Special Edition (August 22, 1952): 4.

Huxley, Julian. "Evolution and Genetics." In *What Is Science? Twelve Eminent Scientists and Philosophers Explain Their Various Fields to the Layman*, edited by James R. Newman, 256–89. New York: Simon and Schuster, 1955.

Internet Speculative Fiction Database. http://www.isfdb.org/cgi-bin/ea.cgi?6.

Jameson, Fredric. *Postmodernism; or, The Logic of Late Capitalism*. Durham, N.C.: Duke University Press, 1991.

Jeter, K. W. Interview by Les Escott. *Interzone* 22 (Winter 1987): 29–31.

Jonas, Gerald. "Of Things to Come." *New York Times*, July 20, 1975.

Joyce, James. *Finnegans Wake*. Oxford: Oxford University Press, 2012.

Knight, Damon. "Beauty, Stupidity, Injustice, and Science Fiction." *Monad: Essays on Science Fiction* 1 (October 1990): 67–88.

———. Review of *The Stars My Destination*, by Alfred Bester. *Infinity* 2, no. 6 (October 1957): 105–7.

Koestler, Arthur. "The Boredom of Fantasy." *Harper's Bazaar* (August 1953). Reprinted in *Science Fiction: The Future*, edited by Dick Allen, 307–10. New York: Harcourt Brace Jovanovich, 1971.

Langford, David. "Shaggy God Story." In *SFE: The Encyclopedia of Science Fiction*, edited by John Clute and Peter Nicholls. 2011. Available at http://www.sf-encyclopedia.com/entry/shaggy_god_story (accessed January 1, 2013).

———. "Zapping Uri Geller." *White Dwarf* 43 (July 1983). Reprinted in *The Complete Critical Assembly*, 23–25. Holicong, Penn.: Cosmos, 2002.

Langford, David, Peter Nicholls, and Brian M. Stableford. "Telepathy." In *SFE: The Encyclopedia of Science Fiction*. Edited by John Clute and Peter Nicholls. 2011. Available at http://www.sf-encyclopedia.com/entry/telepathy (accessed April 2, 2013).

Lévi-Strauss, Claude. *The Savage Mind*. Translated by George Weidenfeld and Nicolson Ltd. Chicago: University of Chicago Press, 1966.

Malzberg, Barry N. *The Engines of the Night*. Garden City, N.Y.: Doubleday, 1982.

Malzberg, Barry N., and Mike Resnick. "The Resnick/Malzberg Dialogues X: Good Influences." *Bulletin of the Science Fiction and Fantasy Writers of America* 150 (Summer 2001): 41–44.

McCarthy, Patrick A. "Science Fiction as Creative Revisionism: The Example of Alfred Bester's *The Stars My Destination*." *Science-Fiction Studies* 10, no. 1 (March 1983): 58–69.

McHale, Brian. "Popular Genres." In *Teaching Narrative Theory*, edited by David Herman, Brian McHale, and James Phelan, 181–94. New York: MLA, 2010.

"Meet the Author." *Thrilling Wonder Stories* 13, no. 2 (April 1939): 64.

Merwin, Sam, Jr. "Universe in Books." *Fantastic Universe* 1, no. 2 (August-September 1953): 190–92.

Meyrink, Gustav. *The Golem*. Translated by Madge Pemberton. New York: Houghton Mifflin, 1928.

Miéville, China. "China Miéville in Da Lair." Interview by Angela Slatter, January 2012. Available at http://www.angelaslatter.com/china-mieville-in-da-lair (accessed February 19, 2012).

———. "Forward Thinking." *New Yorker* (June 4 and June 11, 2012): 80–81.

Miller, P. Schuyler. Review of *The Demolished Man*, by Alfred Bester. *Astounding* 52, no. 4 (December 1953): 149–50.

———. Review of *The Stars My Destination*, by Alfred Bester. *Astounding* 60, no. 3 (November 1957): 148.

Moorcock, Michael. "Play with Feeling." *New Worlds* 129 (April 1963): 2–3, 123–27.

Moskowitz, Sam. "Perpetual Cadenza." *Science-Fiction Plus* 1, no. 5 (August 1953): 27.

———. *Seekers of Tomorrow: Masters of Modern Science Fiction*. Cleveland: World, 1966.

Nicholls, Peter. "Alfred Bester: New York, 2175 A.D." *Washington Post*, May 25, 1980.

Nolan, William F., ed. *The Human Equation*. Los Angeles: Sherbourne, 1971.

Nomad, Ali. *Cosmic Consciousness: The Man-God Whom We Await*. Chicago: Advanced Thought, 1913.

Ouspensky, P. D. *Tertium Organum: The Third Organ of Thought*. Translated by Nicholas Bessaraboff and Claude Bragdon. Rochester, N.Y.: Manas, 1920.

Panshin, Alexei. "Alfred Bester—The Irritating Charmer." *Yandro* 13, no. 1 (1965): 16–19.

Phillips, Rog. "The Club House." *Amazing Stories* 23, no. 2 (February 1949): 145–49.

Philomathean Society of the University of Pennsylvania. "Roll of Moderators." Available at http://www.philomathean.org/alumni/philograds/past-moderators (accessed December 15, 2014).

Platt, Charles. "Attack-Escape: An Article about Alfred Bester." In *New Worlds Quarterly #4*, edited by Michael Moorcock, 210–20. New York: Berkley Medallion, 1972.

———. *Loose Canon*. Gillette, N.J.: Cosmos, 2001.

Pohl, Frederik. "Alfie, Part 2: When Bester Was the Best." *The Way the Future Blogs*. Available at http://www.thewaythefutureblogs.com/2011/03/alfie-part-2-when-bester-was-the-best (accessed February 10, 2012).

———. "Alfred Bester: 1913–1987." In *The SFWA Grand Masters* (vol. 2), edited by Frederik Pohl, 311–13. New York: TOR, 2000.

———. Introduction to *Galaxy: Thirty Years of Innovative Science Fiction*. Edited by Frederik Pohl, Martin H. Greenberg, and Joseph D. Olander, ix–xiii. New York: Playboy, 1980.

———. *The Way the Future Was: A Memoir*. New York: Ballantine, 1978.

"The Recorder's Diary." In *The 1935 Record*, edited by Victor T. Ehre, 376–93. Philadelphia: University of Pennsylvania Senior Class, 1935.

Reinsberg, Mark. "Future of Breath Catching Pace: Life of Dread and Joy in 24th Century." *Chicago Tribune*, March 22, 1953.

Robinson, Spider. Review of *Golem[100]*, by Alfred Bester. *Analog* 100, no. 8 (August 1980): 173.

Rose. Review of "Lost Child." *Variety* 175, no. 8 (August 3, 1949): 32.

Santesson, Hans Stefan. Review of *The Stars My Destination*, by Alfred Bester. *Fantastic Universe* 8, no. 2 (August 1957): 113.

Schwartz, Julius. With Elliot S. Maggin. "The Bester Years of My Life." *Amazing Stories* 68, no. 4 (July 1993): 55–59.

———. With Brian M. Thomsen. *Man of Two Worlds: My Life in Science Fiction and Comics*. New York: HarperCollins, 2000.

Schweitzer, Darrell. *Windows of the Imagination*. Berkeley Heights, N.J.: Wildside, 1999.

Searles, Baird. Review of *The Computer Connection*, by Alfred Bester. *Science Fiction Review Monthly* 3 (May 1975).

———. Review of *Golem[100]*, by Alfred Bester. *Asimov's* 4, no. 7 (July 1980): 20.

Spinrad, Norman, ed. *Modern Science Fiction*. Garden City, N.Y.: Anchor, 1974.

———. Review of *Golem[100]*, by Alfred Bester. *Destinies* 2, no. 3 (Summer 1980): 255–58.

Stableford, Brian M. "Androids." In *SFE: The Encyclopedia of Science Fiction*, edited by John Clute and Peter Nicholls. 2011. Available at http://www.sf-encyclopedia.com/entry/androids (accessed June 6, 2014).

———. Review of *Golem[100]*, by Alfred Bester. *Foundation* 21 (February 1981): 98–99.

Sterling, Bruce. Preface to *Mirrorshades*. 1986. Reprint, New York: Ace, 1988, ix–xvi.

Stockwell, Peter. *The Poetics of Science Fiction*. New York: Routledge, 2014.

Sturgeon, Theodore. Review of *Golem[100]*, by Alfred Bester. *Twilight Zone Magazine* (September 1981): 8.

Tucker, Wilson "Bob." Review of *The Demolished Man*. *Science Fiction News Letter* 29 (July 1953): 10–11.

Turner, George. "The Double Standard: The Short Look, and the Long Hard Look." *Australian Science Fiction Review* 10 (June 1967). Reprinted in *SF Commentary* 76 (October 2000): 16–20.

Walker, Paul. *Speaking of Science Fiction*. Oradell, N.J.: Luna, 1978.

Walton, Jo. "Telepaths, Murder and Typographical Tricks: Alfred Bester's *The Demolished Man*." *Tor.com*. October 22, 2010. Available at www.tor.com/2010/10/22/telepaths-murder-and-typographical-tricks-alfred-besters-the-demolished-man (accessed July 1, 2012).

Warren, George. "Plugged In: An Essay-Review." *Science Fiction Review* 16 (February 1976): 28–30.

Warner, Harry, Jr. Letter. *Tangent* 7/8 (Summer 1977): 125–27.

Weiler, A. H. "Noted on the Local Screen Scene." *New York Times*, December 5, 1954.

Wendell, Carolyn. *Alfred Bester: Starmont Reader's Guide* 6. Mercer Island, Wa.: Starmont, 1982.

Westfahl, Gary. *The Mechanics of Wonder*. Liverpool: Liverpool University Press, 1998.

"Who and Where." Uncredited editorial. *Holiday* 16, no. 4 (October 1954): 33.

Williams, Paul. Introduction to *The Stars My Destination*, by Alfred Bester. Boston: Gregg, 1975, v–xv.

Wollheim, Donald A. Introduction to *Novels of Science*. Edited by Donald A. Wollheim. New York: Viking, 1945. vii–xiii.

Wolfe, Gary K. Review of *Virtual Unrealities*. *Locus* 39, no. 5 (November 1997): 59–60.

INDEX

JAD SMITH is a professor of English at Eastern Illinois University and the author of *John Brunner*.

MODERN MASTERS OF SCIENCE FICTION

John Brunner *Jad Smith*

William Gibson *Gary Westfahl*

Gregory Benford *George Slusser*

Greg Egan *Karen Burnham*

Ray Bradbury *David Seed*

Lois McMaster Bujold *Edward James*

Frederik Pohl *Michael R. Page*

Alfred Bester *Jad Smith*

THE UNIVERSITY OF ILLINOIS PRESS
is a founding member of the
Association of American University Presses.

Composed in 10.75/14.5 Dante
with Univers display
by Kirsten Dennison
at the University of Illinois Press

University of Illinois Press
1325 South Oak Street
Champaign, IL 61820-6903
www.press.uillinois.edu